I0826928

Very sincerely,
R. C. Dodds

# Elisha the Man of God.

BY

R. CLARENCE DODDS, D. D.,

Pastor First Presbyterian Church,
Lansing, Michigan.

WIPF & STOCK · Eugene, Oregon

Wipf and Stock Publishers
199 W 8th Ave, Suite 3
Eugene, OR 97401

Elisha the Man of God
By Dodds, R. Clarence
Softcover ISBN-13: 978-1-6667-6199-3
Hardcover ISBN-13: 978-1-6667-6200-6
eBook ISBN-13: 978-1-6667-6201-3
Publication date 10/11/2022
Previously published by The Winona Publishing Company, 1909

This edition is a scanned facsimile of the original edition
published in 1909.

*To her who walks by my side,*
*whose companionship has ever proved a benediction,*
*Sarah, my beloved wife,*
*this volume*
*in fond admiration and affection*
*is inscribed.*

# CONTENTS.

# PREFACE.

IN NO character of the Bible, perhaps, is the life of Jesus, the SON of God, so perfectly mirrored as in Elisha, the MAN of God. His gentleness of spirit and holiness of life; the patience and faithfulness which must have characterized his teaching; and, above all, the marvelous and beneficent character of his miraculous deeds; were a prophecy in actual life of him who spake as never man spake, "who went about doing good"; and whose miracles proclaimed him to be "the Son of God with power." The desire to direct the attention of students of the word of God with deeper interest to the beautiful and Christ-like character of the son of Shaphat, and thus incite to greater holiness of life, a more perfect consecration to the service of God, has led to the preparation of these chapters. The aim has been to make due acknowledgment, in the proper place, of authors and works quoted from. It seems proper however, that special mention should be made of the History of Elisha, by Dr. Krummacher; Lectures on History of Elisha, by Rev. Henry Blunt; The Prophet Elisha, by John M. Lowrie, D. D.; Elisha the Prophet, by Alfred Edersheim, D. D.; the Pulpit Commentary; and Lange's Commentary.

R. C. D.

Lansing, Mich., January 1, 1904.

# ELISHA.

## CHAPTER I.

### A PROPHET'S CALL.

"So close is glory to our dust,
So near is God to man—
When duty whispers low, thou must,
The youth replies, I can."

Among the grandest characters of sacred or profane history the impartial judgment of the ages has accorded a prominent position to Elijah, the Tishbite, the Prophet of God. The deep mystery which veils his life previous to his sudden and startling appearance at the court of the wicked Ahab; the sublime character of his mission; his courageous performance of duty; his god-like departure from earth in the chariot of fire; and his reappearance, in the shining garments of heaven, upon the mountain of transfiguration, have all contributed to invest the brief history of his life with a peculiar interest, an interest which is intensified rather than diminished by the passing away of centuries. One of the most important events in the life of the great Prophet was the trial upon Carmel when he was called to appear as the sole representative of true religion in Israel, and, as such, to be the principal actor in one of the most sublime scenes that have ever been presented upon the stage of the world's activity. Never was there a more courageous champion of any cause than Elijah proved himself to be upon that memorable occasion.

But, lest he should be exalted above that which he was able to bear, he was permitted to fall from that height of glory upon which he then stood. After that he had faithfully and fearlessly fulfilled his mission as the forerunner; after he had pointed out to others "the Lamb of God who taketh away the sin of the world," John, from the mountain prison of Machaerus, sends two of his trusted disciples to Jesus with this inquiry, "Art thou he that should come, or look we for another?" So long as he was permitted to be active in the service of God, John could rest in the evidence given him that Jesus was the Christ; but when he was shut up in the lonely prison cell, doubts seem to have arisen in his mind. In like manner many of the most worthy servants of God in subsequent times, have had their seasons of spiritual depression, when the eye of faith has seen dimly. Such was the experience of Melancthon, Fuller, Cowper, Brainard, and scores of others, eminent in spiritual attainment and in Christian service. How touching are those words of the good Dean of Carlisle, written to an intimate friend, "Though I have endeavored to discharge my duty as well as I could, yet sadness and melancholy of heart stick close by and increase upon me. I tell nobody, but I am very much sunk indeed, and I wish I could have the relief of weeping as I used to. My days are exceedingly dark and distressing. In a word, Almighty God seems to hide his face." Whether due in whole or in part to his physical condition at the time; to the reaction consequent to the extraordinary degree of spiritual exhilaration which he had experienced; or to the increased energy with which Satan renewed his attacks upon him, Elijah lost sight of the fact, for the time, that his life was in God's keeping. When the threat of Jezebel to make his life as the life of one of the prophets of Baal whom he had slain, or caused to be slain, reached his ear, he arose and fled for his life. Instead of commending himself to God whose care he had hitherto enjoyed, he sought safety in the wilderness, nor ceased to flee until he had reached Horeb, the mount of God, where, centuries before, amid thunderings and lightnings, the law for which he had shown such zeal had been delivered to Moses. Here God addressed him, and directed him to return, and to anoint Hazael to be king of Syria, Jehu to be king of Israel, and Elisha the son of Shaphat of Abel-meholah, to be his successor in the prophetic office.

To what extent Elijah obeyed his instructions, we are not informed. It is evident, from the inspired record, that neither of these persons was formally anointed by him. We may not doubt, however, that the duty with which he was charged was performed in such a manner as to meet the Divine approval. By him Elisha was symbolically called to be a prophet, if not formally anointed. Arriving at Abel-meholah, the home of Elisha, the name means, "the meadow of the dance," referring, perhaps, to the fertility of the soil or the exquisite beauty of scenery, he found Elisha plowing with twelve yoke of oxen before him, and he with the twelfth. The meaning of this statement seems to be that Elisha had charge of twelve plows, eleven of which went before him while he himself guided the twelfth. The busy scene must have charmed the eye of the Prophet, but he pauses not to contemplate it.

Before the plowmen are aware of his presence he approaches Elisha, casts his mantle upon him, and presses on as though the act were no part of his mission, and void of significance. Not a word seems to have been spoken by the Prophet, but Elisha recognizes that which had been done to him as a call to holy service. Dr. Taylor, quoting from Dr. Jamison's Eastern Manners, says, "This ceremony has always been considered by eastern people an indispensable part of the consecration to the sacred office. It is in this way that the Brahmans are still invested with the priestly character, a yellow mantle being thrown across their shoulders, which is buckled round the waist with a sacred ribbon. It is in this way, too, that the Persian Sufis are appointed. The master, in anticipation of death, selecting one of his favorite pupils, bequeaths his antiquated garment to the youth who, by that act, is publicly recognized as his successor, and looked upon as inheriting with the mantle, the virtues and powers of his venerable precursor." The call which came to Elisha was a call from God. Whether Elijah had any previous acquaintance with Elisha, whether he had any preference as to who should succeed him as prophet in Israel, we do not know; but we do know that God explicitly directed him to anoint Elisha.

Those who are God's servants in the truest sense of the term, are not made such by chance, their call to service is not dependent upon the will of man. At the same time, it is to be observed that God usually calls men into his service through his accredited representatives. Moses must anoint, and consecrate, and sanctify Aaron and his sons that they may minister unto the Lord in the priest's office. He must lay his hand upon the head of Joshua that he may be recognized as his successor as the leader of the people. Barnabas and Saul must be separated for the work whereunto God had called them, by prayer, and the laying on of the hands of those who ministered to the Lord in the church of Antioch. By the hand of Elijah, the call to the prophetic office comes to Elisha. God has a work for every man to do, and a man for every work which he designs to accomplish by human instrumentality. When the time was come that the children of Israel should be freed from bondage, the man who, above all others, was competent to lead them was found in the person of Moses.

When the Gospel was to be carried for the first time to the gentile world, Paul, whose mental endowments, whose zeal and energy marked him as the man of his generation best fitted for the work, is impressed into the Lord's service. When the reformation was to be ushered in, when the dark cloud of ignorance, superstition, and prejudice which for centuries had hidden the Son of Righteousness from the minds and hearts of men, was to be riven asunder, Luther is at hand, a man whose equal for the great work to be performed not all the generations from that of Paul to his own had produced. Elijah's glorious ministry must end, but the accomplishment of God's purposes, and the welfare of God's people demanded that the exercise of the prophetic office should not cease. God had a work to be done, and he found the man to do it in the person of Elisha. God's work must go on, and while he may employ human agency in accomplishing it, he is in no sense dependent upon any man. As one falls at the post of duty, another is found to take his place and carry on the work. God takes care that there shall be no break in the line of succession of those who do service to him. Moses is not called to Pisgah's summit, until Joshua is prepared to take his place as leader of the people. Stephen is stoned to death, but the young man, Saul, at whose feet the witnesses laid down their clothes, is already partially prepared to take up the work which the first of Christian martyrs has laid down. Elijah may be nearing the close of his ministry, but Elisha is in training to succeed him. Elisha was called to a special work. While he was to be the successor of Elijah, his mission was different in many essential features from that of his stern predecessor. Elijah was pre-eminently an exponent of the terrors of the law. He was the rod in Jehovah's hand for the punishment of sin. God spoke by him in the sudden and condign punishment which he visited upon the wicked, and the people, from the king upon the throne to the humblest subject, must have learned to fear him. But we see in Elisha more of the characteristics of the evangelist. He came to cultivate and to reap that which Elijah had sown, to reveal the forgiving love of God to those who had been aroused by the thunders of the law. For such a work, he was fitted intellectually and spiritually, as his predecessor was for the sterner, yet not less important, work which had been given him to do. Elijah appears as the prototype of John the Baptist; while Elisha, of gentler spirit and kindlier deeds, reminds us of him of whom it is recorded that he "went about doing good." "Elisha rose upon his people like a serene and placid moon, bearing only gentleness and peace, after the majestic setting of that glittering and burning meteor, which had shone upon Israel in Elijah. His was not the dazzling and destructive glare of the lightning; it refreshed and gladdened all whom it reached." (Krummacher.) That the work of one of these two great prophets was more glorious or more important than that of the other, it seems to me ought not to be affirmed. It was as important that the people should hear the thunders of the law, as that they should be wooed by the gentle voice of love. There are those who insist that the Christian minister ought to preach a gospel of love only, but God has provided that men should be warned to flee from wrath to come, not less faithfully than they are told that God is love. The time was propitious for the performance of the service to which Elisha was called. It was, comparatively speaking, a period of peace. The minds of the people were free from the distractions which war brings and, to such an extent at least, open to receive the truth which the Prophet was sent to teach. Is it too much to affirm that every man is born into the world at the time and in the circumstances which are most favorable to the accomplishment of the work which God has for him to do? I love to think that I live in an age in which it is possible for me to serve God better than I could have done in any previous age; better than I could do in future ages. The prophetic office was not sought by Elisha. In this case the true order obtained, the office sought the man rather than the man the office. It would seem sometimes as though God acted in an arbitrary and capricious manner in selecting those who are to be employed as instruments in the accomplishment of his purposes. Elijah was not told why he was to anoint Hazeal to be king of Syria and Jehu to be king of Israel. We see, however, in the light of subsequent events, that these men were eminently fitted to be the rod in God's hand for the punishment of Israel and the wicked house of Ahab. God's choice of men and means is always governed, "by deep and sufficient reasons though we may not be able to discover them." Perhaps nothing was farther from the mind of Elisha, as he followed the plow that day, than the thought that the prophet's mantle should fall upon him. Yet God made no mistake when he said to Elijah, "anoint Elisha to be prophet in thy room." By mental and spiritual endowments, and the judicious and patient instruction of god-fearing parents he was fitted to adorn the high office to which he was called. So it has ever been, the Lord calls those to serve him who are fitted for his service. Sometimes the needed preparation comes through the gentle and hallowed influences of a Christian home, as in the case of Elisha; sometimes it comes through trials and afflictions. "Whom the Lord loveth he chasteneth, and scourgeth every son whom he receiveth." Perhaps no two persons are called of God in precisely the same manner, for the reason that no two persons are precisely alike in mental temperament and conformation of brain. Yet I believe it to be incontrovertible that every man who has accomplished any great and permanent work for God and humanity has been more or less deeply impressed with the conviction that he was Divinely called to such work. It was this conviction which impelled Paul to say, "Necessity is laid upon me; yea, woe is unto me, if I preach not the gospel." It is with such conviction that the missionary of the cross goes to the most distant lands, to the most inhospitable climes, and among the most degraded and savage people. Every true reform has had its origin in such conviction. God's call came to Elisha while he was engaged in the performance of his duties, he was following the plow and directing the labors of his servants who were engaged with him in tilling the soil. God has set the stamp of his approval upon honest industry. Even in a state of innocence, the first of men was put "into the garden of Eden to dress it and to keep it." And the Divine decree is, "The hand of the diligent shall bear rule; but the slothful shall be under tribute." Idle men are never called into God's service. The man who is too indolent to earn an honest living, to win success in a secular calling, cannot be a profitable servant to the Lord. The Devil secures his servants from the great army of idlers, but when God would call a man to do a great and noble work, he seeks him among those who have something to do in life, and who are willing to do it. "Gideon was found by the angel at his threshing-floor, when he was made the leader of his people against their Midianite oppressors. David was sent for from following the sheep in the fields of Bethlehem to receive the anointing oil from Samuel's horn. Amos was taken from tending his herd at Tekoah, when he was sent to Israel with a message from the Lord." (Dr. W. M. Taylor, in Elijah the Prophet.) Peter and Andrew were casting their net into the sea, James and John were mending their nets, and Matthew was sitting at the receipt of custom, when Jesus called to follow him. The call which came to Elisha was a call to promotion. He had proved himself faithful and efficient in the obscure position which he had hitherto occupied, now God calls him to a position of prominence and honor. We sometimes grow restive, and aspire to promotion for which we have not proved ourselves fitted. Others are called to positions of prominence and responsibility, and we ask ourselves the question, why should not we receive such recognition? Let us remember that it is to those only who have been faithful over a few things, that God says, "I will make thee ruler over many things." If, in a humble position, we have not shown a capacity to attend to the King's business, will he advance us to a more important station? Elisha's response to God's call was prompt. He does not ask that he be permitted to tarry until he has finished plowing his field and sowing the seed upon it, but he immediately leaves all, and runs after the Prophet. His only request is that he be permitted to kiss his father and mother, a request which is not denied him. With a like promptness should men respond to the gospel call.

Christ says, "Follow me." But multitudes reply, "At a more convenient season, I shall obey thy call. After I have made a fortune; after I have enjoyed the pleasures of the world a little longer, I shall follow thee." And with such promises, multitudes in every generation have paved the way to eternal death. But Elisha's response to the Divine call was not less decisive than prompt. His decision was final and unqualified. Henceforth he is to devote himself to his sacred calling, renouncing all secular employment. In token of this he slays a yoke of oxen, probably the one which he himself had been driving, and, boiling their flesh upon a fire made of the plows and yokes which he had been using, gave a farewell feast to his friends and neighbors. The bridges are burned behind him. No more is he to return to the former life. O, that the Christian of to-day were thus wholly separated from the world, and consecrated to the Master! Though Elisha must have recognized the call to the prophetic office as a promotion, he could not be insensible to the fact that to obey this call involved a great sacrifice on his part. To become the follower of Elijah, he must bid farewell to his beloved parents, turn his back upon the dear home of his childhood, endure hardships and privations, and encounter the malignant hatred and persecution of an idolatrous court. Our Lord says, "Whosoever doth not bear his cross, and come after me, cannot be my disciple." To each one of us Jesus says, as he said to Simon Peter, "Lovest thou me more than these?" And, if we are his, we shall answer, "Yea Lord," and by our lives, wholly consecrated to him, demonstrate the sincerity of our profession.

"Once to every man and nation comes the moment to decide,
In the strife of Truth with Falsehood, for the good or evil side;
Some great cause, God's new Messiah, offering each the bloom or blight,
Parts the goats upon the left hand, and the sheep upon the right:—
And the choice goes by forever, 'twixt that darkness and that light." (James Russell Lowell.)

## CHAPTER II.

### THE LAST JOURNEY WITH ELIJAH.

"Down in the valley with the Savior I would go,
Where the flowers are blooming and the sweet waters flow;
Everywhere he leads me I would follow, follow on,
Walking in his foot-steps till the crown be won.

Down in the valley with my Savior I would go,
Where the storms are sweeping and the dark waters flow;
With his hand to lead me I will never, never fear,
Dangers cannot fright me if my Lord is near.

Down in the valley or upon the mountain steep,
Close beside my Savior would my soul ever keep,
He will lead me safely in the path that he has trod
Up to where they gather on the hills of God."

(W. O. Cushing.)

PERHAPS ten years had passed since that memorable day on which Elijah the Prophet had cast his mantle upon the young plow-man of Abel-meholah. To Elisha they had been years of humble service, as seems evident from the language of II Kings 3:11, which describes his as the one who "poured water on the hands of Elijah." Although a servant, in that he thus ministered, he was more truly the disciple and companion of his illustrious master. To sustain such a relation to Elijah as is described in these words of the servant of the king of Israel, would not be considered undignified in Elisha. To the contrary, it would be esteemed an honor to be permitted to perform the light servile duties pertaining to such a position. Of the two men Elisha must have been much the younger. Without the light of any positive evidence upon the subject, it is generally supposed that his earlier advantages were superior to those of Elijah. The one brief view which we get of his childhood home gives the impression that his parents were in comfortable circumstances, if not affluent. That Elijah should be regarded as of humble origin, is due, possibly, to the fact that he was dependent, for a season, upon the food furnished by the ravens, and upon the widow's handful of meal and all but exhausted cruse of oil for his daily bread. But God sometimes requires his servants to make social and financial sacrifices in order that they may serve him. This was true of Paul the Apostle. While it cannot be affirmed with entire certainty that he was born and reared in opulent circumstances, we are made acquainted with certain facts which afford presumptive evidence of this. His father, though a Jew by birth, was a Roman citizen. This distinction might have been conferred gratuitously upon him by the proper authority; but in ordinary circumstances it was purchased by the payment of a large sum of money. The strong prejudice against the Jew renders it highly improbable that the father of Paul obtained the coveted prize of citizenship without paying the price thereof. Whether the parents of the Apostle were wealthy or not, he seems to have enjoyed more than ordinary advantages, and to have occupied a high social position. Yet, as the one whom God chose to send to the Gentiles, he was called to sacrifice the social standing which he enjoyed among his fellow-countrymen, to suffer ostracism, and the loss of earthly possessions. Though he may have been nourished in the lap of luxury he was made to suffer, at times, from lack of the bare necessities of life. In declaring to the Corinthians the things which he had been called to endure as the herald of the Gospel, he adds these words, "In weariness and painfulness, in watchings often, in hunger and thirst, in fastings often, in cold and nakedness." There are scores of men in the Christian ministry today, living upon meager salaries, who are conscious that they possess the ability to acquire wealth and honor, had they chosen another calling. Many, indeed, have given up honorable and lucrative positions to enter the ministry. Many have separated from kindred and friends, have left home and native land, and have sought the most distant and inhospitable shores, that they might be heralds of the Gospel to degraded and, in many respects, repulsive peoples.

The attention of the Christian world has been turned to Miss Annie Taylor, a Presbyterian missionary to Thibet. Wealthy and cultivated, she decided, in spite of the opposition of her friends, to give herself to mission work. She studied medicine, and worked as a nurse in a hospital, to prepare herself for her work. She likewise acquired a knowledge of dentistry. Largely at her own expense, she went to China, assumed native costume, settled on the borders of Thibet, and began to learn the language of that fierce people, among whom Christian missionaries have not yet obtained a foothold. Having thoroughly prepared herself, she made an entrance into the country, and has lived there for some time. She has been exposed to the most terrible dangers but the people have spared a woman where they would not have spared a man. Several times the chiefs have tried to poison her. She was made a prisoner. She was exposed, unprotected, to rain and snow and intense cold, sometimes sleeping at night in a hole dug in the ground. Of a similar character has been the experience of many others who have chosen "rather to suffer affliction with the people of God, than to enjoy the pleasures of sin for a season."

The fact that Elijah seems to have been homeless, and, at times, destitute of the necessities of life during the period of his prophetic service is not sufficient to justify the assumption that he was of humble origin. We do not know but that he was required to make great sacrifices that in exeperience and character he might approach the nearer to him who, though he was rich, yet for our sakes became poor, that we through his poverty might be rich. Who, though he was Lord of heaven and earth, must say, "Foxes have holes and birds of the air have nests; but the Son of Man hath not where to lay his head." Their peculiar and prolonged association together, developed between Elijah and Elisha a friendship of the deepest and the purest character. But the hour of their separation has come, even as it must come to all earthly friends. God has revealed his purpose to receive Elijah into glory. Whether this revelation was made directly to each or to Elijah only and through him to Elisha, the record does not enable us to say. Neither is it certain that they were informed as to the place of separation, or the manner in which it was to be effected. With that same fearless courage which has characterized every act of his public life, save one, Elijah begins to set his house in order. He was now at Gilgal. From this place, the location of which is unknown, God sent him to Bethel, the ecclesiastical or religious center of the ten tribes. It is probable that it was not until they had arrived at Bethel that the Lord directed Elijah to go to Jericho; and when they had reached this city he received further direction to cross the Jordan. Step by step the Lord directs his servants, as each act of service is accomplished, revealing to them some new duty to be performed. Before beginning this last journey, and as he comes to enter upon each successive stage thereof, Elijah earnestly entreats Elisha to tarry behind. But as often as this strange request is pressed, it is resolutely refused. Was it the desire to spend the last hours of his earthly pilgrimage alone with God that led Elijah to make this request? Such may have been the case. Dr. W. M. Taylor observes, "We know that extreme agony or great anxiety produces in the soul this longing for solitude, and it may be that at the other end of the scale this same law holds good, and that the highest raptures of triumph isolate a man from others as really as do the deepest trials." To me, however, it is pleasing to think that the attachment which bound together these two servants of the Lord was mutual; that the thought of separation was not more painful to the one than to the other; that the desire of Elisha to be permitted to remain with his master till the final moment arrived in which he should bid adieu to earth, was not more intense than the desire which Elijah cherished that his companion, and Divinely appointed successor should not leave him alone in that supreme moment. It is recorded that because of the statements which our Lord made upon a certain occasion, "Many of his disciples went back and walked no more with him." As these disaffected followers were withdrawing with many and loud protestations of disapproval, Jesus turned to the twelve and said, "Will ye also go away?" This question was not asked because the master doubted the love of his chosen apostles, "for he knew what was in man," knew the answer which his question would elicit. The design was simply to prove them; to give them another opportunity to think seriously, to count the cost of adhering to him when others were deserting him. Not only so, but in such an hour the heart of Jesus must have yearned for some expression of love, of sympathy, of attachment. And in that marvelous answer of Peter, "Lord to whom shall we go? thou hast the words of eternal life. And we believe and are sure that thou art that Christ, the Son of the living God," he must have found needed comfort and encouragement. In like manner the request that Elisha should tarry behind, was designed to test him, to prove his attachment to Elijah, to reveal what manner of spirit he was of. It gave him an opportunity to decide whether he would go with Elijah or, consulting his own ease and comfort, remain where he was. It demonstrated that he was meet to enjoy the distinguishing privilege of witnessing the glorious departure of his master from earth. "It is not every one who has the spiritual meetness for being a witness of sacred scenes. Jesus took only Peter, James, and John with him to the Mount of Transfiguration, into the house of Jairus, and into the recesses of Gethsemane." (Dr. J. Orr, in Pulpit Commentary.) Elisha was now about to succeed to a position of the highest honor and of the greatest responsibility, and God submits him to this final test. Not every one who professes a willingness to serve the Lord is fitted for every kind of service. God sometimes has special work to be performed which requires special qualifications in his servants. When God would smite the Midianite hosts which had invaded the land of Israel, not one in ten of the thirty-two thousand who responded to the call of Gideon had the courage and faith which would warrant his retention among those by whom the victory was to be won. Gideon is directed to say in the hearing of all, "Whosoever is fearful and afraid, let him return and depart early from Mount Gilead." when twenty-two thousand withdraw, thus confessing their fear, their lack of faith in God, and revealing their unfitness for the special service which God required.

It was a wearisome journey that lay before Elijah, but Elisha was willing to share its hardship if, by so doing, he might prolong for a few hours that intercourse which had proved so delightful and helpful to him. The nearer the hour of separation came, the more precious seemed the society of his master; and with all the earnestness of his nature he protested against the thought of tarrying behind while that master journeyed from place to place. "As the Lord liveth, and as thy soul liveth, I will not leave thee." This vehement language of Elisha recalls to mind the story of Naomi and Ruth. After a long sojourn in the land of Moab, during which she is bereaved of husband and sons, Naomi determins to return to her kindred in her native land. As she sets forth upon the journey she is accompanied by her two daughters-in-law, Orpah and Ruth. In the same spirit in which Elijah urged that Elisha should not accompany him on his last journey, she advises them to return to their own people. Orpah is persuaded, fondly kisses her mother-in-law and turns back, doubtless to spend the remainder of her days and to die under the blighting and destroying influences of heathen idolatry. But Ruth answers, "Entreat me not to leave thee, or to return from following after thee: for whither thou goest, I will go; and where thou lodgest, I will lodge: thy people shall be my people, and thy God my God. Where thou diest, will I die, and there will I be buried: the Lord do so to me, and more also, if ought but death part thee and me." It was not in the spirit of disobedience, of revolt against the authority which he had recognized for years, that Elisha refused to accede to the request of his master. His language is the expression of the most intense and abiding love. The sacred historian doubtless gives us but an epitome of the conversation which passed between Elijah and Elisha upon this occasion. Reasons would be assigned why Elisha should forbear to accompany his master. It might have been urged that the journey was long and tiresome; that he had no duties which called him to any of the places to be visited. But Elisha will not be diverted from his purpose. In spite of all entreaty, he persists in sayiny, "I will not leave thee." No consideration could induce him to consent to a separation so long as his master remained upon earth. Last things are usually most precious to us, and make the most permanent impression upon memory. The last words of friends whom we have left behind or who have gone before us to the heavenly home are enshrined among the most sacred treasures of memory. The last moments of the earthly life of one whom we love, may be unspeakably sad, but they are not less precious to us. Then, as never before, we come to know how much that life has been to us, how much it has contributed to our happiness and joy, how great the loss which we sustain in its taking away. It was not rebellion against the manifest will of God, but the remembrance of that happy and blessed friendship which he had known in past days, and the thought of a future which seemed dark and cheerless, in prospect of the separation at hand, which led Elisha to persist in saying, "I will not leave thee."

To his disciples whose hearts were filled with sorrow by his announcement that he was to leave them, to return to the Father, our Lord said, "Nevertheless, I tell you the truth; it is expedient for you that I go away; for if I go not away, the Comforter will not come unto you; but if I depart I will send him unto you." To the disciples it seemed an irreparable loss that the Master should leave them. The three years which they had spent as his disciples had developed a sense of dependence upon him, and evoked the profoundest love and admiration for him. He had not only been their teacher, but their protector, their defender, as well. When assailed by the Pharisees and scribes with questions which they were not able to answer, he had answered for them, and had put to silence their accusers. A feeling approaching to despair must have taken possession of them when he told them that he was soon to leave them. But subsequent experience convinced the disciples that the Master's words were true, that it was best for them that he should go away. It was not until the promised Comforter came that they were endued with power from on high, and thus fitted to do the Master's service. That Elisha might enter upon that long and glorious service for which God had raised him up, it was expedient that his master, Elijah, whose earthly mission had been fulfilled, should be taken from him. Elisha could not receive a double portion of his master's spirit until that separation should take place. In refusing to consent to it, he was rejecting the greater for the lesser blessing. That he might lead them into a richer and fuller Christian experience, into enlarged fields of service, the loving heavenly Father has removed from many of his dear children those whom they have most loved and cherished. It is our privilege, it is our duty, to pray for the recovery of those who are sick, but we should guard against falling into the sin of dictating to God. Our desires must be made subordinate to the Divine will. We are ignorant, and consequently liable to fall into error. Especially are we ignorant of the future. We know not what a day may bring forth. It is impossible for us to lift the veil that hides the future, to see what lies beyond the narrow present to which we are shut up. Hence it may be that when we ask God to spare those to whom death seems imminent, we crave a curse rather than a blessing. While we are ignorant, and know not what to pray for as we ought, God is infinite in knowledge and in goodness. He declares the end from the beginning, and doeth all things well. O, that we might learn to trust him more fully, and in every circumstance of life, seek for grace to say, "Thy will, not mine, be done." Many times God's ways seem mysterious to us, but he who has been made an heir of God, a joint-heir with Jesus Christ, is ever ready to say; "Though he slay me, yet will I trust him." To such an one the words of Jesus to Peter are a source of enduring comfort, "What I do thou knowest not now, but thou shalt know hereafter." As they journeyed to the place of their final separation, in time, Elijah and Elisha trod historic ground and looked upon scenes and objects which might have reminded them of many of the most sublime and important events in the history of the chosen people. It was at Gilgal, the point of departure, that Israel, preceded by the ark of the covenant, had crossed the Jordan dry-shod. Here might be seen the twelve stones, placed as a memorial of the marvelous power and favor of God, which was manifested in dividing the swollen floods that the people might pass through them. It was while he lay asleep at Beth-el, with stones of the place for his pillow, that Jacob dreamed of that wonderful ladder reaching from earth to heaven. Upon the site of the city of Jericho which they visited, had stood the ancient Jericho whose walls had crumbled and fallen after the army of Israel had marched around them thirteen times, according to the Divine direction.

It seems unnatural to suppose, as some eminent writers have done, that the two prophets observed a solemn silence as they journeyed. The last moments of the earthly life of our Lord were spent in instructing and directing his disciples, and his hands were lifted up to bless them when he was parted from them. So, doubtless, these last moments of Elijah were spent in comforting and counseling his successor, in exhorting him to faithfulness, and in answering the many earnest questions with which he pressed him. At Beth-el, and again at Jericho, the sons of the prophets, who had been apprised of the great event so near at hand, came forth to meet them. It was doubtless after greeting Elijah, and receiving a kind salutation from him, a parting word of counsel and exhortation, that they whisperingly inquired of Elisha if he was aware that the Lord was to take away his master from his head that day. Their question seems to have been prompted by that morbid desire to communicate bad news, by a disposition to pry into that which did not strictly belong to them. Illustrations of this are not wanting in our day. It was displeasing to Elisha to be approached in such a manner, and especially so, at such a time, and he rebukes his inquisitors, saying, "Yea, I know it; hold ye your peace." But the end of this remarkable journey draws near. The feet of the prophets have touched the brink of the swiftly flowing Jordan. Still the word of Divine command is, forward, and they hesitate not a moment in obeying. Undismayed by the apparent impossibility of obeying such a requirement, Elijah takes his mantle, wraps it together, and with it smites the waters, when, lo, they are divided hither and thither, and they two pass over on dry ground. O, the mighty power of faith! By it the arm of Omnipotence becomes our ally. Our Lord said to his disciples, "If ye have faith as a grain of mustard seed, ye shall say unto this mountain, Remove hence to yonder place; and it shall remove; and nothing shall be impossible unto you." "In the most deeply solemn sense we all must stand by the brink of Jordan. Have we the mantle of Elijah wherewith to divide the waters? Can we pass over dry-shod? In that hour, be it ours to remember that the Lord is nigh unto all such as call upon him, to such as call upon him in truth." (Edersheim.)

## CHAPTER III.

### ELISHA'S REQUEST.

"No man is born into the world whose work
Is not born with him; there is always work,
And tools to work withal, for those who will,
And blessed are the horny hands of toil."

ELIJAH and Elisha now stood upon the eastern bank of the Jordan. Those waters, which for the second time had felt a grasp mightier than that of natural law, had resumed their flow to the sea. Conscious that but a few moments of time remained to him, Elijah invited his companion, who had now demonstrated his fitness to succeed him in the prophetic office, to ask what he should do for him before he should be taken away from him. It was the moment, it would seem, for which Elisha had waited. With a promptness which suggests premeditation, he prefers a request which his master had not anticipated and for which he was not prepared. No limitation was placed upon Elisha's asking, yet we are sure that Elijah was free from every feeling of arrogance in the matter. He did not claim to be possessed of infinite power. When the two sons of Zebedee came to our Lord with the request that they might be permitted to sit, one on his right hand, and the other on his left hand, in his glory, he declared that it was not his to give. So Elijah felt with reference to the request of Elisha. Had that request been for any of his personal effects, such as his miracle-working mantle, or for a parting benediction, he would have complied with it at once, but it was for that which he felt it was not his to give, and he leaves it for God to decide how it shall be. "If thou see me when I am taken from thee, it shall be so unto thee; but if not, it shall not be so." We shall find much to interest and to instruct us, if we consider the nature and motive of Elisha's request, "Let a double portion of thy spirit be upon me." Evidently he refers to the Holy Spirit by whom Elijah was so richly endowed. The third person of the Holy Trinity is designated in the Scriptures by various names. He is called the Spirit of God; the Spirit of Jehovah; the Spirit of your Father; the Spirit of his Son; the Spirit of truth; the Holy Spirit; the Comforter. Elisha says, "thy spirit," meaning the spirit by which Elijah was possessed, by which his thoughts, words, and acts were controlled, even the Spirit of God. The Old Testament Scriptures do not give that prominence to the personality and work of the Holy Spirit which is accorded by our Lord and his apostles, yet the prophets, the sacred historians, and psalmists are not silent with reference to this important subject.

The Spirit's agency in the work of creation is recognized when in the second verse of the first chapter of Genesis it is said, "The Spirit of God moved upon the face of the waters." And Job says, "By his Spirit he hath garnished the heavens." The Spirit's work of striving with men, of persuading and enabling them to do right, is set forth when it is said, in Genesis 6:3, "My Spirit shall not always strive with man." Elisha's long association with Elijah, as servant and companion, had enlarged his knowledge of the Spirit, and had impressed upon his mind this truth, that to be God's servant in the fullest and most precious sense of the term, we must be possessed by the Spirit of God. Hence his request that a double portion of the spirit of Elijah, that same Spirit which had made Elijah all that he was, which had endued him with wisdom and courage for the great work which it was his glory to accomplish, might be upon him.

Elisha did not ask for a two-fold measure of the spiritual power by his master, that he might be so much greater than he, but that he might be dealt with according to the law which provided that the eldest son should be allowed a double portion of his father's estate. In the schools of the prophets, some of which he may have established, all of which he had fostered and developed, Elijah had many spiritual sons. To these he had communicated rare and precious blessings as he had taught them by precept and example. To each he had given a final portion, as in that last interview he had spoken to them of things eternal, had exhorted them to be faithful and zealous in God's service, and had breathed upon them his parting benediction. Elisha did not undervalue the legacy thus left to his brethren, yet he is moved to ask that his portion shall be twice as great as theirs. What induced Elisha to prefer such a request as this? What was the motive which lay back of it? If he had no worldly ambition to gratify, why did he not ask that he might be permitted to share in the glory of his master's translation? That, since they had been so long and intimately and lovingly associated in the Lord's work, they might not now be separated. It has been the feeling of many hearts, as the eyes of loved ones have closed in the sleep of death, that it would be a blessed privilege to depart with those loved ones. To many of us the thought has come, what a joy it would be to quit this world of sorrow and disappointment, of toil and conflict, and to enter into the rest and peace of heaven with those who have gone before. But Elisha was persuaded that God had a great work for him to do upon the earth. Doubtless he had been apprised of the fact that he was to be the successor of Elijah, and although, like the Apostle Paul, he may have had "a desire to depart" he was willing to abide in the flesh, as being more needful to the cause of true religion in the earth. But the thought of the vast responsibilities which were to rest upon him so soon must have occurred to him. As the successor of his master he was to take up the work which he laid down, to bear aloft the banner of truth. At the same time a consciousness of his own weakness could scarcely have been wanting in him. Though he must have recognized that the years which he had spent with Elijah were years of preparation for the exercise of the prophetic office, yet, doubtless, during all these years he had been cultivating a feeling of dependence upon him. Now he was to be deprived of that strong arm upon which he had leaned, and, humanly speaking, to be thrown upon his own resources. It would seem, indeed, as though he were shut up to this one request, as though no other desire ought to find a place in his heart than that a double portion of the Holy Spirit might rest upon him.

He was not only conscious of the magnitude of the duties before him, and impressed with a sense of his inability to meet the great responsibilities which were to fall to him, but at the same time he was inspired with a high and holy ambition to be an efficient servant of God; to be the honored instrument in God's hand of bringing many souls into glory. Hence the request, "let a double portion of thy spirit be upon me." Not in any spirit of selfishness does he crave this; not that his fame shall be greater and more lasting than that of his brethren, but that God's glory may be advanced. Solomon, when he came to the throne of Israel, asked not for riches, or honor, or long life, but for wisdom to administer his kingly office. So Elisha asks for that only which will fit him for the service to which he has been called. As the professed servants of the Lord; as parents, charged with the duty of training, in the nuture and admonition of the Lord, the children who have been given to us; as members of the church, as office-bearers in the church; as teachers in the Sabbath School; as citizens of the state, we are confronted by duties, in view of which we may well exclaim in the language of the Apostle, "Who is sufficient for these things," and for the performance of which we do well to seek a double portion of the Holy Spirit. What Elisha felt he needed for the great work which had been given him to do, God's servants need today, if the honor of his name is to be maintained, and his kingdom built up and established in the earth. To combat and to overcome the forces of skepticism, rationalism, and infidelity; to liberate mankind from the bondage of ignorance, prejudice, and mammon; to drive dishonesty and fraud from the marts of commerce, from legislative halls and courts of justice; to bring to naught the machinations of anti-christ; to defend the home against the attacks of intemperance and impurity; to disarm the red hand of socialism and anarchy which is lifted up against the state; to preach the gospel to every creature under heaven, is the mission of those who are upon the Lord's side. For such a work they need much of the spirit of Elijah; the spirit of devotion to the truth as it is in Christ, the spirit of fidelity to duty, the spirit of courage and fearlessness in the presence of opposition and danger, the spirit of love for God and for all men. We must commend the wisdom of Elisha's request. Few of us, if placed in similar circumstances, would choose so wisely as he. It is evident, however, that he had yet to learn that God is the only source of spiritual power; that no mere man, not even excepting Elijah, has the power to bestow spiritual blessings. This truth has been more fully revealed to us than it was to Elisha, yet do we not often fall into the same error with which he seems justly chargeable at this time? Many persons seem to think that the pastor by his faithfulness and zeal, will in some way make atonement for their neglect of the means of grace. It seems to be the feeling of many that when a pastor has been settled in a congregation, all personal activity on the part of the individual member may be dispensed with. Let us remember that while men may help us in seeking after spiritual blessings, God alone is the source of such blessings. The minister can bless us only in the way of becoming the instrument in God's hand in leading us to the fountain of blessing. Not only has God revealed to us the truth that he only has power to bestow spiritual blessings, but he holds out to us every encouragement to come to him, that we may receive of him. How full and free are his invitations thus to come! By the mouth of the Prophet he says, "Look unto me, and be ye saved, all the ends of the earth; for I am God and there is none else." And our Lord's words are, "Whatsoever ye shall ask in my name, that will I do." Again he says, "Ask, and it shall be given you; seek, and ye shall find; knock, and it shall be opened unto you: for every one that asketh receiveth; and he that seeketh findeth; and to him that knocketh it shall be opened."

As Elijah invited the son of Shaphat to ask what he should do for him; so God invites you and me to ask what he shall do for us. Elijah was obliged to confess his inability to bestow the blessing for which he was asked. Though one of the greatest of the Prophets, his power to bless was limited; but God is possessed of infinite power, and is more willing to give good things to them that ask him, than human parents are to give good gifts to their children. O, that we may be divinely taught to covet the best gifts, and by prayer, which of all things human, comes nearest to being omnipotent, to seek them from our heavenly Father's hand. Elisha made his request boldly. There was no fear in his heart as he announced his desire. Why should there be, since he had been invited to say what should be done for him. So the child of God is encouraged to come boldly unto the throne of grace, that he may obtain mercy, "and find grace to help in time of need." Elisha makes his request with the confidence of that faith which "believeth all things, hopeth all things." He seems to have felt assured that his master was able and willing to do all that he desired him to do. In the exercise of a like implicit faith, the Christian is to ask of God "who giveth to all men liberally and upbraideth not." This is the promise of the Master, "All things, whatsoever ye shall ask in prayer, believing, ye shall receive." The granting of Elisha's request was made contingent upon his seeing Elijah when he should be taken from him. "If thou see me when I am taken from thee, it shall be so unto thee; but if not, it shall not be so." This should be not only a token that his request had met with Divine approval, but evidence that his spiritual attainments were already of a high order, if, indeed, he was not even now in possession of the blessing which he craved. The Apostle John says, "If we know that he hear us, whatsoever we ask, we know that we have the petitions that we desired of him." To behold that splendid pageant, the chariot of Israel, and the horsemen thereof, and his beloved master who, "in a moment, in the twinkling of an eye," had been changed, had laid aside the image of the earthy, and assumed the image of the heavenly, required a degree of spiritual vision such as none then upon the earth, save Elisha, possessed.

Only the spiritually enlightened could behold such a vision. If, instead of standing to view afar off, the sons of the prophets had stood upon that now consecrated spot, Elijah would have vanished from their view, even as the risen Lord vanished out of the sight of the two disciples at Emmaus. Elisha saw Elijah, as, wrapt in glory, he was borne heavenward; and thus the token was given him that his request was granted. As to the manner in which the blessing which he sought was bestowed, the record is silent. May it not be that some measure of that blessing, at least, was found in the increase of faith in the unseen realities of a holier and happier state which the Prophet experienced in consequence of the vision which he was permitted to enjoy? How many are the instances in which the faith of God's children in the reality of heavenly things has been strengthened, as they have watched by the bedside of those who were entering into glory! A friend of mine, a prominent physician in one of our western cities, once told me this story. A young lady, of rare attainments in the Christian life, was smitten with that dread disease, pulmonary consumption. One evening he received a note from her stating that she desired to see him. He was surprised, as he had visited her during the day and had left her as comfortable as usual. but he hastened at once to her bedside. Fixing her eyes upon him, she said, "Doctor, do you think I am going to get well? I want to know just what you think." "No, Grace," he replied, "you can never be well. You can live but a few months at most. All the medical skill in the world could not save your life." "I thought as much," said she, "but I am perfectly satisfied." "Now, Doctor," she continued, "if you were in my place, and I in yours, and you were to ask me the question which I have asked you, and I should answer you as you have answered me, what would your feelings be? Do you feel that you would be ready to die?" It was the turning point in the Doctor's life. Though not an unbeliever he had never given himself to Christ. He confessed that he was not prepared to meet death, and kneeling by that bedside he sought and obtained forgiveness and acceptance through the blood of Jesus. When it was all settled, Grace said, "I have read that some persons when about to die, have been permitted to look into heaven, to behold its glories. Now I do not know how it will be with me, but I want you to be near me when the last moment comes, and if such a vision is granted me, I shall try to let you know it." It was agreed between them, that if she were too weak to speak, she should turn her eyes toward him if she saw anything of that which lies beyond. Weeks passed away, during which they held sweet counsel together. Slowly, but surely, the work of the destroyer progressed. As the end approached, the doctor spent much of his time in her company, and when the angels came to bear her to the fold on high, he was watching by her side. Suddenly opening wide her eyes, and lifting her hands, she whispered, "Beautiful! beautiful!" Then her eyes sought the doctor; she smiled faintly, and the spirit was gone. Since that moment, said my friend, I have felt perfectly assured that there is a heaven, for I know that Grace beheld its glories. Let us cultivate that faith which lays hold upon the things that are unseen and eternal. In so doing peace shall be multiplied unto us abundantly, and a double portion of spiritual power be given us for service. There is deep significance in the words of Elijah, "Ask what I shall do for thee before I am taken away from thee." Obviously he felt that it would be impossible for him to render any act of service, after his departure from earth. The word of God nowhere sanctions the practice of praying to departed saints; it affords us no warrant to believe that they are able, in any way, to help us. On the contrary, it teaches that a man's work on earth is forever ended when he is called hence. We need the counsel and the instruction of God's servants, but let us ask what they shall do for us before they are taken from us. If, on the other hand, we would render any service to our fellow-men, let us be up and doing, remembering that our Lord has said, "The night cometh, when no man can work."

# CHAPTER IV.

## ELISHA BEREFT.

"'Twas at high noon, the day serene and fair,
Mountains of lum'nous clouds rolled in the air,
When on a sudden, from the radiant skies,
Superior light flashed in Elisha's eyes;
The heavens were cleft, and from the imperial throne
A stream of glory, dazzling splendor shone:
Beams of ten thousand suns shot round about,
The sun and every blazoned cloud went out:
Bright hosts of angels lined the heavenly way,
To guard the saint up to eternal day."

(Benjamin Coleman.)

ELIJAH had given his prophetic response to the unexpected request of Elisha, and, while the angel messengers who were to bear him above tarried, the two prophets continued their journey, talking as they went. Very different must have been the thoughts and feelings of the master from those of the disciple in those solemn moments. In the case of the former there was the consciousness that life's work had been accomplished, that he was done forever with toil and conflict, with hardship and privation. He had the assurance of immediate and triumphant entrance into glory. The loss of earthly friends was to be compensated by fellowship with the saints, in the presence of God, amid the splendors of the heavenly home. In the case of the latter, the great responsibilities of the prophetic office were now to be assumed. Elisha doubtless realized that, as the servant of God, trials and persecutions awaited him. More absorbing, however, than any such considerations as these, would be the thought of the great bereavement which he was about to suffer in the taking away of his master. The time was all too short for the many questions which he had yet to ask Elijah, for receiving the counsel and instruction which he yet sought. Each succeeding moment seemed more precious than its predecessor as the words of comfort and encouragement fell upon his ears. But the "sharp decisive moment" comes at last, and the messengers of God are at hand. A chariot of fire, drawn by horses of fire, parts the two friends "asunder" and Elisha beholds his master carried, as by a whirlwind, into heaven. We should not fail to note the place of this separation. It may have been the summit of Pisgah, where five centuries before, Moses, the greatest of all the prophets, had stood to view the promised land ere he should be gathered unto his people. No intimation is given as to the direction in which the prophets journeyed after crossing the Jordan, nor of how long they continued the journey thereafter. If their course lay eastward, and this is not improbable, the mountains or hills would be reached in a short time. Strange coincidence, indeed, that from the same locality, at least, if not from the identical spot, Moses and Elijah should take their departure from earth; the one the representative of the law, the other of the prophets, and both to be honored by being permitted to reappear upon the earth, after the lapse of centuries, to stand beside the Redeemer in his transfiguration glory, the former a type of those who shall be raised from the dead at the coming of the Lord, the latter a type of those who being alive upon the earth at the day of his coming, shall be caught up to meet the Lord in the air. But aside from its historic character, that region east of the Jordan must have been peculiarly dear to the heart of Elijah, for he was a Tishbite. Amid those mountains of Gilead he had his birth; here he had been imbued with that bold and courageous spirit which so frequently distinguishes the mountaineer, and which, with one exception, characterized every act of his ministry. It may have been in answer to prayer that, here where his earthly life began in obscurity, it was to terminate in the glory of translation. The time of Elisha's bereavement was of Divine appointment. "When the Lord would take up Elijah into heaven." The Lord has fixed the limit of every human life. Every man's days are numbered, and the number can neither be increased nor diminished. God has a special purpose in calling each individual person into the world. To each one is assigned a work, for which he is specially fitted, and no man is taken out of the world until God's purposes concerning him have been accomplished; and, on the other hand, no man is left in the world longer than is necessary to accomplish God's purposes concerning him.

We sometimes find ourselves wondering why persons of prominence and usefulness are taken away, while others whose lives seem to be of little use at all, perhaps only a burden to themselves and to friends, are permitted to live. Yet God has a purpose in sparing the feeblest life, and, as we may think, the least useful life. We talk about accidental death. Our statistics deal largely with the subject. The causes of accidental death have been analyzed and classified, and statistics are gathered each year showing the number of deaths traceable to these various causes. Insurance companies are organized for the purpose of insuring their policy-holders against accident. But from God's point of view there are no accidents, no premature deaths. It matters not by what means a man is taken away; whether, like Elijah, he passes into the beyond without having tasted death; or yields to the destroyer after a lingering illness; whether he be smitten down by a murderous hand, or with his own hand sends the fatal bullet crashing through his own brain; it is God's time to remove him hence. We mourn the death of some men as untimely, and speak of them as taken away in the midst of their days, but as God sees, this is not true. By the Spirit Job is moved to ask this question, "Is there not an appointed time to man upon earth? Are not his days also like the days of an hireling?" and again he says, "Thine hands have made me and fashioned me, yet thou dost destroy me." In harmony with such statements are the words of the Psalmist, "Thou turnest man to destruction; and sayest, Return ye children of men." It is said that the ancient Turks believed that it was written on every man's forehead, at his birth, when he should die. Hence they exposed themselves recklessly to every danger in war, to the attack of every pestilence, and, in consequence, needlessly perished by thousands. If expostulated with, they would point to their foreheads in justification of what they did. Such belief we call fatalism. It must be distinguished clearly from that faith which accepts the teaching of the word of God that the life of every living thing is in the Lord's hands, that the time of a man's death is appointed of the Lord; yet, at the same time, recognizes the importance of the Divine command, "Thou shalt not kill," and the duty therein implied, namely, that we are to use all lawful means to protect and to preserve our own lives and the lives of others. "In the case of every man there is going on constantly a process of ripening, either for glory or for the shame of eternal punishment. The fruit will not fall till it is fully ripe. The patience and long-suffering of God waiteth till the measure is accomplished. There is a measure of wrath to be accomplished, or else a cup of blessing to be filled. Then cometh the translation, either upward to heaven, or downward to hell." (Edersheim.) What a deeply solemn thought that each moment of time as it passes, makes either for our eternal happiness, or our eternal woe. It is said that the Chinese have in their courts two great books, the one is called the book of life, the other is called the book of death. When a man is tried and found innocent, his name is written in the book of life, but if he is found guilty, his name is written in the book of death. We do not read in God's word of the book of death, but we do read of the book of life. Is it not a legitimate inference that if God keeps a book of life he must also keep a book of death in which to record those names which may not be written in the book of life? However this may be, the evidence is accumulating day by day which shall declare the justice of God in recording our names in the book of life or in refusing them a place there. Elisha's bereavement came not unexpectedly. He knew that the time was at hand when the Lord would take up his master. Every preparation for the great event had been made. The last duty with which the Lord had charged Elijah had been faithfully performed. For the last time he had visited the schools of the prophets, and had spoken his last words to the young men there in training for the great work of teaching the truths of revealed religion. Up to the last moment he had been diligent in redeeming the time. What a lesson these closing hours of the earthly life of the great prophet afford us! He seems to feel no anxiety, save to finish the work which had been given him to do. "When John Knox, the Elijah of Scotland, was on his death-bed, he said to those who stood around him, Serve the Lord with fear, and death shall not be terrible to you." All his days Elijah had lived near to God, and now when the hour of his departure had come, he had no fear. If, like Elijah, we would be ready when the Lord calls us to go hence, we must imitate him in improving the time. If we would spend our last hours peacefully, each day must be spent as though we knew it to be our last day upon earth. A lady once asked John Wesley how he would spend the day if he knew it would be his last day. She expected to receive some rules for pious meditation in preparation for death, but he replied, "Just as I expect to spend it madam." The best preparation for death is a constant living in the discharge of duty. "So long as God gives us health and strength to work for him, it is best to do as Elijah did, to live in the harness to the last moment."

Although apprised of the fact for days, perhaps weeks, beforehand, the moment of separation came suddenly to Elisha. Like a flash of lightning from a clear sky, the charioteers of heaven swept down upon the two prophets, even while they talked, and parted them asunder. No time to complete that half-uttered sentence, no time even to say farewell. Before Elisha has recovered from his consternation, his master has departed. More swiftly than speed the wings of the morning light, he mounts upward until lost to sight in the etherial blue.

"Servant of God, thy fight is fought;
Servant of God, thy crown is wrought;
Lingerest thou yet upon the joyless earth?
Thy place is now in heaven's high bowers,
Far from this mournful world of ours,
Among the sons of light, that have a different birth.

"Thy human task is ended now,
No more the lightning of thy brow
Shall wake strange terror in the soul of guilt;
As when thou wentest forth to fling
The curse upon the shuddering king,
Yet reeking with the blood, the sinless blood, he spilt.

"And all that thou hast braved and borne,
The heathen's hate, the heathen's scorn,
The wasting famine, and the galling chain,
Henceforth these things to thee shall seem
The phantoms of a by-gone dream;
And rest shall be for toil, and blessedness for pain."
(Winthrop Macworth Praed.)

How many sudden separations take place in the world every day. Perhaps in a majority of cases, death comes suddenly to men. How frequently we hear of the fond husband and father who, pleasantly taking leave of his loved ones as he goes to his business in the morning, is brought home a corpse before the day is done. Apoplexy, heart failure, explosion, collision, murder, are terms which occur with remarkable frequency in our mortuary reports. Every year flood and fire and tempest carry off their thousands, adding an awful emphasis to those words of the Savior, "Watch, therefore, for ye know neither the day nor the hour wherein the Son of Man cometh."

God is not limited as to the means to be employed in our translation from time to eternity. Elijah was taken up to heaven by a whirlwind. Never before nor since has any man quitted the shores of time in like manner. Those who are alive upon the earth at the coming of the Lord, are to be caught up to meet him in the air; but until that time, God has ordained that all must pass to the future world through the portal of death. From this decree there is no exemption. It is said of the great Cardinal Henry Beauford that he cried out upon his death-bed, "Why should I die, having such riches? If the whole realm would save my life, I am able by policy to get it, or riches to buy it. Will not death be hired, will money do nothing?" But death cannot be bribed to stay his stroke. Neither the time nor the method of his attack can be anticipated, nor is any armor sufficient to withstand his assault. He rides upon the storm-cloud, or steals upon his victim in the gentle zephyr which cools the feverish brow. The flaming thunderbolt and the invisible microbe are alike his messengers. Somtimes he resorts to siege, as it were, and succeeds in reducing the citadel of life only after long and painful sickness has wasted the vital forces. Again he executes a surprise movement by which the silver cord is suddenly severed, the golden bowl instantly broken. But whatever may be the manner of death, we may rest assured that it is Divinely chosen, and that it is the best suited to promote God's glory and the welfare of his children. Although for many days Elisha had been looking forward to this parting moment, he was not prepared for it when it came. "Trials are never really expected; the reality always takes us by surprise." (Edersheim.)

Stunned by the suddenness of his bereavement the Prophet is for the moment, speechless. Then, recovering himself, he cries, as with tear-dimmed eyes he gazes upon the rapidly vanishing form of his master, "My father, my father, the chariot of Israel, and the horsemen thereof." And as he came to realize more fully the loss which he had sustained; as that feeling of loneliness came over him, which none can know, save those who, like him, have been profoundly bereaved, "he took hold of his own clothes, and rent them in two pieces." This is one way in which the people of Oriental countries give expression to the feeling of indignation or grief. We may feel disposed to censure Elisha for the grief which he thus exhibits. If ever there was an instance in which grief over the taking of a person out of this world was uncalled for, it is to be found in the translation of Elijah. That he had entered into glory, Elisha could not doubt. Why then this great grief? The same question might be asked those who bathe with their tears the faces of loved ones who have fallen asleep in Jesus. Elisha mourned not for Elijah's sake, but for his own sake. There is much of truth in the oft repeated statement that a man's worth is never fully recognized until after his death. Elijah never was so great and good in Elisha's estimation as when he came to realize that he "should see his face no more." Our Lord's words, "Ye build the sepulchres of the prophets, and your fathers killed them," are as applicable to other generations, as to the Jews of his day. Many of the great reformers whose memory we delight to cherish, whose monuments adorn our parks and public squares, were hated, maligned, and mobbed while living. Not a few of those whose fame is immortal were persecuted even to death. Let us seek to appreciate the worth of our friends while they are living, nor wait until they are taken from us, to learn how good and kind they are, and how much they minister to our happiness and welfare. It will make our memory of them so much sweeter when they are gone. Elisha's cry was a lamentation. It seems to be the expression of a conviction that he had sustained an irreparable loss; that with Elijah the defense of Israel had vanished. Elisha seems to have felt that no one could fill the place left vacant in his own heart and life, and in the nation's life, by the taking away of his master. So it often is with us in the first moments of some great personal or national bereavement. When a friend in whom we have trusted, and upon whom we have depended, is taken from us; when some trusted leader in the councils of the church or of the state, falls by the hand of death, we are disposed to give way to despair; to forget that though human friends may be removed, and those who have proved themselves to be public benefactors fall at the post of duty, God still lives and reigns. The recognition of this truth brings comfort to the bereaved heart, dispels our doubts and fears, and imparts strength and courage. When the news of the assassination of President Lincoln was flashed over the wires, the hearts of loyal men and women were filled with consternation and forebodings of evil to come. The feeling seemed to prevail everywhere that there was no longer hope for the nation. "What next?" was the anxious inquiry of patriotic hearts. Amid the gloom of a nation's bereavement, a brave man who was himself to fall by the assassin's hand, and to be borne to the tomb amid the tears of the nation, stood upon an improvised platform in one of the great thoroughfares of our metropolis, and, lifting up his voice, cried to the almost frenzied multitudes which surged around him, "Fellow citizens, God reigns, and the government at Washington still lives." The effect was magical. The feeling of despair gave way to that of hope, and confidence in God. Brave men regained courage as they were led to reflect that he who controls the destiny of nations, as of men, still had his hand upon the helm. Let us, in the hour of bereavement, cherish, for our comfort and encouragement, the assurance, that he who hears the young ravens when they cry, who gives to the lily its beautiful dress, will provide all things necessary to the comfort and welfare of his children.

## CHAPTER V.

### THE FALLEN MANTLE TAKEN UP.

"The Prophet's mantle ere his flight began,
Dropped on the world, a sacred gift to man."
(Campbell.)

On the eve of his departure from Carthage to begin the conquest of Spain, Hamilcar, one of the greatest military geniuses of antiquity, led to the altar of sacrifice his son Hannibal, a child only nine years old, but whose fame was to surpass that of his illustrious father, and caused him to swear that he would be the implacable enemy of Rome. Hamilcar, in this manner, sought to perpetuate his own hatred of Rome; to provide that resistance to her rapacious designs should not cease with his death. In pronouncing the words of that solemn vow which his son was to take upon him, he bequeathed to him his purpose to destroy the powerful rival of his country which had grown up upon the banks of the Tiber. When one who has been distinguished for his public services, for his wisdom, his eloquence, his power, is removed by death or retires from active life, and another of equal or superior ability succeeds him, it is popularly said that the mantle of the former has fallen to the latter. This beautiful and expressive figure may have had its origin in this incident in the life of Elisha which we now consider. It might seem, at first thought, that the falling of the mantle of Elijah, as he began his heavenward ascent, was a trivial feature of that remarkable event. Yet it was not without its significance. It suggests that with our translation from time to eternity there comes deliverance from many of the needs and limitations which we experience in this life. Elijah no longer had need of the mantle which fell from him. Henceforth the glorious vesture of heaven was to be his. Of the inhabitants of that "better country, that is an heavenly," to which he was borne, the Apostle John in the Apocalypse declares, "They shall hunger no more, neither thirst any more; neither shall the sun light on them, nor any heat." Those ofttimes distressing problems which confront men in this life, "What shall we eat? or, What shall we drink? or, Wherewithal shall we be clothed?" cannot enter into the life beyond. As the mantle of Elijah fell from his shoulders, so the burden of care and perplexity must fall from our hearts and minds when this mortal shall put on immortality. Elijah, stripped of his mantle which descends to his successor, affords an illustration of Paul's words to Timothy, "We brought nothing into this world, and it is certain we can carry nothing out." However great the distinctions which appear among men with respect to worldly possessions, they vanish as the portal of death is entered. Though we should gain the world we can retain possession of it for but a few brief years at most. "Wise men die, likewise the fool and the brutish person perish, and leave their wealth to others." All that man can carry with him from time to eternity, is his character. In the light of such truth how significant those words of our Lord appear! "Labor not for the meat which perisheth, but for that meat which endureth unto everlasting life." The falling of the Prophet's mantle was likewise a symbol of his release from the responsibilities which had rested upon him. As we have already observed, the mantle was regarded as the insignia of office.

To most minds official position is attractive; yet, in many instances, it involves responsibilities of the gravest and most burdensome character. As the Lord's prophet, Elijah had been honored above all his contemporaries, but with the great honor which he enjoyed had come responsibilities which, in their magnitude, were sufficient to have crushed a less resolute spirit; and in the presence of which he well might have exclaimed, as did the Apostle of the Gentiles, "Who is sufficient for these things?" The period of his prophetic service was marked by the culmination of Israel's apostasy from the true religion. His mission was that of a reformer. He was sent to preach righteousness to the people whose moral and religious reformation seemed all but hopeless. The task set before him was that of winning Israel back to her allegiance to Jehovah, and, in this way, overthrowing the idolatrous practices which state-craft had introduced, and human depravity had nourished and developed. To the accomplishment of this mighty task he had devoted every energy of his being. Without reserve he had laid his life upon God's altar. From the inception to the close of his public life, he encountered the cruel hatred and the relentless opposition of the corrupt and the corrupting court of Samaria. But with undaunted courage, save upon one occasion, and with unflagging fidelity, he held his course. Whether, in the vehemence of his fiery and impetuous spirit, he flings "the gage of defiance" at the feet of the king and his idolatry-loving and blood-thirsty consort; or, by Divine direction, hides himself by the brook Cherith, to be fed by the ravens; meets the prophets of Baal and of the grove, before assembled Israel, in that momentous and sublime contest upon the heights of Carmel; flees for his life to the wilderness, where in the moments of weakness, discouragement, and despair, he makes request that he may die; wraps his face in his mantle while God is manifested to him in the "still small voice" in the cave before Horeb; pronounces judgment upon Ahab and his house for the murder and robbery of Naboth; or calls down fire from heaven to consume the captains with their fifties, sent to apprehend him, he is animated by the same high and holy purpose to be faithful to him who had called him, to meet his responsibilities to God and to his fellow-men. But as the mantle fell from his shoulders, his earthly responsibilities were terminated. From that warfare to which he had been called, and which he had conducted with such courage and fidelity, he was now discharged, and, at the same time, promoted to the rank and service of those who surround the throne that is set in heaven. As we view it, Elijah's ministry was not preeminently successful. He did not succeed in producing any marked reformation in the religious life of Israel. Despite his earnest and persistent efforts, idolatry continued to abound on every hand up to the day that the Lord took him to glory. And yet at no time does he seem to have felt that his labors were in vain. Not even when, in despair, he prays that his life may be taken away, does he utter a word of self-reproach. Conscious that he had performed his duty faithfully, he was satisfied; and God set his seal to his ministry in granting him a triumphant and glorious departure from earth. In the unprecedented honor bestowed upon him in his translation, God said to him, "Well done, good and faithful servant." Elijah sowed the seed, others reaped the harvest. We are too much given, perhaps, to estimate success by apparent results; and have need that this truth be more firmly pressed upon our hearts, that a life devoted to God must be a success, cannot be a failure. Let us seek to do our duty faithfully, in whatsoever sphere we may be called to labor, and God will take care of the results. The final moment must come to every child of God, even as it came to Elijah, when the mantle is to be laid aside. God has fixed a limit to the time during which the responsibilities of the life which now is, are to be borne. To those who are faithful to the charge which has been committed to them, this assurance brings comfort and joy. However burdensome may seem the demands which the Master makes, his words are, "Look up, and lift up your heads; for your redemption draweth nigh." As, in imagination, we behold the mantle of the Prophet wafted earthward from his flaming chariot, we are reminded of those who were, but are not; of those moments in which, with eyes dim with tears, we beheld the mantle fall from the shoulders of those whose care we were in infant days, who had been the guide of our youth, whose willing hands had provided for our comfort and safety. While we rejoice in the blessed assurance that their translation was their eternal gain, God's way of promoting them to immortal honors and glory, a feeling of sadness comes over us as we contemplate the empty chair, the silent corner, the vacant pew. If, in thought, we, who are comparatively young, turn to the neighborhood or community in which our childhood days were spent, we shall note the absence of many a familiar face. Those who were bearing the burden and heat of the day when children's toys and youthful sports claimed our attention have departed, one by one, for the other shore, until few are left to us. "The fathers where are they?" Many of them have put off the mantle to receive the crown, while those who remain are calmly waiting the coming of the chariots which are to bear them home. Soon the burdens of life must drop from their weary hands. As the mantle of Elijah, unclasped it may have been by the hands of an angel, fell at the feet of Elisha, he recognized it as a token that he was Divinely called to become the successor of his master. It was a symbol of his investure with prophetic authority and power. The act of taking up that mantle was in itself a declaration of his willingness to assume the duties and responsibilities which now devolved upon him.

It partook of the nature of a promise to be true to the religious principles of which his master had been the exponent; to take up the great work to which he had devoted his life. God has never lacked a seed to do him service, nor shall he ever experience such lack. "God buries his workmen, but his work goes on." As one servant, as one generation, puts off the mantle, another is prepared to take it up. The triumph of truth over error, of good over evil, is not dependent upon the life and service of any one man. We sometimes think so, but God has furnished abundant evidence that such is not the case. Elisha doubtless felt, as he beheld his master borne away from earth, and cried after him, "My father! my father! the chariot of Israel, and the horsemen thereof!" that God's cause had suffered an irreparable loss; yet under his own ministry the truth was to prevail to a greater extent than under the ministry of Elijah. That stern, courageous, impetuous champion had been taken away, but God's cause was not to suffer. Soon the enemies against whom Elijah had been called to contend were to be cut off, and with their destruction the persecutions of God's people were to cease for a season. In the less troublous times which followed, that little company which had not bowed the knee to Baal, nor kissed his image was increased manyfold. God may preserve and prosper his cause by raising up an Elijah to defend it, or by cutting off an Ahab or a Jezebel who would destroy it. It is frequently said, when a great and useful man falls at the post of duty, "There will be none to take his place." But God never takes one servant away, until he has provided another to occupy the place left vacant. When Aaron was summoned to repair to Mount Hor to die, Moses was directed to strip him of his priestly garments and to put them upon Eleazar, his son, who was to be priest in his stead. And when the time drew near that Moses himself should go up to Pisgah's summit, there to die according to the word of the Lord, the Divine command was given that he should lay his hand upon Joshua, the son of Nun, and in the presence of Eleazar, the priest, and of all the congregation, transfer the leadership of Israel to him. David, forbidden to build a house for God, because he had been a man of blood, is comforted in his disappointment by the Divine assurance that his son shall carry out the long cherished design. Stephen is honored with the martyr's crown, but Saul of Tarsus, as mighty in deed and word as he, is at once called from the ranks of the enemy to take his place. Impious hands may burn the bones of Wycliffe, and throw their ashes into the Swift, but in his own time God will raise up a Luther to occupy the place left vacant by the going out of that "Morning Star of the Reformation." Thus it has always been, thus it will continue to be, until God's purposes concerning our race have all been accomplished. Individual men die, generations of men pass away, but the race abides; believers die, but the church remains; ministers may be called away, pastorates may end, but not until every soul whom the Father hath given to the Son shall have been brought into glory, is the ministry of God's own appointment to cease from the earth. The mantles of our fathers have fallen at our feet. Having run the race that was set before them, they have rested from their labors and the responsibilities which were theirs, have been transferred to us. One of the theories which have been advanced concerning the construction of the great pyramid of Egypt, is that it is the product of successive builders, the monument of successive dynasties. One Paraoh would resume the work of construction at the point where his predecessor had left off building, and thus the structure was carried to completion. Whether this be a correct theory or not, it may serve to illustrate the manner in which one generation succeeds to the labors and responsibilities of the generation which precedes it. Thus it is that God's work is carried on in the world. When that great temple, the Church Invisible, which Jehovah is rearing to the honor and glory of his name, stands complete, when the last living stone shall have been set in his place, it will be found that of God's workmen each generation has furnished its contingent, that the finished structure is the product of no one age, but of all the ages. One generation enters into the labors of all its predecessors. In the working out of those great problems which concern the final destiny of our race, we begin where our fathers left off. With their mistakes, as so many light-houses, to warn us of the lurking-places of danger, and with all the fruits of their scholarly research which have been transmitted to us, it is but reasonable that we should be expected to build more wisely and successfully than they. Let this be remembered ever, ability and opportunity are the measure of responsibility. Our Lord lays it down as a great principle of his kingdom that, "Unto whomsoever much is given, of them shall much be required." The mantle which has fallen at our feet cannot be neglected by us with impunity. We must take it up or suffer the consequences. "That servant which knew his lord's will, and prepared not himself, neither did according to his will shall be beaten with many stripes." On the other hand, let us remember, for our comfort and encouragement, as we take up the mantle of responsibility, that he who has called us to bear this mantle gives strength for every duty which he imposes upon his servants. As he said to his servant Paul, so to us he says, "My grace is sufficient for thee: for my strength is made perfect in weakness." And by and by, if we are faithful, we shall hear him say, "Well done, thou good and faithful servant: thou hast been faithful over a few things, I will make thee ruler over many things: enter thou into the joy of thy Lord."

## CHAPTER VI.

### PROVING HIS ARMOR.

"As a little child relies
  On a care beyond his own,
Knows he's neither strong nor wise,
  Fears to move a step alone,
Let me thus with thee abide,
As my Father, Guard, and Guide."

WHILE memory lasted, that spot of earth from which his master had been swept into glory, must have remained sacred to the heart of Elisha. As those who have laid their dead out of their sight love to linger by the new-made grave, so, doubtless, he fain would have lingered near the scene of his bereavement. But the King's business was urgent. He must dash away his tears, and prepare to enter at once upon the great work to which, henceforth, he was to devote his life. Reverently clasping to his bosom the precious mantle, he retraced his steps until he stood once more by the Jordan, that river which so often has been made a type of that which separates between time and eternity. Duty called him to cross those turbid waters, for Jericho, where he was to begin his prophetic ministry, lay beyond. But will God provide a way for him as, when with his master, he had sought to pass hither from the other shore? Will the mantle prove as potent in his hand as in the hand of

Elijah? To know the worth of his armor, he must prove it. "The best way to prove the power of Divine grace, is to exercise the gifts we have. Neglect not the gift that is in thee. We shall not accomplish much in the world, if we stand gazing into heaven." (C. H. Irwin.)

Doubtless wrapping the mantle together, as he had seen Elijah do, he smote the waters with it, crying as he did so, "Where is the Lord God of Elijah, even he?" The effect is instantaneous and marvelous. Again that glittering stream is cut asunder, and through the midst of its waters Elisha passed over dry-shod." It is worthy of note that the mantle of Elijah is not mentioned again by the sacred historian after this incident. Having served its purpose, every trace of it is lost. May it not be that God thus provided that it should not prove a snare to the people? Had it been preserved, it might have been made an object of idolatrous worship, as was the brazen serpent which Moses made. God would not only save the people from this, but he would teach them that the power exercised by his servants, the prophets, did not reside in the mantle. It was a time of extreme loneliness and dejection with Elisha when this, his first miracle, was wrought. His master had just been taken from his head, and he felt as though God himself had forsaken him, as seems evident from the words which fell from his lips while in the act of smiting the waters, "Where is the Lord God of Elijah?" It is but another way of saying, If God has not left me alone and helpless in the world, let it now be made manifest. In the miracle of cleaving the waters before him, God graciously answered his anxious inquiry. As Elisha beheld those waters part hither and thither, his doubts were dispelled, and his sorrowing and discouraged heart was comforted. In the way which was thus provided for him, was the evidence that, although he had been bereft of his earthly companion and guide, God was with him, by his Spirit to uphold and guide him. How frequently does God, by some special token of his presence and love, thus comfort the hearts of his children when trials and bereavements come upon them. The Psalmist could sing, "When my father and my mother forsake me, then the Lord will take me up." And again, "My flesh and my heart faileth, but God is the strength of my heart, and my portion for ever." Our Lord has said, "Lo, I am with you always, even unto the end of the world." And again he says, "I will pray the Father, and he shall give you another comforter, that he may abide with you for ever; even the Spirit of truth." How has the assurance that these blessed promises were fulfilled to them, cheered the hearts, and made strong the arms of the hands of God's people when flesh and heart have failed because of sore persecutions. Paul and Silas, though suffering from the wounds which they had received at the hands of their persecutors, and fastened in the stocks of the prison dungeon, could sing praises unto God at the midnight hour, because assured that the Lord was with them. As one has said, "Perhaps the most trying moments in the life of Elisha were those in which he retraced the distance from the place of Elijah's ascension till he reached the brink of the Jordan. A whole life of faith was again to be summed up in one experiment of God's faithfulness." (Edersheim.) Elisha had seen Elijah when he was taken from him, and in the vision had received Divine assurance that his request that a double portion of the spirit of Elijah might rest upon him had been granted. The mantle which had fallen to him was an additional confirmation of this. But he was unaccustomed to act upon his own responsibility. For the first time, perhaps, in his life, he was now thrown upon his own resources. Though he had probably reached the years of manhood before leaving his father's house, yet in all important matters, doubtless, he had been advised and directed by his father. Not only so, but the years which he had spent as the companion and disciple of Elijah, had contributed to develop still further this spirit of dependence. Now he is left without any to advise or to direct him. No audible voice from heaven, no words from human lips, indicated to him the path of duty.

Hitherto, perhaps, he had leaned upon the faith of Elijah. Now that he had departed, Elisha was called to exercise a personal faith. "There is a time in the history of each one of us when we make, as it were, the first trial of our faith; when for the first time we kneel down to plead the promises, and to pray, believing that all which is written is literally true, that we are accepted in Christ and shall be heard for his sake." (Edersheim.) Elisha was conscious of faith within the heart, yet he scarcely knew how to use it. He was like the little child just learning to walk, whom the loving mother has placed in the center of the room, and then, withdrawing her supporting hand from him and retiring a few paces, bids come to her. The child has the limbs necessary for locomotion, and a certain degree of strength in them, but he does not know how to use them. He is afraid to attempt to exercise the power which he possesses. Elisha had asked for spiritual power, and had received it; nevertheless anxious thoughts must have arisen in his heart, as he came to exercise this power for the first time. Sometimes God requires us to walk alone in Christ, and to this end places us in circumstances in which no human aid is available. There may have been a tinge of disappointment in the experience of Elisha at this time. He may have expected that, in receiving a double portion of the spirit of Elijah, he would experience an immediate and radical change in his character and feelings. He may have expected to become like his master; to receive something of that courage and boldness of spirit which distinguished him. If so, his expectations were not realized. So far as his feelings were concerned, no change had been wrought in him. He thought and acted as he had ever done. Questioning, as he may have done, the genuineness of his own faith, because his experience did not correspond to what he thought the experience of Elijah must have been, it may have been with some degree of anxiety as to the result, that he prepared to make the test which should reveal the character and the measure of his faith. We choose a false standard, when we measure our Christian faith and character by those of any mere man. The fact that your experience does not correspond in every respect with that of some person whom you may believe to be a Christian, is not to be regarded as proof positive that you, my brother, have not been born of God. The operations of the Spirit in the human heart are compatible with the widest diversity of gifts. The Apostle declares that, "There are diversities of gifts, but the same Spirit. For to one is given by the Spirit the word of wisdom; to another the word of knowledge by the same Spirit; to another faith by the same Spirit;

to another the gift of healing by the same Spirit; to another the working of miracles; to another prophecy; to another discerning of spirits; to another divers kinds of tongues; to another the interpretation of tongues: but all these things worketh that one and the selfsame Spirit, dividing to every many severally as he will." The Holy Spirit who dwells in all believers, manifests himself in one way in one person, and in another way in another person. Let us guard against the thought that to be a Christian, it is necessary to become like to any man, save "the man Christ Jesus." Certainly the profoundest feelings of joy which the human heart can know, are those which arise from the assurance of God's acceptance. Such joy Elisha must have experienced, when, having smitten the waters of the Jordan, he saw them part before him, and stand like a wall on either hand until he had passed through the midst of them. Henceforth he could not doubt that he had been chosen and called of God, for the Divine seal was in this manner placed upon his ministry. Though no record is left us of the fact, we may well believe that Elisha "exulted in spirit" when he beheld this great thing which the Lord had done for him; that the deep feelings which thrilled his soul, must have found expression in words of adoration and thanksgiving. During all the years of his long and eventful life he would doubtless look back with feelings of delight and assurance to the moment when he saw the waters begin to part when smitten by his hand. Many things may minister to our happiness in this life, "but one thing is needful," it is to be assured, as was Elisha at the very beginning of his prophetic ministry, that we are right with God; that we are engaged in the work which he would have us do. Were every man and woman assured of this, earth would be transformed into Paradise, and human happiness would be complete. This assurance is possible to all who seek for it. As Elijah ended his ministry, so Elisha began his. The last act of the one was the first act of the other. In a manner precisely similar, each wrought the same miracle. It was thus made manifest to the people that Elisha was to be the successor of Elijah. The divided waters of the Jordan were God's credentials to him. "When the sons of the prophets which were to view at Jericho saw him, they said, the spirit of Elijah doth rest on Elisha. And they came to meet him, and bowed themselves to the ground before him." The natural inference is that they had witnessed the mighty miracle which God had wrought by him, and, by it, were convinced that God was with him. Our Lord appealed to the works which he did as a reason why men should believe in him. His words are, "If I do not the works of my Father, believe me not." When warning his followers against false prophets, he said, "Ye shall know them by their fruits." Men universally accept this as the true standard by which character is to be measured. The world demands, and it has a right to demand, that every man who professes to be a disciple of Christ shall present the necessary credentials, that his "manner of life be worthy of the gospel of Christ." Brethren, what are our credentials as the followers of Jesus? Are they such as all men must honor? It is not improbable that, in addition to the miracle thus wrought, other facts contributed to produce this conviction concerning Elisha in the minds of the sons of the prophets. It is recorded that when Moses came down from Mount Sinai, where for the second time he had received the commandments of the Lord, and for forty days and forty nights had communed with God, that "the skin of his face did shine." May not the face of Elisha have caught, and still have reflected, something of the heavenly glory which he had been permitted to behold? Where there is fellowship with God, there will be this shining of the face. When the Christ is enthroned in the soul, he will illumine and beautify the countenance. True piety always shines. It was the face of Moses, not any thing which he said or did, that indicated the rapture of soul which he had experienced in the mount. The Jewish Sanhedrin, before which Peter and John were brought, "took knowledge of them that they had been with Jesus." If we have been with Jesus, if we have learned of him, the world will take knowledge of the fact without any flourish of trumpets on our part. There is one kind of diamond which, after it has been exposed for some minutes to the light of the sun and then taken into a dark room, will emit light for some time. On a small scale, it becomes the source of light. So those in whose hearts God hath shined, "to give the light of the knowledge of the glory of God in the face of Jesus Christ," become sources of light in this dark world. "Moses wist not that the skin of his face shined." To a certain degree, at least, the true child of God is unconscious of the glory which inswathes him. The faith of Elisha has stood the crucial test to which it has been subjected; his patience is now to be tried. Patience has been discribed as the queen of the Christian virtues. Its possession is necessary to the attainment of the best results in the present life. Stevenson, the inventor of the locomotive, declared that he surpassed the majority of mankind in patience only. Newton ascribed his ability to read nature's laws, solely to his patience. When asked how he had discovered the law of gravitation, he replied, "By incessantly thinking about it." To the Christian, patience is indispensable. "Patience," said F. W. Robertson, "wears out the world." Without it there can be no stability of Christian character and life; since, even with those who are devoted to the Master's service, there is a constant liability to excess, in one direction or another, because of the temptations which beset, the trials which come in the form of provocations, persecutions, losses, afflictions, and bereavements. The Apostle James says, "My brethren, count it all joy when ye fall into temptations, knowing that the trying of your faith worketh patience. But let patience have her perfect work, that ye may be perfect and entire, wanting nothing." Centuries before him, Solomon had said, "The patient in spirit is better than the proud in spirit." "That the man of God may be perfect, thoroughly furnished unto all good works," the grace of patience must be developed in him. No sooner had the sons of the prophets recognized Elisha as their master, than they began to urge that a party of fifty strong men be sent to search for Elijah upon the mountains and in the valleys. These sons of the prophets were not the children of the prophets, but their pupils, students in the schools of the prophets.

It is probable their course of study was confined to so much of the Scriptures as had then been given. It seems impossible to justify this request, or suggestion, upon any principle whatsoever. Had those who made it been mere children, or men whose religious education had been neglected, it might have been condoned. But it is the request of men of mature minds, of men who have enjoyed superior advantages in the way of religious training. In many respects it must have been peculiarly irritating and disheartening to Elisha to be met by such a request. In the first place, it indicated a lack of confidence in him. He must have told them, before they thus addressed him, of that marvelous event which he alone had been permitted to witness, of how he had seen Elijah carried into heaven. Yet they say, "Let these fifty strong men go and seek for thy master." Only a lack of confidence in his veracity, or of respect for his intelligence could have prompted them to make such a request. It requires the possession and the lively exercise of a large measure of the grace of patience to endure such aspersion without resentment. This request displayed a spirit of officiousness likewise which, in the circumstances, must have been exceedingly distasteful to Elisha. It was an impertinence for these young men to suggest to him what should be done, and especially to insist so strenuously on having their way. In so doing, they assumed to have greater knowledge than he possessed, to be competent to advise him. Much of the advice which is thrust upon the attention of the Church, and especially of the clergy, to-day, is of this officious character. One of the many things which the faithful herald of the gospel may regard as designed to develop the grace of patience in his soul, is the gratuitous suggestions so frequently offered him by the secular press, political and platform orators, and those who have devoted their lives to the stage, as to how and what he should preach. This request was due, in a large measure, to a spirit of unbelief. As the narrative shows, these sons of the prophets had been apprised of the fact that the Lord was to take Elijah up into heaven. Yet, now that the prediction has been fulfilled, they propose to search for him, lest "the Spirit of the Lord has taken him up, and cast him upon some mountain, or into some valley." It is impossible for the unregenerate heart to honor God by trusting him, by believing the word of his promise. Had these men been able just to take God at his word, how much anxiety and useless toil they might have been spared! Could we, with implicit confidence, rest upon the promises which God has given us in Jesus Christ, how much greater would be the measure of our peace and joy! Unbelief robs us of many a precious blessing, and binds upon us burdens which the mighty Lord yearns to bear for us. Notwithstanding this severe test, Elisha's patience remained unshaken. He seems to have suffered no word of resentment to have escaped his lips. He does not even upbraid them for their unbelief, as, very properly, he might have done. In a dispassionate manner he simply tells them not to send the searching party. "Ye shall not send." This may be but the substance of his reply. He doubtless attempted to explain to them why he refused his consent, that it was useless and improper to do as they proposed. Be this as it may, they would not take no for an answer. Vehemently they pled with him, until he was ashamed to persist in his refusal, and yielded. He doubtless felt that not to do so, would be to bring suspicion upon himself and to deprive them of a much needed lesson.

Not even when, after three days weary and fruitless search, they returned to him to report their failure does he chide them, further than to remind them that he had counseled not to start upon such an errand. How lovely appears the life of Elisha in the light of this incident of his life. O, that, in our hearts, patience may have her perfect work; that we may able to say,

> "We take with solemn thankfulness
> Our burden up, nor ask it less,
> And count it joy that even we
> May suffer, serve, or wait for thee,
> Whose will be done!"
>
> (Whittier.)

## CHAPTER VII.

### THE WATERS OF JERICHO HEALED.

> "But man feels a burden of care and of grief,
> While plucking the cluster and binding the sheaf.
> In the summer we faint, in the winter we're chilled,
> With ever a void that is yet to be filled.
> We take from the ocean, the earth, and the air.
> Yet all their rich gifts do not silence our care."
> (Miss Gould.)

SOME five or six miles west of the Jordan, and about the same distance north of the dead sea, is a squalid village which the natives call Eriha. It stands in the midst of a plain which is thirteen hundred feet below the level of the sea, and is supposed to mark the spot where stood the far-famed city of Jericho, the city of palm-trees. The blighting hand of Islam has wasted the munificence of nature which led ancient writers to describe Jericho as, "a very garden and paradise of eastern beauty." The palm-tree, the rose, the fruitful vine, and the balsam, once a source of vast revenue, have all disappeared. The fields where the wheat and barley once waved in luxuriance, and whitened for the harvest, are now, for the most part, desolate and waste. But Jericho has an imperishable history. It is first mentioned by the inspired historian in indicating the place where the children of Israel pitched their camp after completing the conquest of

Bashan. As Moses stood upon Pisgah's lonely height and viewed the promised land which he was not permitted to enter, his eyes rested upon Jericho.

Hither Joshua sent the two spies, the record of whose concealment by Rahab and their subsequent covenant with her, reads like romance. It was while Joshua stood by Jericho, doubtless to reconnoiter and to determine the best method of attack, that the Captain of the Lord's host appeared to him to make known the Divine plan of campaign. Jericho was the first city taken by the Israelites west of the Jordan. When, for the thirteenth time, the city had been compassed, according to the direction which Joshua had received, and the priests had blown a long blast with trumpets, the people shouted with a mighty shout; and those massive walls, which hitherto had bidden defiance to every assailant, crumbled, and, with the noise of an avalanch, fell flat to the ground. The city was totally destroyed, and as Joshua viewed its ruins, he uttered this malediction, "Cursed be the man before the Lord that riseth up and buildeth this city of Jericho: he shall lay the foundation thereof in his firstborn, and in his youngest son shall be set up the gates of it."

Five hundred years had passed when Hiel, the Bethelite, in defiance of the Divine interdict, began to rebuild Jericho. In executing this impious project he suffered the penalty which Joshua had foretold. It is recorded that, "he laid the foundation thereof in Abiram his firstborn, and set up the gates thereof in his youngest son Segub." It was in the plains of Jericho that the Chaldean army overtook the fugitive king Zedekiah and made him a prisoner. Only in an incidental way is the city mentioned again in the Old Testament. Sixty-three years before the birth of our Lord, Jericho was taken by the Romans under Pompey who made Palestine a Roman province. Fifty-nine years later the death of Herod the Great, who had adorned and beautified the city, was announced by Salome to the multitude assembled in the amphitheater. At least two important events in the earthly ministry of Jesus occurred at Jericho. It was here, while on his last journey to Jerusalem, that he restored Bartimeus to sight, and became the guest of Zacheus, the publican. It remained for the Turk, the scourge of so many prosperous cities and fair lands, to inflict final and irreparable ruin upon Jericho. In the year eighteen hundred and forty, Ibrahim Pasha, retreating fom Damascus, was attacked by the Arabs at the ford of the Jordan, near Jericho. In revenge for this, he sent a detachment of his army and razed the city to the ground. It must have been but a short time after the work of rebuilding Jericho had been completed by Hiel, that the event occurred which we now consider. For a brief season Elisha had come to tarry in the city, doubtless in the school of the prophets which was established here, to wait for the manifestation of the Divine will as to the service he should undertake. Apprised of his presence, and having heard of the great miracle by which his prophetic character had been attested at the Jordan, the men of the city, representative men, come to him and say, "Behold, I pray thee, the situation of this city is pleasant, as my lord seeth: but the water is naught, and the ground barren." So far as the inspired record shows, these men were content with this brief and simple recital of the evils which they experienced. Perhaps, however, we have but the substance of what was said. Be this as it may, it is evident that Elisha recognized the statement made to him as an appeal for help. In effect these men entreated him as the servant of God, to remove the cause of their distress. The fact that Elisha was thus approached has been cited as an illustration of the contrast between him and his great predecessor. The majestic appearance, perhaps, of Elijah, and the imperiousness of his conduct, were such as to isolate him from his fellow-men.

Though not shunning human society, his life seems to have been that of a hermit. These men of Jericho would scarcely have dared to make their complaint to him, so much did they stand in awe of him. But there must have been something in the appearance and the demeanor of Elisha which drew men to him, which inspired the belief that he cherished kindly feelings toward all, and that he was ready to help in time of trouble. More, perhaps, than any other of the Old Testament worthies, Elisha resembles our Lord in character and ministry. Like him, he "went about doing good." O, that there were more like him in the world to-day! How much one such character in the community, in the congregation, in the home, contributes to smooth the rough places in life's pathway, to dispel the darkness and gloom of doubt, and assure our faith! How truly typical of human experience was the experience of the inhabitants of Jericho at this time. But recently built, their city must have been fair to look upon. The situation was beautiful, and the broad acres adjacent, were of unsurpassed fertility. Still they were unhappy, because dissatisfied with their lot. With all their apparent prosperity, and exhaustless resources, they lacked one of the most important of the necessities of life, the water was "naught." So man has ever found earthly things to be unsatisfying. However great his possessions, he is forever deploring the presence or absence, as the case may be, of something. If the situation is desirable, the water is naught; if the waters are sweet, the situation is unfortunate. The more we get, the more we want; and our cares are multiplied in proportion to our getting. There are few families without "a skeleton of some sort in the closet." Wretchedness and shame have their abode in many a kingly palace, and gorgeous mansion. Beneath silken folds, flashing jewels, and a smiling face, there is often hidden a sad heart or the canker of a guilty conscience. Very important, indeed, is the part which this little word, "but," plays in human history. Had the first of human kind continued in the holy estate in which they were created, this world must have remained forever the abode of perfect happiness and joy; but God was disbelieved, and disobeyed, the tempter's voice was heeded, "sin entered the world, and death by sin." Had the Saracens been victorious in the great battle of Tours, they, doubtless, whould have overrun all Europe, and, from a human point of view, Christianity would thus have been extirpated. But victory perched upon the standard of Charles Martel, the hammer, for God determined her course; the followers of the false prophet were discomfited and put to flight; and the history of the world, as we now read it, became possible. Had the Spanish Armada proved itself worthy the proud title "Invincible," the design to stamp Protestantism out of Europe might have succeeded. But the stars in their courses fought against King Philip and his allies, as truly as they fought against Sisera in the days of old.

Buffeted by the winds of heaven, and assailed by British seamen, as brave men as ever battled for a nation's life, that vast armament was swept from the seas, and England and Protestantism, of which England was then the home, were saved. Had the troops which the keen eye of Napoleon perceived to be deploying on his right in the afternoon of that ever memorable 18th of June, 1815, proved to be those of Marshal Grouchy, he might have won Waterloo. Had such been the result of that great battle, the subsequent history of Europe, and of America perhaps, must have been very different from that which has been written. But they were the troops of Blucher and the day was lost, and with it the empire and freedom of the great Emperor. Had Spain or France succeeded in establishing colonies on the North American continent, between the thirty-first and forty-ninth parallels of latitude, these United States, if they had ever come into existence at all, must have been Roman Catholic in religious faith. But it was Protestant England which laid claim to this vast territory and was first to colonize it. The settlements of the Latin nations were confined to the north and south, and, as a consequence of this, ours is a Protestant nation. It is a testimony to the intelligence of the people of Jericho that they were conscious of the evils which they suffered, and knew their source. The beautiful situation of their city did not render them oblivious to the fact that fruitfulness had forsaken their fields; that the earth cast her fruits before they were matured; that grievous maladies prevailed among the people; that the death rate was alarmingly high. All this they attributed to the unhealthful character of the water. Perhaps this was a result of the curse which Joshua had pronounced upon the city. Whatever the cause, these men of Jericho were convinced that so long as the great spring, issuing from the base of the mountain, hard by their city, continued to send forth its brackish waters they must expect to experience the evils of which they complain. It is of the first importance that men should understand and appreciate their needs. Doubtless many a disease has proved fatal which might have been cured, had its true character been known, and the proper remedies employed at the proper time. One reason why multitudes of men are living in neglect of God's offer of salvation, is to be found in the fact that they have never felt their need of salvation. Many a man is perishing, spiritually, because he is so much absorbed with the contemplation of his brother's shortcomings that he forgets his own. Thinking only of the mote which he has discovered in his brother's eye, he perceives not the beam that is in his own eye. Many a man permits the comforting truth that God is a being of infinite love and mercy to divert attention from the equally important truth that God is just, and cannot but hate sin; that out of Christ God is a consuming fire; that if the spiritual spring within be not healed, the result must be spiritual desolation and death. There can be no profit in attempting to deceive ourselves concerning our relation to God. No advantage can be gained by refusing to believe the truth as God has revealed it. No amount of false reasoning, no denial, however emphatic, can change the truth. If the skeptic were to devote a tithe of the time and trouble which he expends in the effort to fortify himself in his unbelief, to a careful, candid, prayerful searching after reasons why he should believe the statements of God's word, he would be thoroughly relieved of his skepticism. Like the poisoned fountain of Jericho, the human heart is the source of that which produces blighting and death. Our Lord says, "Out of the heart proceed evil thoughts, murders, adulteries, fornications, thefts, false witness, blasphemies: these are the things which defile a man." Men love to talk about heredity and environment. The doctrine that, "circumstances make the man," finds many an adherent in our day. It must be admitted that such teaching contains a certain per cent of truth. The danger lies in pushing our deductions too far, so that we come to regard sin as a "misfortune," rather than as a crime against God. Neither the character of our progenitors nor our environments in life can relieve us of the responsibility which God has laid upon every man. "Let us not judge ourselves too leniently. Circumstances make the man in so far only as we permit them to do so. It is for man himself to say whether his own heart shall be a temple or a kennel." (George Danna Boardman, D.D.) In the light of such truth we see the wisdom of that scripture which says, "Keep thy heart with all diligence; for out of it are the issues of life." Character is of paramount importance in all things. Quantity cannot compensate for quality. Jericho had an abundant supply of water, but these men who come to Elisha say, "the water is naught." As a consequence of this, the ground was barren. The simple fact that they possessed a fountain did not suffice, though its streams were copious and exhaustless. Every man has some kind of a reputation, but the esteem in which he is held by his fellow-men, will depend upon the character of his reputation. There are some persons who insist that it signifies little what a man's religious faith may be, provided he is sincere. Yet the word of God tells us of but one way, the narrow way, that leads to eternal life. The Lord Jesus said, "I am the door: by me if any man enter in, he shall be saved, and shall go in and out, and find pasture." Again he says, "I am the way," not a way, but the way. He then adds these deeply significant words, "No man cometh unto the Father but by me." In harmony with this statement are the words of the Apostle, "Neither is there salvation in any other: for there is no other name under heaven given among men, whereby we must be saved." What men need is not a faith, but the faith. "We must have not merely water, but good water. It is of comparatively secondary importance in whose company we get it, provided the water be living. To attend a ministry of error, because we can attend it in fashionable company, or because the mode of service is in accordance with our predilections, is most dangerous trifling." (Edersheim.) The appeal which the men of Jericho made to Elisha was opportune. God's time had come to remove the evil from which they suffered. His chosen servant was at hand to execute his purpose. The exercise of Divine power for their deliverance only awaited their cry. In an important sense, God could not bless them until they felt their need and sought the blessing at his hand. Had they not invoked God's aid through Elisha, had they not done so at this particular time, the waters, so essential to their happiness and welfare, never might have been healed. It is a great thing to be able to discern the time of our visitation. It is possible to neglect the things which belong to our peace to such an extent that they are forever hidden from our eyes. God says,

"My spirit shall not always strive with man." His words are, "Seek ye the Lord while he may be found, call ye upon him while he is near." The implication of this exhortation is that there may be a time when the Lord cannot be found, a time when he is not near, does not hear the cry addressed to him. In response to the appeal made to him, Elisha directs that a new cruse be provided, and that salt be put therein. To this extent, at least, those who had sought his aid were associated with him in the healing of the waters. In most instances, God requires some service on our part, as a preliminary step in answering our prayers. Such service is a test or proof, if nothing more, of the sincerity of our requests, of the earnestness of our desire. In this manner God likewise honors us, by making us workers together with him. We cannot heal the poisoned waters, the power is of God, but we may provide the cruse, and put the salt therein. We cannot make the dead to live, but we may take away the stone from the door of the sepulcher. We may loose the bands with which those who have been made alive in Christ Jesus are still bound. We may help to remove the napkin of ignorance, prejudice, and doubt, which excludes from their eyes so large a measure of the light of truth. Their hearts are bound with the habiliments of sorrow and care; their hands and feet trammeled by evil habits, and allegiance to the world. It is ours to loose them and let them go. The thoughtful reader of the inspired narrative is ever impressed with the simplicity, even seeming incongruity, of the means employed by the Prophet in the miraculous purification of the waters of Jericho. He calls for a new cruse, doubtless because he felt that the vessel to be employed in such a service should be free from every impurity, from all defilement which previous use might impart. It was to be new that the people might be convinced that he had imparted no magic properties to it; that it contained no talismanic potion. Salt is the symbol of that which is pure, purifying, and savory. Because of its preservative properties, it is invaluable to man. To his disciples our Lord says, "Ye are the salt of the earth." The thought is that they are the purifying and preserving moral element in the world. Frequently in the Scriptures reference is made to salt as a purifying, preserving, and savoring element. Paradoxical as it may seem, salt has been regarded, likewise, in all ages, as the symbol of complete destruction, of perpetual desolation. It was a custom with the ancients to sow salt upon such places as they devoted to endless ruin. Water when charged with salt becomes unfit for use, destructive of vegetable life. With this fact the people of Jericho, living so near the Dead Sea, must have been thoroughly familiar. The very fact, however, that the agency employed must have seemed so incongrous would contribute to render the impression produced by the miracle more profound and abiding than it could have been otherwise. The truth would thus be impressed upon the hearts of the people that the excellency of the power was of God, and not of means. Many times the means which God is pleased to employ do not seem to us commensurate to the results sought. But God can render any means effectual. "He is able to bring to pass his wonderful designs either with means or without means or with means which seem wholly unsuited to his purpose." (Blunt.) A blast from seven trumpets of rams' horns, followed by the shout of the armies of Israel, was sufficient to throw down the strong walls of Jericho. By putting clay on the eyes of a blind man, Jesus restored him to sight. With but five loaves and two fishes, he fed five thousand hungry men, and, doubtless, as many women and children besides. "It pleased God," says the Apostle, "by the foolishness of preaching to save them that believe." How great the encouragement we have to trust in the Lord. "With God all things are possible." The fact that Elisha was directed to go to the spring of the waters, is not without significance. The salt of purification was to be cast into the fountain whence the poisonous waters issued. If the stream of man's life is to be purified, the salt of Divine grace must be cast into the heart, which is the source of all moral and spiritual impurity. The tree may be pruned, but, so long as the trunk retains life, other branches will put forth, similar in nature to those you have removed. A man's life is not made pure by forsaking this or that sinful habit, or by the practice of any particular virtue, however commendable. Character may be greatly improved by such a course, but to make life what it ought to be, what God requires it to be, the heart must be purified from sin. Elisha takes none of the glory of this great miracle to himself. His only concern seems to have been that God might be glorified, and that the welfare and happiness of those to whom he was sent might be promoted. As he casts the salt into the spring, he utters these words, "Thus saith the Lord, I have healed these waters." Like John the forerunner, he was content to be but a voice, to be recognized as God's instrument, merely. God seeketh such to serve him. The more nearly we can forget self, in our desire and endeavor to serve God, and to benefit our fellow-men, the more acceptable our service becomes. To be honored of God, we must yield all the honor and the glory to him. We are to seek to hide behind the cross, not to hide the cross behind us; to preach Christ, not self. Those servants to whom the Lord when he cometh, shall say, "Well done," are ever found saying, "Not unto us, O Lord, not unto us, but unto thy name give glory."

## CHAPTER VIII.

### THE MOCKERS OF BETHEL.

"Upon the just God keeps his eyes;
His ears are open to their cries:
Against the wicked sets his face,
From earth their memory to erase."

How varied are the experiences of human life! No two successive days, perhaps, are precisely alike with us. The sunshine and cheer of to-day may be succeeded by clouds and storms to-morrow. After the summer, with its life-giving warmth, its green-robed forests and fields, its fragrant flowers, its ripening fruits and waving harvests, comes the winter with its chilling blasts, its leafless trees, its ice and snow. To-day we may rejoice "as a strong man to run a race," to-morrow may find us faint and sick and ready to die. To-day the heart may be buoyant, filled with hope, to-morrow it may be cast down, and filled with despair. The voice of friends may cheer us to-day, and appreciative words be the reward of honest effort; but to-morrow may find us in the very camp of the enemy, where naught but harsh words and menacing acts greet us. By the miraculous healing of the waters of Jericho, Elisha had doubtless won the respect and gratitude of her citizens. He had proved himself a public benefactor, and thousands, we may believe, were found to rise up and call him blessed. But while yet his praise was upon the lips of all, he was directed by the Spirit to go to Bethel, which stood on the highlands of Benjamin, some twelve or fifteen miles to the northwest. The steep and long ascent of the mountain slope has been accomplished; the gate of the city has been reached, almost; the heart of the Prophet yet thrills as he recalls the benedictions of the grateful people whom he has left in the plain below, when, suddenly, scores of voices greet him and startle him with the wild, contemptuous cry, "Go up, thou bald head; go up, thou bald head." Who were these mockers? Perhaps we have in the margin of the Revised Version, the best translation of the Hebrew word by which they are described as "young lads," boys from twelve to eighteen years old. The contention of some that the persons who are here spoken of as, "little children," were in fact adults is not unworthy of notice. The word child is frequently used in such a sense. Isaac is called a lad, or child, when he must have been a young man. The same term is applied to Joseph, when called to interpret the dream of Pharaoh; to Joshua, when acting as the assistant or prime minister of Moses.

Solomon speaks of himself as a little child, when he must have been twenty years old, and sat on the throne of Israel. Jeremiah speaks of himself in the same manner, when called to be the Lord's prophet and after he must have reached the years of manhood. It will be conceded, however, that the term is commonly applied to infants and to persons who have not reached the years of maturity. And, since the conduct of this mob which Elisha encountered is so inconsistent with that which might be expected of men, even lawless men, it seems the most reasonable conclusion that it was composed of rude, disorderly boys.

"Such mischievous youths are among the chief nuisances of Oriental towns; they waylay the traveler, deride him, jeer him, are keen to remark any personal defect that he may have and merciless in flouting it; they dog his steps, shout out their rude remarks, and sometimes proceed from abusive words to violent acts." (Rev. G. Rawlinson.) These jeering, hooting young ruffians, came from Bethel. Many centuries before this, the patriarch Jacob, as he journeyed from Beersheba to Haran, had visited the site of this city. Overtaken here by the night, he had made for himself a pillow of the stones of the place, and, lying down to peaceful slumbers, had seen in vision a ladder stretching from earth to heaven, and the angels of God ascending and descending upon it; and had heard from God who stood above it, these gracious words, "I am the Lord God of Abraham, thy father, and the God of Isaac: the land whereon thou liest, to thee will I give it, and to thy seed. And, behold, I am with thee, and will keep thee in all places whither thou goest, and will bring thee again into this land, for I will not leave thee until I have done that which I have spoken to thee of." Awaking from his sleep, Jacob said, "Surely the Lord is in this place, and I knew it not." And, seized with fear, he said, "How dreadful is this place! this is none other than the house of God, and this is the gate of heaven." Arising with the first dawn of the morning, he took the stone which he had put for his pillow, and, setting it up for a pillar, "poured oil upon it and called the name of the place Bethel." After the promise which was made to Jacob had been fulfilled, and his descendants had acquired possession of the land of Canaan, Bethel became a place of great prominence. "In the troubled times when there was no king in Israel, it was to Bethel that the people went up in their distress to ask counsel of God." (Smith's Bible Dictionary.) For a number of years the ark of the covenant remained at Bethel in charge of a priest of the Aaronic order. With other cities of Israel, Bethel was visited by the Prophet Samuel at stated times. It was doubtless the history of the city, as well as its geographical position, which determined the crafty and wicked Jeroboam to make it one of the centers of the idolatrous worship which he introduced among the ten seceding tribes of Israel. Eighty years' schooling in idolatrous practices, had produced its legitimate effect upon the inhabitants of Bethel. They had become thoroughly estranged from the worship of Jehovah, and, to a corresponding degree, attached to the prevailing religion. The city had forfeited the glorious appellation, Bethel, the house of God, and deserved henceforth the odious distinction, fastened upon her by a prophet of a later date, in the name Beth-aven, house of vanity.

Mercenary motives doubtless contributed in no small measure to intensify the zeal of the idol-worshipers of Bethel. To the presence of the golden calf the preeminence and prosperity of their city was largely due. "People easily forget principle when their eyes are fixed on profits." (Dr. Lowrie.) The fact that such a mob could be collected is evidence of the complete demoralization which had taken place in Bethel. Parents cannot be held to be wholly responsible for the character and conduct of their children. Despite the most careful and faithful training, the child may go astray, may disregard the fond entreaties of the parent to walk in wisdom's ways, and, instead, choose a life of sin and shame. Nevertheless, children furnish an almost infallible index of the character of the home, of the influences which are brought to bear upon them. We may determine, with a good degree of accuracy, the mental and social culture of the parent, by the language and conduct of the child. We do not need to be told that the parent is illiterate, when we find the child unable to read or write, although old enough to have mastered such subjects; when we hear him habitually violating the rules of grammar and pronunciation. When you see a young man or young woman who is ill-behaved, who has no respect for person or place, who whispers and giggles in the house of God, to the annoyance and pain of others, strive to pity such an one, for you may rest assured the training at home has been wrong or neglected. Could our young men and young women realize what a tell-tale their public life is, they would learn to be more thoughful and careful. Family pride, if nothing else, should induce us to walk circumspectly before the world. It is but fair to conclude that, had the home-training of these boys of Bethel been of a proper character, they would not have lent themselves to such disgraceful and lawless acts.

This cry of mockery was directed against an unoffending man. We may well believe that Elisha in no way provoked such an attack upon himself. His character, as revealed to us, forbids such a thought. He was a man of peace, by nature averse to harsh measures. His ministry, with few exceptions, was one of gentleness and consolation. Solomon says, "To every thing there is a season, and a time to every purpose under the heaven: a time to keep silence and a time to speak." With this truth Elisha was familiar. Led by the Spirit which he had invoked, he knew when and how to speak, and was not to be decoyed into the error of casting pearls before swine. He knew well that such creatures are liable to turn upon those so doing, and to rend them. There are many good Christian people who are continually getting into trouble through failure to remember our Lord's injunction concerning this matter. God's servants should not fear to reprove sin wherever found; but there is such a thing as choosing an inopportune time in which to perform this duty. For instance, to reprove a man for profanity when he is in a towering rage, is like adding fuel to the flame, or attempting to mend an old garment with a piece of new cloth. "That which is put in to fill up, taketh from the garment, and the rent is made worse." It is worse than useless to upbraid the drunkard for his sin and folly, when he is in a state of intoxication. To have attempted to rebuke these youthful idolaters while banded together for mischievous purposes, could have resulted only in provoking their resentment, hence the Prophet would be disposed to pass them by, to avoid saying or doing anything which would precipitate a conflict with them. But this cry of mockery was directed against Elisha more particularly as the servant of God. It is in his representative character that he is thus assailed. As the recognized head of the Divinely appointed prophetic order, and, hence, the leader of those who still adhered to the true religion, he was preeminently obnoxious to the priests of the false worship, who may have instigated the rabble to insult him. He may not have known his assailants, but it is evident that they were not ignorant as to who he was. Doubtless they had seen him many times in company with Elijah, and had been informed that he had become his successor. It seems evident that they had been apprised of his purpose to visit their city, and had prepared themselves to receive him. Relieved of the fear which Elijah had inspired, they seek to improve the first opportunity to manifest their hatred of him by the abuse of his friend.

It is an attempt to triumph over the translated prophet. The insolence of the cry with which Elisha is greeted, is seen when we remember that among Oriental people, baldness is looked upon as a disgrace, because supposed to be a mark of uncleanness. Not infrequently, it was the result of leprosy. Elisha may have been bald. But as he was yet a young man, comparatively, it is probable that the term, as applied to him, did not declare a fact, but was used simply to express contempt. He is thus branded as an unclean person, a leper, and therefore to be despised and shunned. The offense of these mockers lies chiefly, however, in their ridicule of a Divine act. In the call to Elisha to "go up," there is evidently a reference to his account of the translation of Elijah, and an avowal of their disbelief of the same. Not content with malinging the person of the Prophet, they assailed his veracity, and challenged him to furnish proof that he is the successor of the Tishbite by doing as he had done. In effect they say, "You assert that your master was taken up into heaven, and that you have succeeded him as the Lord's prophet in Israel. Prove that all this is true by ascending to heaven yourself. Call now for the horses and chariot of fire and go up, as you say Elijah did. Then we shall believe your story, and recognize your claim, but not otherwise." The contemptuous cry of the mockers of Bethel, brings to mind those taunting words which, many centuries later, were to fall upon the ears of the dying Savior of men. "He saved others; himself he cannot save. If he be the king of Israel, let him now come down from the cross, and we will believe him." This challenge to Elisha likewise expressed the contempt which his assailants cherished for him, and for his office. We would be rid of you too, is the animus of their insolent cry. But above all, this cry is the expression of unbelief in the God of Elisha. His story of the translation of his master is disbelieved and ridiculed, because these idolaters do not believe that Jehovah possesses the power and the wisdom necessary to perform such a mighty act. Neither do they believe that he is even now present with his servant, able to protect him, and to avenge their insolent treatment of him. That unbelief in the miraculous which is so loudly vaunted by many in our day, which would explain upon scientific principles the miracles of the Bible, or regard them as harmless deceptions, originates in the same spirit of unbelief in God. To those who endure as seeing him who is invisible, all things are possible with God. Swift and sore was the punishment visited upon these mockers. As they dogged the steps of the Prophet, hooting and jeering him, "He turned back, and looked upon them, and cursed them in the name of the Lord. And there came forth two she bears out of the wood, and tare forty and two children of them." Perhaps not all who had participated in this impious attack upon the Prophet fell a prey to the instruments of God's wrath. From the narrative it would seem that the forty-two who were punished constituted but a part of the band. It may be that the leaders only suffered. It is not a necessary conclusion, though it may be natural and well-nigh universal, that there was any destruction of life. The record is that the bears "tare forty and two of them," which may mean simply that they were wounded.

However this may be, the punishment was sufficiently severe to accomplish the purpose for which it was sent. The assertion of a recent expositor of this portion of the word that the action of the Prophet was too hasty, and "cannot be defended from a Christian point of view;" that Elisha should have been more tolerant, is as unjust as it is unwise. We are to remember that in this transaction the Prophet was acting as God's representative; that he did not utter these words of execration in his own name or by his own authority. As when, by beneficent miracle, the waters of Jericho were healed, he had disclaimed any share of the glory, ascribing all the power and the glory to God in the words, "Thus sayeth the Lord, I have healed these waters," so now he speaks in the name of the Lord. Whether or not he knew what the result was to be, he spoke from a sense of duty, in response to the Divine leading, rather than out of any feeling of personal resentment. "He cursed them in the name of the Lord." That God approved, aye inspired, the sentence pronounced upon these evil doers, is evident from the fact that it was at once executed, and that by messengers which no human foresight could have provided or could have anticipated. While the Syrian bear, which still inhabits part of Palestine, is remarkable for its strength and ferocity, it is said to be of a cowardly disposition, and seldom attacks man, unless maddened by hunger or by loss of its young.

In the latter circumstances, the female becomes frantic with rage, and has been known to attack a band of armed men. Whatever may have aroused the fury of the two beasts whose bloody work now claims our attention, we cannot doubt that God made them his instrument in the vindication of his faithful servant, and the punishment of sin. The attempt to establish a distinction, as to spirit and motive, between God's acts under the former dispensations, and his acts under the present dispensation, has no warrant in the word of God. From of old, even from everlasting, all God's acts "may be defended from the Christian point of view," because in harmony with his infinite holiness and justice. He changes not; but is the same "yesterday, to-day, and for ever." Now and then, in the onward sweep of time, it has seemed necessary that, "By terrible things in righteousness," God should impress upon the minds of men, great and salutary lessons which they would not learn otherwise. Such acts have characterized no one dispensation exclusively. The judgment visited upon Ananias and Sapphira in New Testament times was not less signal than those which were sent upon men in Old Testament times for a similar purpose. At the very outset of Elisha's ministry, the enemies of God, and of the true religion, sought to discredit him, to make him a laughing-stock, and his name a by-word among the people. Had they succeeded, the results must have been disastrous. His moral influence would have been destroyed by depriving him of the respect and confidence of the people. His very life would have been in constant jeopardy, and his ministry rendered ineffective. "His whole usefulness depended upon his prophetic office being acknowledged and felt to be real; and hence, however incongruous with the rest of his life, his second public appearing must be in judgment and not in mercy." (Dr. Edersheim.)

Let me close this chapter with a quotation from the pen of Dr. Arnold. "I take this story as teaching us what I think we very much need to be taught, namely, that the faults of our youth, and those which are most natural to us at that age, are not considered by God as trifling. You may hear grown-up people talk in a laughing manner of the faults which they committed at school, of their idleness, and their various acts of mischief, and worse than mischief. And when boys hear this, it naturally makes them think it really does not matter much whether they behave well or ill, they are just as likely to be respectable and amiable men hereafter. I would beg those who think so, to attend a little to the story in the text."

# CHAPTER IX.

## ELISHA IN THE CAMP OF THE ALLIED KINGS.

"Better to trust the Lord Most High,
Than on the help of man rely.
Better to trust Jehovah's grace,
Than confidence in princes place."

EASTWARD of the possession of Benjamin, with only the Jordan separating, lay the land of Moab. Its inhabitants were of the lineage of Lot, and, consequently, kindred to the descendants of Abraham. Notwithstanding the Lord had said to Moses, "Distress not the Moabites, neither contend with them in battle," Moab, by the fortunes of war, became tributary to Israel during the reign of David. When the dilaceration of the kingdom of Israel occurred, the conquered province seems to have fallen by mutual agreement, to the ten seceding tribes. Unless the resources of the land were surpassingly great, the tribute imposed by Israel must have been excessive and burdensome, especially if, as seems probable, it was paid annually. We read that "Mesha, king of Moab, was a sheepmaster, and rendered unto the king of Israel an hundred thousand lambs, and an hundred thousand rams, with the wool." Driven to desperation, it may have been, by the exaction of such a crushing tribute, Moab awaited a favorable opportunity to throw off the yoke of allegiance, and to assert her independence. The decisive moment seemed to have arrived when the warrior king Ahab breathed his last. Then the standard of revolt was raised, and throughout the land the cry of defiant hosts was heard. During the short and weak reign of Ahaziah, who succeeded Ahab, the rebellion was permitted to go unpunished and to become thoroughly established. But when Jehoram succeeded to the throne, he immediately adopted measures looking to the subjugation of the revolting people. After mobilizing his own forces, he seems to have become convinced that he was unable to put down the rebellion without aid. But he thinks of man's aid only. He relies entirely upon an arm of flesh. Not for one moment do his thoughts seem to have turned to the living God,

"On whose sustaining arm depend,
To earth's and sea's remotest end
  All men, in every age.
Who, girt with strength, sets fast the hills,
Who roaring seas and billows stills,
  Who calms the nations' rage."

Governed by such considerations only as are suggested to the carnally minded, he appeals for assistance to Jehoshaphat, kind of Judah. The vanity of such assistance, though freely and unreservedly granted, he was soon to experience. It may have been the consciousness that his heart was not right with God which deterred king Jehoram from seeking Divine direction and assistance at this important juncture in his life. Though his impiety seems to have been less daring than that of his parents or of his brother; though he instituted certain religious reforms;

it is recorded that, "he wrought evil in the sight of the Lord," that "he cleaved unto the sins of Jeroboam, the son of Nebat, which made Israel to sin; he departed not therefrom." God says, "Your iniquities have separated between you and your God, and your sins have hid his face from you that he will not hear." Righteousness can have no fellowship with unrighteousness; light can have no communion with darkness. There is a state of heart which forbids communion with God; which hides his glory from us, and makes us ashamed and afraid to cry to him for deliverance in the time of trouble. God's hand is not shortened that it cannot save; neither is his ear heavy that it cannot hear. He abideth faithful and omnipotent. We are not straitened in him, but in ourselves. It is sin that forbids appeal to God; that comes between our praying lips and his hearing ear; between us, in all our need and helplessness, and his omnipotent hand. If we will not have God to reign over us, if we stubbornly, and haughtily reject that salvation which he offers us in Jesus Christ, we have no right to cry to him for deliverance when trouble comes. Not only so, but from a spiritual point of view, this becomes impossible. A very small cloud is sufficient, if its position be favorable, to hide from us the face of the sun. A celebrated astronomer found that a silk thread, stretched across the object glass of his telescope, would hide a star entirely from view; that a silk fiber, however small, if placed upon the same glass, would cover so much of the heavens, that a star, if a small one and near the pole, would be hidden for several seconds. The infinite distance between God and unholiness makes it possible for those faults in us which we are pleased to esteem of little consequence, secret sins, incipient doubtings, to become obscuring fibers, dark clouds, which hide from us the face of our heavenly Father. Jehoshaphat at once complies with the request of Jehoram. Without seeking to know God's will in the matter, he replied, "I will go up; I am as thou art, my people as thy people, and my horses as thy horses."

Doubtless Jehoshaphat meant no more by this statement than that he was in sympathy with the purpose to invade Moab, and ready to aid in such an undertaking to the extent of his ability. Indeed he must have felt personally interested in the result, for it was but the year before, perhaps, that the Moabites, in alliance with the Ammonites and other tribes, had come up against him. God had given him a signal victory over them, and their forces had been utterly destroyed, yet still he must have felt that, as an independent nation, they would prove a constant menace to his kingdom, and, consequently, he would be disposed to regard the acceptance of an alliance which promised the permanent humiliation of such a dangerous foe, as a master stroke of policy. Well had it been for Jehoshaphat had he been less hasty in the matter, had he taken time to ask counsel of the Lord before giving answer. God's servants are never advantaged by striking hands with the wicked, by adopting the principles, the plans, and methods of the world. His word is, "Come ye out from among them, and be ye separate." For the believer to fall short of this, is to work injury to his own soul, and to the cause of righteousness. Firmly, yet not in an ostentatious manner, not in a self-righteous spirit, the follower of Christ should refuse to be "unequally yoked together with unbelievers." Matrimonial alliances, business associations, with the unbelieving or with those of a contrary religious faith, as a rule, are not conducive to the believer's growth in grace. It is frequently said by persons who enter into such relations, "We have agreed to disagree concerning the subject of religion, and to abstain from discussing it." But in all such circumstances, the believer is placed under restraints which cannot but prove injurious to the spiritual life. He is deprived of that spiritual communion and fellowship, that interchange of views as to the teaching of God's word, as to the path of duty in the varying circumstances of life, so inspiring and helpful. We soon lose interest in religious principles and convictions, however profound, which must be banished from the daily life. Any lowering of religious standards, on the part of the church or of the individual believer, to meet the demands of the world, to obliterate, in any measure, the line which separates between the believer and the unbeliever, must result in the diminishing of spiritual power. To do as the world does, is simply to be of the world, no matter what our profession may be. Two persons cannot walk together, except they be agreed. The specious plea that by associating with the unbelieving and wicked, we may be able to exert a good influence upon them, and lead them to a better life, is seldom justified by the results. The familiar modern fable is apropos. Two ladies had each a parrot. One of the birds had learned to speak profanely, the other had learned the words of prayer. The two birds were brought together with the hope that the profane one might learn to pray and forget its profanity. The result, however, was that the praying bird learned to speak profanely, while its companion was nothing improved. While the desire to be freed from an enemy which threatened the peace and safety of his kingdom, was commendable in the good king of Judah, he should have sought assurance that the method proposed was approved of God.

Too frequently God's people act upon the assumption that the end justifies the means. Methods which are questionable, to say the least, are sometimes employed to obtain money to carry on the work of the Church at home and abroad. The numerous protests from almost every quarter, against modern church fairs, and lottery schemes to raise money to liquidate church debts and support missionaries, is one of the hopeful signs of our day. Money which is obtained without value rendered therefor, had better be applied to the purchase of the potter's field, than converted into the Lord's treasury. When the combined armies of the three kings were ready to take the field, it became necessary to determine by what route they should march. From a human point of view, the success or failure of the expedition depended upon the answer to the question, "Which way shall we go up?" How pressing the need of Divine guidance at this moment! Yet these royal commanders, surrounded by their armed hosts, seem to have been wholly unconscious of their need. Neglecting to take counsel of God before entering upon the campaign, they do not turn to him now. But let us be slow to condemn them, lest our Lord's words become a rebuke to us. "Let him who is without sin cast the first stone." Every one of us is constantly confronted by questions like these, "How shall we go?" "How shall we do?" But do we always seek to be divinely guided in obtaining the answer? Is it not true that habitually we neglect to seek counsel of God as to how we shall direct our steps? Especially is this true of us in business affairs. As a result of this council of war, it was determined that the march should be through the wilderness of Edom. Doubtless the decision was well taken from a military point of view. A shorter route might have been found, but marching by the one chosen, they would be able to strike the enemy at the most vulnerable point. In addition to this, they would be better able to maintain an efficient surveillance over Edom which was a dependency of Judah. The line of march may have been determined by sound military principles, but while "man proposes, God disposes."

A contingency which no human wisdom could have foreseen, or could have provided against, well-nigh proved disastrous. After marching seven days, during part of which time, at least, they must have experienced great hardships, they reach the borders of Moab, where, it seems evident, they expected to find water. Dr. Robinson suggests that they had probably reached the Wady-el-Ahsy, which is considered a perennial stream. What then must have been their consternation, when, instead of the gleaming and joy-inspiring waters for which they craved, they beheld the dry, parched bed of the stream, and realized that in all the wide waste there was no fountain or cistern to afford relief. How vain must have seemed man's pomp and pride to that famishing host! In letters of living fire which seemed to burn into the very soul, they read that, "God ruleth in the army of heaven and among the inhabitants of earth," that battles and wars are decided, not by human power or sagacity, but according to God's sovereign will. It is instructive to note the contrast between the conduct of Jehoram and the conduct of Jehoshaphat in the presence of the appalling danger to which they were now alike exposed. Jehoram is seized with terror and despair. Courage, if he ever possessed any, deserts him. An aroused conscience leads him to conclude that the righteous judgments of the Almighty are about to be visited upon him. Impliedly confessing his utter impotence to deliver himself, he cries, "Alas! that the Lord hath called these three kings together, to deliver them into the hand of Moab! Hitherto God had had no place in all his thoughts; but now, in his humiliation and distress, he thinks of him; yet it is only to murmur against him, and to charge him with being responsible for that which he himself, above all others, was responsible.

How often it is that the sinner seeks to make others responsible for his shortcomings. God had not called Jehoram and his associates to undertake this campaign against Moab. So far as they had been able, they had not permitted God to have any thing to do with it. Without taking him into their counsel, they had marshaled their armies, and had chosen the line of march which had led to this critical pass. No! no! God had not called these three kings together. The whole matter was of their own planning. Neither was Jehoram's prediction of what was to occur, less out of harmony with the facts, than his statement of what had already occurred. It was not God's purpose to deliver them into the hand of Moab. To the contrary, he was about to deliver Moab into their hands. There is a day coming when all men must think of God. To the believer, it will be a day of joy, for the Son of Man shall be seen coming in the clouds of heaven to receive his own. To the unbeliever, that day must be full of terrors, for he shall behold God coming in judgment. Filled with dismay when called to stand before that awful presence, he shall call upon the mountains and the rocks to fall on him, and hide him from the face of him that setteth on the throne, and from the wrath of the Lamb. But while Jehoram fears, despairs, and murmurs against God, Jehoshaphat asks for a prophet of the Lord that he may inquire of the Lord. He has no complaint to make. He has no one, save himself, to blame for the calamities which have come upon him. Above all it should be noted that he has no fears to express. Calmly, hopefully, he asks, "Is there not here a prophet of the Lord, that we may inquire of the Lord by him?" That it was a gross neglect of duty not to inquire of the Lord before engaging to assist the king of Israel, he doubtless felt most deeply. But present duty may not be neglected because of past shortcomings and offenses. He feels that God still waits to be gracious. It is ever thus with the true believer. He stands undismayed in the presence of dangers which fill the boasting unbeliever with fear and alarm. He is "perplexed, but not in despair." The balm for a wounded conscience, he finds in a speedy and sincere repentance of sin; and in the time of trouble, his help is found in God. Notwithstanding Jehoshaphat's foolish words to Jehoram, "I am as thou art," he was not the same as Jehoram in God's sight, neither did he appear the same in the sight of men. He was smitten with the same rod which fell upon his wicked ally, and, yet, as Krummacher asserts, God did not deal with the two kings in the same spirit. "Jehoram was punished, Jehoshaphat only endured the stroke of love. Anger and curse have nothing more to do with the children of God." The Apostle declares, "There is therefore now no condemnation to them who are in Christ Jesus." "Whom the Lord loveth he chasteneth, and scourgeth every son whom he receiveth." God may chasten, may scourge, his chosen, but he cannot be said to punish them. Once for all, the believer was punished for sin in Jesus Christ, his representative, who hath endured the curse for him, borne his sins "in his own body on the tree." This blessed truth is not to be perverted into a license or an indulgence to commit sin. Rather should we find in it an incentive to holiness.

John says, "Whosoever is born of God doth not commit sin; for his seed remaineth in him: and he cannot sin, because he is born of God." Ideally, and potentially, the Christian life is one of freedom from sin. In proportion as a man yields himself unto God, permits the Holy Spirit to possess him, the ideal is realized. It is possible for the believer to be so filled with the Spirit, as to be guided by him in all things, and, where this is the case, there can be no sin. It is a servant of the king of Israel who replies to the inquiry of king Jehoshaphat, "Here is Elisha, the son of Shaphat, who poured water on the hands of Elijah." The name of this person, like that of many another who has proved himself a benefactor of his fellow-men, is unknown. He may have occupied a very humble position, but there was glory enough for one life in the simple act of directing attention to Elisha in a time of such dire distress and imminent peril. However lowly our station in life, let us be persuaded that it is possible for us to do some really great thing. If our hearts be right with God, we may point the weary and the heavy laden to a greater than Elisha, and who giveth rest. We may tell the perishing around us of the Lamb of God, who taketh away the sin of the world. We do not know how long Elisha had been in the camp of the allied kings; whether he arrived about the time the king was moved to inquire for a prophet of the Lord, or had been with the army since the march began. The fact that Jehoshaphat was ignorant of his presence in the camp, would seem to favor the first supposition. Such ignorance would seem scarcely possible, in view of the prominence which Elisha had already acquired. But of this we may be assured, Elisha was in the camp by Divine direction. The heart of the pious king of Judah leaps with joy when the announcement of Elisha's presence is made to him. Whether or not he had had any previous knowledge of the prophet, he is convinced that God will speak by him, and exultingly exclaims, "The word of the Lord is with him," meaning, he is such an one as we desire, a prophet of the Lord. "God, who at sundry times and in divers manners spake in time past unto the fathers by the prophets, hath in these last days spoken unto us by his Son, whom he hath appointed heir of all things, by whom also he made the worlds." Do we appreciate this truth as we should?

## CHAPTER X.

### ELISHA'S AID INVOKED BY THREE KINGS.

"My steps have pressed the flowers,
That to the Muses' bowers
The eternal dews of Helicon have given:
And trod the mountain height,
Where Science, young and bright,
Scans with poetic gaze the midnight-heavens;
Yet have I found no power to vie
With thine, severe necessity!"
(Thomas Love Peacock.)

WITH a withering sun above them; and burning sands beneath their feet; frenzied with thirst, to quench which no water might be found; and almost suffocated by the sirocco, the armies of the allied kings of Israel, Judah, and Edom, lay encamped upon the borders of the land of Moab. Like the condor which, from the lofty mountain summit, watches the staggering movements of the famished traveler, waiting the favorable moment to attack and to destroy him, the sentinels of the enemy might be seen in the distance. To advance promised no relief, indeed such a movement could but intensify the distress already experienced. To attempt to retreat seemed even more perilous. Whilst certain destruction must be the result, if the armies remained in the position which they now occupied. Ofttimes God thus shuts men up to seek his aid. Until brought to this wretched strait, even the pious Jehoshaphat had prosecuted the campaign without inquiring of the Lord. Now, however, when destruction seems inevitable, he hastens with his associates to the tent of the Prophet. For the time, the custom of kings is disregarded, every question of precedence forgotten. Instead of summoning Elisha into their presence, they determine humbly to go to him. How marvelous the change which has taken place in the circumstances of this farmer boy of Abel-mehola! Out of the obscurity in which his childhood days were spent, and from the humble occupation of pouring water on the hands of Elijah, he has come to be sought of kings. To him the great ones of the earth now turn as "their last and only refuge in distress." To a less thoroughly sanctified heart, to one whose consecration to God was less perfect, such honors must have proved perilous. Success and honor are sometimes as hard to bear, as failure and the denial by the world of that recognition to which merit entitles a man. But Elisha is not elated nor flattered by the honor shown him. He is not permitted to forget his dependence upon God, and the duty of ascribing all the honor and the power and the glory to his name. Neither is he abashed nor terrified in the presence of these great dignitaries. With a fearlessness and firmness which must command our admiration, and which appears most remarkable when we consider the despotic power possessed by kings in ancient times, he rebukes the king of Israel. With intense indignation, he denies the right of this man, who had persisted in following after the sins of Jeroboam, to come to him as the Lord's prophet with an appeal for help when in distress. "What have I to do with thee?" he reproachfully asks.

Which is but another way of asserting that there is nothing in common between him and the king; that, as the Lord's servant, he owes the king nothing; that he has no just claim upon him. In terms of the keenest irony and which must appear heartless and cruel, did we not know that he spoke as the Spirit of God moved him to speak, he bids the king seek counsel of the prophets of his father, and the prophets of his mother. By the former, he doubtless means those court-prophets through whom the lying spirit spoke to persuade Ahab that he might "go up and fall at Ramoth-gilead." By the latter, he must mean the prophets of Baal, whose predecessors Elijah slew by the brook Kishon. Despite the repellent attitude of the Prophet toward him, the king of Israel continues to plead his cause, and repeats the impious charge that the Lord is responsible for the perilous position in which the three kings, with their armies, were placed, a position from which no human power could save. "Nay: for the Lord hath called these three kings together, to deliver them into the hand of Moab." Persuaded, doubtless, that discussion would avail nothing; that any attempt to convince the king of his folly and sin, must prove futile, Elisha contents himself with the emphatic and disdainful rejoinder, "As the Lord of Hosts liveth, before whom I stand, surely were it not that I regard the pressence of Jehoshaphat the king of Judah, I would not look toward thee, nor see thee." How greatly to the advantage of a company, or a community the presence of a righteous person may prove! Even the unbelieving and godless may be sharers in such advantage. Had there been ten righteous persons in Sodom, the terrible destruction of the city would have been averted. But for the presence of the pious, though for the time erring, Jehoshaphat, Elisha had refused to intercede in behalf of this imperiled host. Were righteousness to perish from the earth, God would refuse to look toward our apostate race. It is the presence of those who fear him which enlists the favor of God in behalf of a world which lies in wickedness, which delays the coming of the end of time. For Jehoshaphat's sake Elisha is entreated, but his spirit has been too greatly perturbed to enter into communion with God. Even righteous indignation unfits a soul for this. Anger is incompatible with the profoundest spiritual aspirations and experience. That he might receive and deliver God's message the spirit of the Prophet must be calmed. To this end he calls for a minstrel, one who plays upon the harp, and who may have accompanied the tones of his instrument with some of those words of song which the Psalmist had been inspired to teach the people. "There is no feeling, perhaps, except the extremes of fear and grief, that does not find relief in music." (George Eliot.)

"Music religious heat inspires,
It wakes the soul and lifts it high,
And wings it with sublime desires,
And fits it to bespeak the Deity."
(Addison.)

Every man, no matter how religiously inclined, must feel at times the need of some aid to devotion. We are not always in that frame of mind which makes it possible for us to engage with pleasure and profit in the worship of Almighty God. The cares and vexations of life, the disappointments which come to us daily, and even the realization of our hopes and expectations, may serve to divert the mind from that which is heavenly, even while we wait before God in the sanctuary. But music, which Carlyle has characterized as "the speech of angels," has power to soothe the troubled breast; to arrest the wanderings of the mind; to inspire holy and reverent thoughts; and it thus serves as an aid in bringing the mind into a proper frame to commune with God.

> "Music the fiercest grief can charm,
> And fate's severest rage disarm:
> Music can soften pain to ease,
> And make despair and madness please:
> Our joys below it can improve,
> And antedate the bliss above."
>
> (Pope.)

As the sweet strains of David's harp fell upon the ear of King Saul, the evil spirit which troubled him departed. The power of music to impart inspiration to do and to dare, has ever been recognized. Marvelous, indeed, have been the effects produced by the playing of some stirring air at a critical point in the march of an army, or when the result of battle has trembled in the balance. In crossing the Alps, Napoleon Bonaparte's army came to a pass where the rocks could not be surmounted by the ammunition wagons. Napoleon went to the leader of the band and asked for his portfolio. Receiving it, he turned over the pages until he came to an inspiring march, "Play that," he said to the leader. The whole band joined in rendering the music, and over the rocks went the ammunition wagons. At a critical moment during the battle of Waterloo, Wellington discovered that the Forty-second Highlanders began to waver. On inquiring as to the cause of a thing so unusual, he was informed that the band had ceased to play. He instantly gave command that the pipes be played in full force. The effect was magical. The wavering Highlanders rallied, and, with tattered colors and blood-drenched swords, they pressed forward to win the hard contested field. "All history," says a writer in the Youths' Companion, "reveals the fact that music, wedded to stirring and patriotic words, has in every age had a powerful influence on the course of public events. Nor is this true of civilized people alone. Among almost all savage races, the warriors excite themselves to martial ardor by songs which thrill their souls. The war dances alike of our North American Indians, of the African Negroes, and of the semi-civilized races which dwell in Asia, are accompanied by songs which, though wild and incoherent to us, have an inspiring influence upon themselves. Lord Wharton boasted, it is said, that his political ballad, "Lilliburlero," sung James the Second out of three kingdoms. The effect of the "Marseillaise" in arousing and exciting the revolutionary spirit of France is one of the prominent facts in the history of that country. To it in no small degree is attributed the success of the French arms against the allies who assailed the young republic. So potent indeed was it felt to be in kindling the patriotic passion, that both the Napoleons forbade its being sung or played in France during their reigns. In the same way, the great patriotic Hungarian song, the "Bakoczy March" was prohibited in Austria, since, as it was said, the very sound of it made Hungarian swords leap from their scabbards. Can it be doubted that the fire of Scottish patriotism has long been fed by Burns's clarion song, "Scots wha hae"? that the Briton feels the love of country swelling in his heart as he hears the familiar strains of "Rule

Britannia" or "Ye Mariners of England"? or that American souls kindled to the same emotion when greeted with "America" or "The Star-Spangled Banner"? To the soldier of the cross, whose citizenship is in heaven, the song of thanksgiving to God, of adoration and trust, has proved a source of strength and courage when called to do battle against temptation, when trying duty has been laid upon him, when the heart has been filled with discouragement and forebodings, when the hands have been weary and the knees feeble. May the Church come to recognize music more fully as a Divine gift to man, and seek to avail herself of its power. May the sanctified effort never cease to make the music of the sanctuary of such a character as is best suited to fit the soul for communion with God. Martin Luther was wont to say, "One of the finest and noblest gifts of God is music. This is very hateful to the devil, and with it we may drive off temptations and evil thoughts. After theology I give the next and highest place to music. It has often aroused and moved me, so that I have won a desire to preach."

As Elisha yielded himself to the soothing influences of music, "The hand of the Lord came upon him," "the veil which hides from human view the future, was withdrawn, and he saw what should shortly come to pass." The minstrel ceases to play, and he gives this strange direction, "Make this valley full of ditches." In explanation of this direction, and with the intent that those to whom it is given may be the more ready to obey it, the Prophet adds these words, "For thus saith the Lord, ye shall not see wind, neither shall ye see rain; yet that valley shall be filled with water, that ye may drink, both ye, and your cattle, and your beasts. And this is but a light thing in the sight of the Lord: he will deliver the Moabites also into your hands." Preparation was to be made for the reception of the blessing promised, and so much needed. To the men who composed that famishing army the preparation required would doubtless appear ridiculously inadequate. By the majority, doubtless, the Prophet's words would be received with a large measure of incredulity. The idea of digging trenches in those shimmering sands to obtain water, would seem an absurd thing to most minds. It would be insisted that the scorching sun and the withering winds had robbed the earth of all moisture: that the brazen heavens and the absence of cloud afforded no hope of rain. In addition to this, it might have been urged that by reason of hardships already endured, the soldiers would be unequal to such a task. God meant to teach these kings and their subjects a lesson of faith, to impress upon their minds the truth that, strengthened and assisted by him, they were sufficient for every duty. Had they been bidden to seek to propitiate God by sacrifices and penances; had Elisha cried to God in their behalf; or had there been any promise of rain; the task set before them might not have seemed so unreasonable and hopeless. But they must simply accept the word of the Prophet, and trust God for strength to do as they had been directed. We need not speculate as to what would have been the result, had they refused to do this. Their only hope lay in obedience. Every other hope had vanished. Thus it is with the sinner. No hope is left him, save that which is set before him in the Gospel. To turn away from this hope, is to refuse life. "Neither is there salvation in any other: for there is none other name under heaven given among men, whereby we must be saved." As we may imagine the men of Israel and Judah to have reasoned and spoken concerning God's plan for saving them from a terrible death by thirst or by the hands of the Moabites; so many are found to reason and to speak concerning the plan which God, in infinite wisdom and mercy, has devised to save men from sin. All men are, to some extent at least, conscious of sin. Even the benighted heathen have this consciousness, as is evident from their sacrifices and penances. All men, to some extent at least, recognize the ruinous consequences of sin. Yet unregenerate men are prone to think that God's plan to save sinners is not feasible, at least, it is not the best. To the Jew, it has ever been a stumbling-block; and to the Greek, foolishness. Avowed unbelief proclaims the doctrine of justification by faith to be unworthy the acceptance of intelligent minds. There is no reason, cries the infidel, in such a scheme. Why should God save any man, simply because he believes on the Lord Jesus Christ? Many who profess to accept God's plan, at the same time seek to improve upon it according to their fancy. To some, salvation through grace has seemed too easy, and they have attempted to supplement such a method by self-imposed penances and works of supererogation. To others, God's method of saving sinners has seemed too exacting, to impose too many and too great restrictions. Christ says, "If any man will come after me, let him deny himself, and take up his cross daily, and follow me." Yet professing Christians will say, "why should we deny ourselves, and bear a cross?" God says, "Come ye out from among them and be ye separate." But it is said, "why should we separate ourselves from the world, and appear odd?" Why should we forego the pleasures of the world, and be required to eschew those little acts of dishonesty, and words of deceit which the world recognizes as necessary to success in business?" Our Lord says, "Preach the Gospel," yet how many, even of those who have been ordained to this glorious work, choose rather to preach science and philosophy. In a figurative and spiritual sense these words may be regarded as addressed to each one of us personally. "Make this valley full of ditches." Our hearts are by nature destitute of the water of eternal life. To the woman of Samaria, Jesus said, "Whosoever drinketh of the water that I shall give him shall never thirst; but the water that I shall give him shall be in him a well of water springing up into everlasting life." There is an implied promise in these words that this water of life shall be given. But this promise cannot be fulfilled in us, this blessing cannot be enjoyed by us, until our hearts are prepared to receive the blessing. There must be faith in the word of promise. There must be a willingness, an earnest desire, on our part to be blessed. We must diligently seek to avail ourselves of every means of grace. By prayer, by the study of the word of God, in the Sabbath-School, in the prayer meeting, in the sanctuary, and by a daily life becoming the gospel, we are digging ditches for the reception of the blessings of God's grace. We cannot have too many ditches; neither can these ditches be dug too deeply.

These words admit of a wider application. By every Christian, the community in which he lives, the world at large, is regarded as a waste place, a desert, which must be filled with ditches, that the water of eternal life which God has promised to every soul, to every nation, kindred, and tongue, may be received. These ditches are dug by the Christian when his life is conformed to the pattern which Christ has given; when he lets his light so shine before men, that they may see his good works, and glorify his Father which is in heaven; when by earnest prayer he seeks the outpouring of the Spirit upon the community and upon the world. Those of us who are familiar with the operations in our oil fields, know that it is the custom to make preparation for saving the oil before it is obtained. Before the drill has reached the rock which contains the oil, large tanks are constructed, at a convenient distance from the well, and pipes are laid whereby the oil, when obtained, may be conducted into these tanks, and from thence into still larger tanks. To neglect to make such preparation may be to lose thousands of barrels of oil. Let us seek that our hearts, and the hearts of others, may be brought into such relation to God as to receive and treasure up his saving truth. It seems evident that, however great may have been the measure of their incredulity, the Hebrew soldiers at once began the work of making ditches; and that they rested not until their task was done. Weary from toil, and still suffering from thirst, they sought their tents at even-tide, wondering what the morrow would bring. With the dawn of the new day, all were astir; and as the sun was gilding the eastern sky, indicating that the time had come for the offering of the morning sacrifices, they were startled and gladdened by the sound of surging waves. Looking toward Edom, the direction from which the sound seemed to come, they beheld a mighty flood rolling toward them with resistless force. Onward it rushed until swallowed up by the ditches which they had digged, and the whole valley was filled with water. What wonder, if these famishing men, as they beheld, had felt disposed to question their sense of vision, and to suspect that all this was but a cruel mirage, mocking their distress. But to quaff their fill was to dispel all doubt, and to assure their senses. Fervent must have been the words of thanksgiving, and loud the hozannas which burst from the lips of those to whom this great deliverance had come. We are left to conjecture as to whence this abundant supply of water had come. Josephus states, without giving authority, that a great storm had occurred at a distance of three days journey from the camp of the Israelites. A cloud-burst, or an unusually heavy and protracted rain at some distance from the camp might be sufficient to account for the phenomenon. Yet this does not rob it of its miraculous character. "The salvation of the Israelitish army from the destruction which threatened it, did not consist in a miracle which overruled the laws of nature, but only in this, that God caused the powers of nature which he had prepared, to work in the manner which he had foreordained." (Keil.)

That which brought safety and happiness to Israel, led Moab to the destruction which God had appointed her. As her soldiers stood in armor "in the border," and looked toward the camp of Israel, they saw the water "as red as blood," and instantly concluded that their invaders had fallen out among themselves and had destroyed one another. The desire may have been father to the conclusion. But to this conclusion they would be the more inclined in view of their own experience the previous year. Without taking the precaution to investigate, the cry is raised, "Moab, to the spoil. In wild confusion, they rush forward, only to be met by their now refreshed and confident enemies by whom they are smitten, routed, pursued, and wasted, according to the word of Elisha.

# CHAPTER XI.

## A WIDOW'S CRY FOR HELP.

"And man whose heaven-erected face
The smiles of love adorn,
Man's inhumanity to man
Makes countless thousands mourn."
(Robert Burns.)

THE inspired record of events in the life of Elisha, does not purport to be a detailed and consecutive history. Out of a long and eventful career a few salient acts have been selected, the choice of each being determined, doubtless, by some peculiar didactic value. Years may have intervened between the event which we last considered, and that which is now to claim our attention. During this time, Elisha, with increasing prestige, had devoted himself to the peaceful duties of his sacred office. It may have been while he was visiting one of the schools of the prophets that to him "there cried a certain woman of the wives of the sons of the prophets." We know nothing of this woman, further than that which is disclosed by this cumbersome, yet vague, designation. According to a Jewish tradition, she was the widow of the pious Obadiah who, while occupying a position of honor and responsibility at the court of Ahab, contrived to hide a hundred of the Lord's prophets in a cave, and to supply them with food during the time of their murderous persecution by Jezebel.

According to this tradition, Jezebel was informed of the kindness which Obadiah had shown to the prophets, and of his strong attachment to the true religion, and succeeded in having him dismissed from the king's service. After his dismissal, he took up his abode in one of the schools of the prophets, and thenceforth devoted himself to the work of instructing the people in the truths of Divine revelation. Indirectly, the narrative shows us that the sons of the prophets were not exclusively young men and unmarried, and that their life was not monastic.

We can scarcely conceive of a more pathetic story than that which this woman relates to Elisha. She had been profoundly bereaved. God had been pleased to take her husband from her. That he had been a kind and loving husband is evident from her statement that he "feared the Lord." The godly man honors every position and relation in life. A true Christian makes a good citizen, a kind, considerate, and affectionate husband or wife, parent or child. If the testimony borne to this deceased prophet were true of every man and woman in our land today, the evils which afflict society, which so frequently mar domestic peace and felicity, which endanger the rights and the person of the individual member of society would be unknown. Then we should have no need for bars and locks, for criminal laws and prison houses. To be bereft of such a noble and devoted companion would seem enough for one poor heart to bear. Yet in this case the grief occasioned by bereavement must have known some mitigation. Dark and lonely as the life of this woman had been rendered, her bereavement was not without some elements of comfort. The death of the believer brings joy as well as sorrow to the hearts of those whom he leaves behind.

If they share his faith, they have the assurance that his departure means for him "to be with Christ, which is far better." The vision which faith affords of the land of immortality, renders it possible, and proper, for the believer to consider even death itself as a part of his heritage from God. But sorrow for a loved one departed, was not the only bitter element mingled in the cup which was pressed to the lips of this sorely distressed woman. Her husband, though he had been so good and so true, had not only left her in impoverished circumstances, but had bequeathed to her a burdensome debt. It can serve no useful purpose, perhaps, to inquire how this debt had been incurred, since we are not told and have no means of learning. According to the tradition to which we have already referred, it was the result of the support given to the one hundred prophets while secreted for safety in the cave. Whether this be true or not, it seems safe to assume that neither the deceased prophet nor his now desolate wife, was blamable in the matter. This debt was not the result of extravagant living, nor of dishonest speculation. At the same time we cannot emphasize too strongly that scripture which saith, "Owe no man any thing, but to love one another." Debt is like many a sin, in that it often affects others besides the person who is directly responsible for it. In many cases the innocent suffer more than the guilty. It is to be feared that the conscience of this age is not as sensitive upon this subject as it ought to be, as sober honesty demands it should be. The thirst for riches, the consuming desire to become wealthy, the love of display, and the pernicious credit system of our day, tempt many men to engage in hazardous speculations, and to live beyond their means, to an extent which has proved ruinous in many cases, both from a financial and moral point of view. No intelligent Christian can contemplate with indifference the prospect of leaving his family destitute at his death. By every legitimate means in his power, he will guard against the necessity of bequeathing a debt to the loved ones whom he must leave behind. Mr. Spurgeon, commenting upon the words, "Take no thought for the morrow," began by saying, "I insured my life last week and have thus been able to carry out the injunction of the text, and not to be over anxious for the morrow, for such undue care and anxiety that I had is now laid aside, secure in the knowledge that my forethought has provided for my loved ones." To every honest person, debt brings distress of mind, especially when the means of satisfying it are inadequate or wholly lacking. To such distress there was added, in the case of this woman, the heartless and persistent demands of the creditor for that which was legally due him. Aware of her destitute circumstances, knowing that she did not possess the money nor the property sufficient to satisfy his claim, he had served notice of his intention to avail himself of his legal right to seize and to hold her two sons as bondmen. In primitive times, the methods by which credit and loans are obtained in our day, and which are often so shamefully abused, were unknown. There was no system by which one man could become indorser of another's note, and thus, without value received, jeopard his own business and estate. The loan of money could be obtained upon the credit of the borrower only who was obliged to pledge his person, and, in the event of his failure to pay, he went into servitude. In a modified form this law, perhaps hitherto unwritten, was incorporated in the Mosaic code.

The creditor might take his debtor and make him a bondman, but he was forbidden to rule over him with rigor; neither was the period of servitude to extend beyond the next year of jubilee. To Israel, God revealed himself as the friend and protector of the widow and the fatherless, ready to avenge any wrong that might be done them. As a statute, it was written, "Ye shall not afflict any widow or fatherless child. If thou afflict them in any wise, and they cry at all unto me, I will surely hear their cry; and my wrath shall wax hot, and I will kill you with the sword; and your wives shall be widows, and your children fatherless." Barbarous as this law of the Hebrews concerning the debtor may seem to us, it should be remembered that its provisions for the protection of the unfortunate and the helpless were far in advance of the laws of any of the surrounding nations upon the same subject; and that it was doubtless the best which human society, as it then existed, was able to receive. With her burden of distress, this poor woman comes to Elisha to cast herself at his feet and to implore his aid. Doubtless she felt that there was none other to whom she might go with any hope of obtaining help. It is probable that her neighbors had shown her but little sympathy. They were accustomed to see debtors dealt with as her creditor was about to deal with her, and were therefore oblivious, to a great extent, to the cruelty of such proceedings. Some there may have been who were even disposed to upbraid her for her unwillingness to have the law take its course. But to know that many another had suffered the same fate which now seemed to await her, that the great evil which menaced her already desolate home, had the sanction of law, brought not the least ray of comfort to the breaking heart of this woman. It but served to intensify her grief to feel that long familiarity with such agony as she now endured, had rendered callous the hearts of those about her, and thus deprived her of that sympathy which, though it could not avert, might render her calamity less intolerable. It was in recognition of Elisha as the representative of God, that this friendless and oppressed woman came to him for help. With the Psalmist, she could say, "I am poor and needy, yet the Lord thinketh upon me." God is the "refuge and strength" of the believer, "a very present help in trouble." Other help may fail, but God faileth never. If we find ourselves inquiring why this woman did not go directly to God, we must remember that "the way into the holiest of all was not yet made manifest," that under the former covenant those who worshiped God saw but dimly, and, in many instances, were obliged to approach the throne of grace through prophet or priest because they did not know the way of approach. How vastly greater our privileges as set forth in those triumphant words of the Apostle. "Seeing then that we have a great high priest that is passed into the heavens, Jesus the Son of God, let us hold fast our profession. For we have not an high priest which cannot be touched with the feeling of our infirmities; but was in all points tempted like as we are, yet without sin. Let us therefore come boldly unto the throne of grace, that we may obtain mercy, and find grace to help in time of need." This woman seems to have preferred no definite request. "Without presuming to prescribe, or even to ask a remedy, she simply states her case of utter desolation, and leaves a blank in the hand of her God, to be filled as his mercy and his love shall dictate. She knows the extent of her calamity, but she does not know the extent of God's love, and she is wisely silent, for, in suggesting a remedy, she would probably only have abridged her mercies. The child of God can never be so safe as in his Father's hands. Exceeding abundantly above all that we ask or think, is the only measure by which even an apostle could describe the bounties of our God." (Rev. Henry Blunt.)

The assumption on the part of this woman that the Prophet ought to help her, is based upon the fact that her husband had been an acquaintance, perhaps an intimate friend of the Prophet, and, more especially, upon the fact that he had been a god-fearing man. "Thou knowest that thy servant did fear the Lord." It must always prove an advantage to a man to cultivate the society of God's people. It furnishes an inspiration to uprightness of life and purity of heart, and at the same time secures immunity from the perils of godless associates. But there is vastly greater advantage in being numbered among those who fear the Lord. No higher eulogy could have been pronounced upon this deceased prophet than these words which fall from the lips of her who knew him best, "Thou knowest that thy servant did fear the Lord." Such a good name was a precious legacy to leave to his children. Elisha's Christ-like heart is moved with pity for her who has poured this story of bereavement and distress into his ear. It may have been after he had breathed an inaudible prayer in her behalf, that he was Divinely impelled and directed to minister to her relief. In pursuance of this purpose, he asks, "What shall I do for thee?" This question implies that all his resources were placed at her command, that he was willing to aid her to the extent of his ability. Thus unreservedly are the resources of heaven made subject to the order of the believer when it is said to him, "Ask, and ye shall receive." "If ye shall ask any thing in my name, I will do it." Pausing a moment, perhaps, for a reply, but receiving none, the Prophet again speaks. "Tell me," he earnestly asks, "what hast thou in the house?" Money or its equivalent must be had that this woman might meet the claims of her inexorable creditor, and thus save her sons from bondage. But neither of these did the Prophet possess.

His interposition must therefore be of a miraculous character. He seems to have felt the necessity of something material as a basis for the exercise of the miraculous power which was granted him, hence his question, "What hast thou in the house?" Not always, perhaps, yet in very many instances, our Lord seems to have felt the same necessity, not that such necessity actually existed, perhaps, though it is a question whether even miraculous energy may not be subject to certain limitations, but because it seems to be the Divine purpose to digress as slightly as possible from the established constitution and course of things. When our Lord would supply the lack of wine at the marriage in Cana of Galilee, and manifest forth his glory, he directed that the water-pots should be filled with water, and with this as a basis, he wrought the initial miracle of his earthly ministry. We do not deny the power of the Son of God to have caused wine to fill the cups of those who were present at that marriage supper, but he did not do so. He chose rather to imitate nature to some extent, at least, in the process of making wine. When he would give sight to the man who was born blind, he must needs make an ointment of spittle and clay and anoint his eyes, and bid him, "Go, wash in the pool of

Siloam." When he would feed that hungry multitude out by the sea of Galilee, he takes the scanty supply of food which the disciples had with them, and with this as a "working basis," so to speak, produced food sufficient to satisfy the needy thousands about him. To assert that the few loaves and fishes were not necessary to the result obtained, that Christ could have wrought this mighty miracle without them, is more than our present knowledge will justify. All things are possible with God, and yet we read that our Lord, when in his own country, "could there do no mighty works." Not that he lacked the power, but because the conditions were not favorable for the exercise of that power. Jesus might have commanded that the stones of the wilderness be made bread to feed those on whom he had compassion, but he chose to make bread out of bread, and fish out of fish. There are exceptions, I freely grant, to this rule, at least so far as we are able to observe, but the more we study the miracles wrought by our Lord and his prophets and apostles, the more apparent will become this principle of the use of means. Many times the means at hand appear wholly inadequate, yet God seems to have need of them, and requires nothing more. "Thine handmaid," says this woman, "hath not any thing in the house, save a pot of oil," literally an anointing of oil, that is, so much oil as one person would require for one anointing. It was all she had, but more was not required. At every step in the journey of life, with every duty that is laid upon us, this question demands an answer. "What hast thou in the house?" The young man or the young woman in seeking to determine what shall be the work of life, what calling shall be chosen, should seek, first of all, to be able to give an intelligent answer to this question. Every man is specially suited for some one calling. There have been very few men who have excelled in more than one vocation; but every man is good for something, and success in life depends upon his discovering his special talent, and employing it faithfully.

The talent of many a man has been buried in a calling for which he was not suited. "My father spoiled an excellent mechanic in trying to make a preacher of me," said a clergyman who, after years of honest but disappointing effort, was obliged to retire from the ministry. Many a man has made a dismal failure of life in trying to be a farmer or a mechanic when he might have won renown at the editor's desk, in the pulpit, or on the bench. To us who profess to believe in his name, the Master says, "Go, work in my vineyard." "Go, preach the Gospel." And with such words of command comes the inquiry, "What hast thou in the house." Not with great talents such as we might wish to possess, but with such as we have, we are to be about our Lord's business. No matter how small our talents may be, if they are but consecrated to the service of God, we shall be able to do great things for him and for our fellow-men. Informed as to the extent of this woman's resources, Elisha is no longer in doubt as to what he shall do for her relief. Led by the Spirit, he gives this strange direction, "Go, borrow thee vessels abroad of all thy neighbors, even empty vessels; borrow not a few. And when thou art come in thou shalt shut the door upon thee and upon thy sons, and shalt pour out into all those vessels, and thou shalt set aside that which is full." So far as the record shows, the woman was not told what would be the result of obedience to this direction. She is required simply to trust the Prophet, more truly, to have faith in God who spoke to her through the Prophet. And yet, she must have been led to expect great things because of the Prophet's words, "borrow not a few," "set aside that which is full." God encourages us to ask for much, and to expect much. His words are, "Open thy mouth wide, and I will fill it." Again he says, "Prove me now herewith, if I will not open the windows of heaven, and pour you out a blessing, that there shall not be room enough to receive it." And our Lord says, "If ye abide in me, and my words abide in you, ye shall ask what ye will, and it shall be done unto you." This woman is directed to borrow empty vessels. To have done otherwise would but have increased her indebtedness, and, from a human point of view, would have defeated the Lord's purpose to save her from distress. God would have us come to him empty, that he may fill us. He cannot bless those who do not "hunger and thirst after righteousness." "They that be whole need not a physician." To receive of God's infinite fulness, we must be able to say, as we come to him,

"Nothing in my hand I bring;
Simply to thy cross I cling;
Naked, come to thee for dress,
Helpless, look to thee for grace,
Foul, I to the fountain fly;
Wash me, Savior! or I die."

If God is to fill us with his Spirit, we must be emptied of all self righteousness, of all sin. That which was about to be done, was too sacred a thing to permit the curious gaze of those not directly interested; nor were the minds of the widow and her sons to be diverted from duty by the presence of others; hence she was directed to shut the door upon them while pouring the oil into the vessels which she had borrowed. The world was to be shut out that they might be alone with God who was to work so marvelously for them. We all have need thus to be alone at times with God that we may receive his blessing. Jesus says, "When thou prayest, enter into thy closet, and when thou hast shut the door, pray to thy Father which is in secret." However strange the direction of the Prophet might seem to her, this woman hesitates not to obey it. Having borrowed all the vessels which her neighbors had to lend her, or, it may be, as many as she had faith to borrow, she entered into her house, and, when she had shut the door upon herself and sons, she took the vessel which contained all her earthly store, and proceeded to pour the contents into one of the borrowed vessels. But without diminishing the quantity of oil in her own vessel, the borrowed vessel is filled. It is set aside, and another is handed to her, which is in turn filled. This is continued until all the vessels in the house have been filled. Then only did the oil cease to flow. Had there been more vessels, they too might have been filled. The miraculous supply of oil was limited to this woman's ability to receive it, and to that hour alone. Had she now hastened to her neighbors and secured additional vessels it would have availed her nothing. The oil had stayed. The opportunity to be enriched by the miraculous stream was never to return. God's ability and willingness to bless are infinite; yet his blessings are limited to our ability and willingness to receive, and to the time and place of his own appointment. Opportunities to receive good, which are permitted to pass unimproved, may never return. With a heart throbbing with gratitude, and exulting in the manifestation of God's love for her, this woman, poor no longer, hastens to the Prophet again, to tell him what great things the Lord has done for her, and to ask direction as to what disposition she should make of the oil. It was doubtless that the trial and triumph of her faith might be the more complete that such direction was not given her during her first interview with the Prophet. "Go, sell the oil," he now says to her, "and pay thy debt, and live thou and thy children of the rest." Before appropriating any part of the proceeds of the sale of the oil to her own use, she was to pay her debt. The safety of her children, and her own peace and happiness required this; but fidelity to the principle of honesty likewise required it. How much better it would be for all concerned, if this were the rule today. Before gratifying the desire to travel, to dress elegantly, to live sumptuously, every man should see to it that his debts are all paid. But while we seek to meet our obligations to our fellow-men may this be the honest inquiry of each one of us, "What shall I render unto the Lord for all his benefits toward me?"

# CHAPTER XII.

## HOSPITALITY SHOWN AND REWARDED.

"Nay, thank me not! the kind one said,
'Tis to myself I've given!
Each friendly deed like this, I make
A stepping-stone to Heaven."

It is probable that Elisha had no fixed place of residence after leaving the parental roof to become the disciple and companion of Elijah. During a part, at least, of his ministry, Mount Carmel seems to have been a favorite resort with him, as it had been with his master. Here, when not engaged with the duties of his office, he sought retirement and rest, and found opportunity for study and for communion with God. In consequence of this, Carmel became, in some sense, a center from which he went forth, at stated intervals, perhaps, to visit the various schools of the prophets. As he thus journeyed to and fro, he frequently had occasion to pass through Shunem, now called Solam, a village of Issachar, situated at the base of the Gebel Duhy, or Little Hermon, and on the border of the Plain of Esdraelon, by many described as one of the fairest spots of earth, unsurpassed in fertility of soil and salubrity of climate. In this quiet, but prosperous village, lived a remarkable woman. Her name is not once mentioned in the somewhat lengthy story that is told concerning her;

but that she was a person of note in the community in which she lived is evident from the fact that she is described as a great woman. The inspired narrative affords no warrant at all for the assumption, which seems almost universal, that this woman exceeded her husband in that which contributed to make her great, whatever it may have been. The story relates to her rather than to her husband, hence it is that prominence is given to her while he is mentioned but incidentally. It may have been because she possessed great wealth and lived in a stately mansion, or because she belonged to some distinguished family, that her neighbors called her great; but the story shows her to have been great in the truest and best sense. She was one of God's noble women, one of those angelic spirits whose lives are a benediction to the world. She had observed Elisha as, with weary step and dust-covered garments, he had passed and repassed her door; and, although not personally acquainted with him perhaps, she resolved to invite him to her house, that he might rest, and be refreshed with food. Hospitality cannot be said to be a distinctively Christian virtue. Plato enjoins its practice by declaring that, "the avenging deities are especially severe against inhospitality." A distinguished historian states that, "the Arabs pushed to superstition their respect of hospitality. Their most inveterate enemy found refuge, security, and even protection as soon as he succeeded in touching the cord of their tents, or the gown skirts of their wives." (Lamartine.) Speaking of the aborigines of America, Bancroft says, "The hospitality of the Indian has rarely been questioned. The stranger enters his cabin day or night without asking leave. He will take his own rest abroad that he may give up his own skin or mat of sedge to his guest." Irving observes that, "food is generally open to free participation in savage life, and is rarely made an object of barter, until habits of trade have been introduced by the white men. The untutored savage in almost every part of the world scorns to make a traffic of hospitality."

While man possesses an instinctive appreciation of the duty of hospitality, the religion which God gave to his people, and which received its highest development in the lives and teachings of our Lord and his apostles, enjoins the practice of hospitality. Christian hospitality is an act of obedience to the expressed will of God.

It was not because this woman cherished any desire or expectation of material reward that she showed such kindness to Elisha, but because she feared God, and had respect unto his word. Elisha was invited to enter her house, not because she knew him to be a great man and therefore felt that it would be an honor to entertain him, but because she saw that he had need of rest and food. Much that goes with us under the name of hospitality is nothing more nor less than a refined form of selfishness. That "respect of persons" which the Apostle James forbids, the "gold ring" and "goodly apparel" of which he speaks, have too much to do with the hospitality of most of us. Our Lord says, "When thou makest a feast, call not thy brethren, nor thy kinsmen, nor thy rich neighbors; lest they also bid thee again, and a recompense be made thee. But when thou makest a feast, call the poor, the maimed, the lame, and the blind." But conventional hospitality reverses this order to a great extent, and instead of the "deserving poor," instead of those who have need of our hospitality, we seek to have as our guests those who possess wealth and social standing. But if the hospitality which the Shunammite showed to Elisha was unselfish, it was not less hearty. "She constrained him to eat bread." The statement implies that Elisha was at first unwilling to accept of her invitation but that she pressed it upon him, and would not be denied the privilege of entertaining him. As she came to be better acquainted with the Prophet, by his instruction to be brought into closer fellowship with God, and, through his intercession at a throne of grace, to receive from God that treasure which the mother-instinct craves, she would find abundant and ceaseless reason to rejoice that such importunity had been granted her. "She constrained him to eat bread." The expression calls to mind the account of the two disciples with whom Jesus walked to Emmaus after his resurrection from the dead. It is recorded that when "he made as though he would have gone farther, they constrained him, saying, Abide with us." How much it must have added to their joy of heart, and to their gratitude to God, to reflect, "when their eyes were opened, and they knew him," that they had not been content with a mere formal invitation, that they did not permit the Savior to go his way without tarrying with them. The hospitality of the Shunammite was untiring. Apparently loath at first to accept her kind invitation, Elisha came to feel at home when under her roof. When better acquainted with his benefactress, he came and went without any feeling of hesitancy. And as often as he came, he received a hearty welcome. "And so it was, that as oft as he passed by, he turned in thither to eat bread." Convinced that Elisha was a teacher come from God, this great woman esteemed it a privilege to entertain him as frequently as he chose to come. Christian people should seek to become better acquainted with their brethren. How much of the truest and purest enjoyment which this life affords, how much that would prove helpful and comforting to us, is lost to us because we do not understand one another and, in consequence, keep aloof one from another. There is in many of us a false pride which makes it impossible for us to receive a kindness in the right spirit, to honor a benefactor by receiving in a hearty and unquestioning manner the favor which he finds pleasure in bestowing. The hospitality of the Shunammite woman was likewise painstaking and considerate. She was not satisfied to provide ordinary accommodations for the Prophet, to give him such things as she might have at hand or might be procured without trouble; but she was willing to spend time and money, and to be put to some inconvenience in order that every thing which could minister to the comfort and convenience of her guest might be provided. At her suggestion a "little chamber" is built for him "on the wall," probably on the top of the house. Access to this chamber was doubtless by an outside stair, so that the Prophet might enter and depart without meeting any member of the household if, for any reason, he chose to do so. In this room were placed a bed, a table, a chair, and a lamp. It was furnished not only as a sleeping apartment, but as a study as well. Nothing was obtruded upon the Prophet, which would in any way tend to mar his enjoyment of that which had been provided for him. There was nothing patronizing in the good woman's address or behavior. No word or act of hers reminded the Prophet of how much she had done for him. He was not made to feel that he was an object of charity; to the contrary, his hostess studied how she might show the delight she found in having him as her guest, and how she might prove the deep concern which she felt for his comfort and welfare. There "passeth by us continually" a greater and holier than Elisha. Gladly would he accept our hospitality, and enter in and dwell with us. These are his words to us, "Behold, I stand at the door and knock; if any man hear my voice, and open the door, I will come in to him, and will sup with him, and he with me." "Let us prepare the dwelling for him, and pray every day: Come Lord Jesus, be our guest! and: Remain with us, for the evening is drawing on." (Starke.) The testimony which the Shunammite bears to the character of Elisha should not pass unnoticed. "Behold now, I perceive that this is an holy man of God." There were many false prophets and teachers in Elisha's day, as in our day there are many who without right call themselves Christians, but long and close observation had convinced this woman that Elisha was all that he professed to be. His life was an exposition of the religious principles which he taught. It is the custom of many to leave their religion behind them when they go from home, or to conceal it when in the company of strangers. But Elisha took his religion with him wherever he went. Every true Christian character will bear acquaintance.

The more we come to know of him who is a true disciple of Christ, the more we will be persuaded that he "is an holy man of God." As the followers of the Lord Jesus, we should be very solicitous concerning the impressions which we make upon others. "We should always keep the thought close to us that our spirit and our word and our conduct are watched daily; sometimes kindly, sometimes unkindly, always keenly. If we have been with Jesus, the world will take knowledge of the fact. Something must be wrong if our life as Christians is not so toned and characterized as to arrest attention." (R. T. in Pulpit Com. on Acts.) "Gratus animus est una virtus non solum maxima, sed etiam mater virtutum omnium reliquarum." (Cicero.) "Gratitude is the fairest blossom which springs from the soul; and the heart of man knoweth none more fragrant." (Hosea Ballou.)

Elisha showed his appreciation of the Shunammite woman's hospitality, not only by his willingness to avail himself of it whenever circumstances permitted; but, he gratefully acknowledges her kindness to him and to his servant, and expresses his desire to recompense her to the extent of his ability. "Thou hast been careful for us with all this care; what is to be done for thee? Wouldst thou be spoken for to the king, or to the captain of the host?" He was unwilling to be the recipient of such marked kindness without repaying it in some way.

Elisha was fully persuaded that the kindness which had been shown him had not been inspired by any hope of material reward. This assurance, however, contributed to intensify the desire to render her some service in return. But he does not decide what the reward shall be. He simply suggests such service as he feels himself able to render, and as she might be thought willing to receive, and leaves it for her to decide what shall be done for her. The Prophet's proposal to speak to the king or to the captain of the host in behalf of his benefactress implies that at this time he was in favor at the court, that he exercised such an influence over the king and his ministers as to render it certain that any request which he might prefer would be complied with at once. This influence was due, doubtless, to the great service which he had rendered in the campaign against Moab. No intimation is given, other than that which is contained in the woman's reply to Gehazi, as to what the Prophet had in mind to ask the king or the captain of the host to do for her in his behalf. His purpose was doubtless understood by her, however, since she promptly, yet courteously declined the proffered service. The beauty and wisdom of her reply grow upon us as we study it; and furnish conclusive evidence, if it had been wanting, that in all she had done for the Prophet she had been free from selfish motives. "I dwell among mine own people." It is a simple declaration that her mode of life was according to her choice; that, above everything which the king might be able and willing to grant her, she preferred to live in the quiet village of Shunem, surrounded by her kinsmen and acquaintances. Blessed with ample store from which to satisfy all her own needs, and to minister to the relief and comfort of others as she found opportunity, she was contented with her lot in life, and had no worldly ambition to gratify. What a blessed state of mind this! How many of the wrecks and ruins of life are due to the opposite spirit, the spirit of discontent.

"Sweet are the thoughts that savor of content;
The quiet mind is richer than a crown."
(Robert Green.)

"The shepherd's homely curds,
His cold thin drink out of his leathern bottle,
His wanted sleep under a fresh tree's shade,
All which secure and sweetly he enjoys,
Is far beyond a prince's delicates,
His viands sparkling in a golden cup,
His body couched in a curious bed,
When care, mistrust, and treason wait on him."
(Shakespeare.)

A strange, and in some respects a remarkable, character is first introduced in connection with this story of the woman of Shunem, Gehazi, the servant of Elisha. Where he came from, or when or why he came to sustain the relation of servant to Elisha is not known. He seems to have been a servant, not in the sense in which Elisha was servant to Elijah, that is as a disciple and companion and destined successor, but in a more menial sense. Between the master and servant there seems to have been very little, if anything, in common. In contrast to the child-like and deeply spiritual character of the master, there is presented the shrewd, unscrupulous, and intensely practical character of the servant. From a merely human point of view, aside from any recognition of the divine purpose, it seems no more appropriate that Elisha should choose such an attendant, than that Judas should be numbered among the twelve. For some reason, doubtless good and sufficient, Elisha choose to communicate with this woman through his servant; but he does not seem to have anticipated such an answer as she commissioned Gehazi to return. Evidently it is with some measure of surprise and disappointment that he asks the question, "What then is to be done for her?" He does not abandon his purpose to do something for her as a token of his gratitude for what she had done for him; but he is at a loss to know what he shall do, now that she has declined his generous proposal without intimating that anything else he might propose would be any more acceptable to her.

It is remarkable that Elisha should neglect the privilege and the duty of seeking Divine direction in his preplexity, and that, instead, he should turn to Gehazi for counsel. But God used the native shrewdness of the servant to discover that which the master seems never to have observed, that the one thing which was wanting to render the happiness of that Shunammite home complete was a child.

To be childless was considered a mark of dishonor among the Hebrew people; but to this woman, with a heart over-flowing with mother-love, the lack of one upon whom she might lavish such love would be felt to be a most grievous cross. She was content because persuaded that her motherless state was of the Lord; yet without the boon which the mother-nature craved, "existence remained incomplete." All this the keen eye of Gehazi has observed. He is persuaded that above all other earthly things a child to brighten her home and to gladden her heart would be welcomed by her whose happiness and welfare the Prophet so earnestly desired to promote. As became a servant, he contented himself with a simple suggestion, leaving the Prophet to accept or reject it as he might deem proper. "Verily she hath no child, and her husband is old." Elisha perceived the wisdom of this suggestion, but we must believe that it was not until he had laid the matter before God, and had obtained assurance that it met with the Divine approbation, that he directed Gehazi to call the woman a second time and then, personally addressing her as it would seem, he announced to her that the one desire of her heart was to be granted her, that she should have a son. The promise so far exceeded the fondest hope which she had permitted herself to cherish, that for the moment, she could not but believe that the Prophet was cruelly trifling with her. She could not think that so great a blessing was in store for her. "Nay, my lord, thou man of God," she exclaims, "do not lie unto thine handmaid." "Her words were really not those of unbelief, but of faith asking for greater assurance. When her mind had time to take in the full extent of Elisha's promise, inexpressible joy would chase the last trace of doubt from her soul." (J. Orr, D.D.). Far beyond our present ability to comprehend, are the precious and exceeding great promises which God has granted unto the believer. As we contemplate them we are filled with wonder and amazement. Our weak faith cannot appropriate them in all their fulness. "Eye hath not seen nor ear heard, neither have entered into the heart of man, the things which God hath prepared for them that love him."

"In vain our fancy strives to paint
The moment after death."

Even he who has seen all of heaven which mortal minds can grasp, and more than mortal tongue can tell, who has stood so near the portals of glory that "the skin of his face shone," will be overwhelmed with astonishment as he beholds the glories which lie hidden behind the gates of pearl. As incomprehensible as are the glories and the joys of the heavenly state to even the most spiritually minded, are the blessings of grace which the believer now enjoys, to the soul out of Christ. The preaching of Christ crucified is, "unto the Jew a stumbling block and unto the Greeks foolishness." To him who has not passed from death unto life the fruit of the Spirit is incredible. "The natural man receiveth not the things of the Spirit of God: for they are foolishness unto him: neither can he know them, because they are spiritually discerned." From among the sayings of our Lord not recorded by the inspired historians of his life, the Apostle Paul has saved from oblivion these precious words, "It is more blessed to give than to receive." He who gives in the right spirit, is made more happy, enjoys a greater measure of blessedness, than he who receives. So Elisha must have felt that morning as he departed from the home of the Shunammite.

If the joy of her to whom he had been commissioned to give precious promise was great, much greater must have been the joy which he felt, in that he had been permitted to impart such happiness to others. God gave effect to the words of the Prophet, and, at the time indicated, the Shunammite clasped in fond embrace her own child. That she felt her loved one to be the gift of God to her, and, in recognition of the responsibility which the gift imposed, sought the child's highest welfare we cannot doubt. Would that as parents this thought might possess us more fully, God holds us responsible for the proper training of our children. They are given that they may be fitted for God's service, that they may shine as jewels in the Master's crown. "Sad indeed will be that parent's heart, at the great day of accounts, who shall stand before the tribunal of the Lord, bereft of some once tenderly dear to him, and shall feel, I never labored, I never prayed, I never strove earnestly and perseveringly to bring my children to the knowledge of the Lord Almighty. The world was once the model of my own conduct, and for my children's imitation. I knew no higher, and sought no wiser guide for them; and although God, in his mercy, taught me better things, and snatched me as a brand from the burning, it was all too late for those who had lived a life of utter worldliness beneath my roof, and died in unrepented sin before my eyes." (Rev. Henry Blunt, Lectures on the History of Elisha.)

## CHAPTER XIII.

### BEREFT, BUT NOT IN DESPAIR.

"There is a reaper whose name is death
And with his sickle keen,
He reaps the bearded grain at a breath
And the flowers that grow between."
(Longfellow.)

EVERY human life is like a sum of money which, without counting, is placed in the bank to be "checked out." No man knows the exact amount that is placed to his credit. We can tell how much we have drawn out, and it is evident that the more we draw the less will remain on deposit, but how much remains, we have no means of ascertaining. It is certain that the limit of our credit will be reached some time, though it is uncertain at what time. We are wont to think of death as a future event, but, in reality, we die daily. Every day consumes its portion of life. Each flitting moment leaves us, by so much, nearer the grave. "Death borders upon our birth, and our cradle stands in our grave." (Hall.) Neither rank, character, nor age can insure immunity from the icy touch of death. "Death is a black camel, which kneels at the gate of all." (Abd-el-Kader.) Death enters the gorgeous palace and the wretched hovel, and claims as his own the pure and noble, as well as the base and vicious.

"There is no flock however watched and tended,
But one dead lamb is there;
There is no fireside howsoe'er defended
But has one vacant chair."
(Longfellow.)

With remorseless hand death hurls his shafts at the youthful and the aged alike.

"Leaves have their time to fall,
And flowers to wither at the north wind's breath,
And stars to set; but all,
Thou hast all seasons for thine own, O death!"
(Mrs. Hemans.)

Assiduously, and lovingly, the Shunammite had cared for the child whom God had given her. Nothing was left undone which might minister to his comfort and welfare. With a mother's joy she observed the unfolding of the faculties of mind and the development of bodily strength in her boy; while with her whole heart she sought that the "grace of God" might be "upon him," that he might "advance in favor with God." Each day served to bind him more closely to her heart, and to enlarge her hopes and expectations concerning him. He had escaped the perils of infancy, and was now five or six years old, perhaps. His merry laugh and childish gambols were the cheer and amusement of the household. It was the time of harvest, and the child, doubtless with the consent of his mother, had gone out to his father who was with the reapers. Scarcely, however, had he reached the father's side, when, with the cry, "My head, my head!" he sank unconscious at his feet. It is probable that he was overcome by the intense heat of the sun. One who has spent many years in Palestine as a missionary says, "I know by experience that this valley glows like a furnace in harvest-time." (Land and the Book.) Tenderly the aged parent lifted the prostrate form of his child and, after waiting for a short time, but in vain, for his return to consciousness, he placed him in the arms of a servant who was directed to carry him to his mother. Apparently the father entertained no thought that any thing serious had befallen the lad. He does not accompany him to the house, but resumes his labors, trusting that by the use of some simple home remedy he would soon be restored. But what dismay and grief must have filled the mother's heart as that limp form was laid in her arms. Faintness came upon her as, with blanched cheek, she heard the story of what had befallen her darling boy, and realized how critical his condition was. Bitterly she reproached herself for her imprudence in suffering him to go to the field at such an hour. Though hope must have died within her breast, she spares no effort in behalf of the sufferer. Every means available to her is employed to stay the hand of the destroyer. With a mother's devotion she supports her stricken one upon her knees, unwilling to be separated from him even to the extent of placing him upon his bed. But all her efforts prove unavailing. Her forebodings must be realized. When the sun had reached the zenith,

"Death stole in softness o'er that lovely face,
And touched each feature with a new-born grace;
On cheek and brow unearthly beauty lay,
And told that life's poor cares had passed away."

(Sprague.)

The bereavement which this mother was thus called upon to sustain, was wholly unlooked-for. Her son, an only child, was, in a peculiar sense, God's gift to her. He had been promised to her as a reward for the kindness which she had shown to the man of God. Though it had seemed like hoping against hope that such a promise could be fulfilled, she had been given grace to believe. She trusted in the Lord, and was not put to shame. It would not be strange if she had come to regard the child who had been sent to reward her generous deeds and to gladden her heart and home, as possessed of a charmed life, as under the special care of God, in view of the almost miraculous manner in which he had been given her. A life so obviously the gift of God, might be thought to be less exposed, at least, than others to the diseases and so-called accidents to which flesh is heir. Besides, the morning light had found her little son buoyant in life and health. With a merry heart he had gone forth to find his father among the reapers, with no thought that he should be borne home the next hour to die. How many there are who are thus called unexpectedly to meet death and the judgment. "All the processes of nature are silent and secret. We know the passage of the seasons only by their changes. The precise moment when nature has reached its culminating point and must descend; when her embroidered web has been woven, and must be unraveled, is shrouded in mystery. No boundary line separates the season of life from the season of death; the full vigor and perfection of summer from the feebleness and languor of autumn. One by one the leaves become discolored and drop off. Some of them fade before others, but we cannot tell why. We cannot tell which leaf of all the rich green multitude will be the first to wear the impress of decay. Thus fades the leaf, and so silently do we all fade. The king of terrors comes with a noiseless step, stealthily, silently, with bated breath. He is not seen; he is not heard; he is not suspected, till all at once his cold shadow falls upon us, and his dark form stands between us and the light of the living world." (Macmillan.) This bereavement was as sudden as it was unexpected. The merry laugh of the child was immediately succeeded by the cry of pain which indicated that the destroying rays of the sun had struck him. The great majority of persons, perhaps, anticipate that the approach of death will be heralded in some way so that preparation may be made for his coming. Very few persons live in expectation of a sudden or accidental death. We should be disposed to look upon such a person as in some measure demented, and yet statistics show that more persons die suddenly than of lingering diseases. "We expect the old to die; but our hearts cling tenderly to the young, while we almost refuse to contemplate the possibility of their being taken from us." (Taylor.) It is, however, by no means an unheard-of thing for children to be taken away as suddenly and pathetically as was the son of this woman of Shunem. "Many a parent's bleeding heart can tell of similar wounds." The bereavement of the Shunammite was especially sad. The death of a child, even when it is one of a large family, is a sad event indeed. How the heart of the fond parent clings to the loved one while life lingers, and yearns for him when the vital spark has fled. But in the death of this child all the light and joy of a home had gone out, he was an only child. There was none left to comfort the hearts of his sorrowing parents, none to inherit the love which was cherished for him alone. Silent now must be those halls which, in the happy years forever gone, had resounded with his childish mirth. This bereavement was also a sore disappointment to the mother's heart. It is not unreasonable to suppose that this was a precocious child.

His parents had looked forward to a life of usefulness and honor awaiting him when he should come to manhood's years. Like the God-fearing Hannah, the Shunammite may have dedicated her child to the Lord, with the hope that he should some day succeed to the prophetic office. The hearts of these parents had also been cheered and gladdened, we may believe, by the thought that when the infirmities of old age should render it necessary for them to retire from the active duties of life, their son would care for them, would support and comfort. Now all their hopes and expectations were destroyed. Again, as before the birth of their child, they came to look upon "all around as strangers, and all around as for strangers." How uncertain the things of this life are, and how dark the prospect to him who has nothing better upon which to fix his hope! This bereavement must likewise have been painfully perplexing. Doubtless the mother would find herself asking the question, in spite of her assurance that all was well, Why hath the Lord dealt thus with me? She had not asked that God should give her this child, yet he had been pleased to do so, and now he had taken him away, after she had learned to love him more dearly than she loved any other earthly object, more dearly than she loved her own life. Why had such a trial come upon her? Did she need to be reminded that the child belonged to God who loved him more than it was possible for her to love him?

Had she been making an idol of her boy, loving him more than she loved God who had given him to her? Did she need this kind of discipline? Did she need to be reminded that heaven is not to be enjoyed here upon the earth, that here man can have no continuing city? We cannot say; but of this we may be assured, that by this providence God was glorified and that his faithful servants were blest, for "all things work together for good to them that love God, to them who are the called according to his purpose." Convinced that life was extinct, the bereaved, sorrow-stricken mother bore the body of her child to the upper chamber and laid it upon the Prophet's bed. Perhaps she felt that by so doing she, in some measure, placed it in the care of the Prophet to whom her thoughts seem to have turned instinctively as she realized the sad fact of her bereavement. Passionately kissing once more the cold, mute lips, she calmly shut the door upon her dead. Whatever may have been the motive, she evidently sought to conceal from her husband the fact of the child's death, at least until after she had visited the Prophet.

It may have been with this purpose likewise in view that she chose to lay him in the Prophet's room, and carefully to shut the door upon him. To her husband she makes known her purpose, without assigning any reason therefor, to "run to the man of God, and come again," and requests that "one of the young men and one of the asses" be sent her. To the husband's objection that "it was neither new moon nor sabbath," an allusion, doubtless, to the fact that at such seasons and upon such days the Prophet held religious assemblies at Carmel, she simply replied, "It shall be well." Her request is granted without further parley, and she immediately starts upon her mission. To the servant who is to accompany her she gives this direction, indicative of the urgency of her desire to reach the abode of the Prophet at the earliest moment possible, "Drive, and go forward; slack me not the riding, except I bid thee." The distance from Shunem to Carmel is fifteen or sixteen miles, and it requires from five to six hours to make the journey. The sanguinary temperament of this woman is shown by her willingness to start upon such a journey at an hour when the heat of the sun must have been most intense. Evidently she cherished the hope and expectation that Elisha was able, and would be willing, to restore her son to life. She had heard, doubtless, the story of how Elijah had brought back to life the dead son of the widow of Zarephath and she was encouraged to believe that Elisha could and would do as much for her. And why not, seeing that a double portion of the spirit of Elijah had been granted him, and that his friendship for her had been so thoroughly attested? As we contemplate the eagerness with which this mother seeks the comfort and aid of the Prophet in the time of her bereavement and sorrow, may our thoughts turn to that greater than Elisha in whose ear we may tell our sorrows, to whom we may look for deliverance when the waters threaten to overflow. No long, weary, journey are we required to make that we may find this friend and deliverer. His words are, "Lo I am with you alway, even unto the end of the world." Heedless of danger, hardship, or fatigue the Shunammite pressed forward over the burning sands of the plain of Jezreel, and up the mountain steeps, absorbed with the one purpose, speaking not save, perhaps, to call upon the driver to urge the ass to its utmost speed. At length the Prophet's abode is seen in the distance, and, while she is yet afar off, the Prophet recognizes her. The unseemly time, and the speed of her coming warn him that some great calamity has befallen her. Impatient to learn what it is, and desiring also to show his solicitude for her welfare, he directs his servant, Gehazi, to run to meet her with this anxious inquiry, "Is it well with thee? Is it well with thy husband? Is it well with the child?" "Not one object is omitted which he thinks the thoughts or hopes of his coming visitor are fixed upon, or from which he imagines it possible that her present sorrow emanates." (Blunt.) The Prophet's inquiry is the Oriental form of salutation, equivalent to our common salutation, "How do you do?" "The universality of this question among friends implies the constant presentiment we have, that men are always under impending evil. When we separate for a time, we are like soldiers leaving the bivouac for the battle, and when we meet again, it is as soldiers returning from the conflict, scanning each other's persons for the wounds. Solicitude is necessarily one of the bonds of friendship; and when friendship deepens into love, solicitude deepens into anxiety." (The Homiletic Review.) "Is it well with thee?" "Is it well with thy loved ones?" What momentuous interests are involved in the question which we too often lightly ask and as lightly answer. Eternity itself hangs upon the final answer. Personally, are we prepared to met the Judge of the quick and the dead at his appearing and his kingdom? Do we believe this to be true of those who are nearest and dearest to us? How is it with us as parents? As we think of our children, living or dead, can we say, it is well with them?

It has been suggested that the reply of this woman was of an evasive character. That she did not wish to unburden her heart to him, and, hence, dismissed him with the single word, peace. This would seem, however, to imply that there was a lack on her part of sincerity or truthfulness. It is preferable to regard her answer as the expression of an intelligent faith. Perhaps she did not know as much about the immortality of the soul and the blessedness of heaven, as has been revealed to us in the light of the Gospel; but, as a daughter of Abraham, these glorious truths were not wholly hidden from her. She was persuaded that God had taken her child to himself, and that, therefore, it was well.

As for herself and husband, she might not be able to explain the providence which had left them childless, and desolate, yet she felt in her heart that it was well. And, though her eyes may have been dim with tears, and her voice may almost have failed her as she said it, she hastened to make answer, It is well with my husband; it is well with myself; it is well with the child. The Shunammite replies to Gehazi without drawing rein and presses on until she arrives at the spot where Elisha stands waiting to receive her. Then, hastily dismounting, she casts herself at his feet "in all the eloquence of silent woe." For the moment, utterance is denied her, and the long pent up feelings of her heart find expression in silent tears, and the attitude of humble supplication. There was nothing unusual or what would be considered improper in her conduct toward Elisha. It is said to be the custom in the East, even at the present time, to embrace the feet or the knees in order to add force to supplication. "The falling down, clasping the feet are actions frequently witnessed.

I have had this done to me before I coula prevent it." (The Land and the Book.) For some reason, however, Gehazi regarded the silent suppliant with disfavor and "came near to thrust her away." But the man of God is more considerate and kind. To him, the simple fact that "her soul is vexed within her" is a sufficient apology for any seeming impropriety in her conduct. Jesus says, "Come unto me, all ye that labor and are heavy laden, and I will give you rest. Take my yoke upon you, and learn of me; for I am meek and lowly in heart: and ye shall find rest unto your souls." And again, "Him that cometh to me I will in no wise cast out."

# CHAPTER XIV.

## VICTORY OVER DEATH.

"Death, be not proud, though some have called thee
 Mighty and dreadful, for thou are not so;
For those whom thou thinkest thou dost overthrow,
Die not, poor death.
* * * * * * * * *
One short sleep past, we wake eternally,
 And death shall be no more; Death thou shalt die."
(Donne.)

Elisha was obliged to witness, for a time, the profound grief of the Shunammite, while ignorant of the cause thereof, to listen to her passionate appeal for help, while the nature of her calamity was hidden from him. Perhaps the Prophet had need to be reminded that he was not omniscient; while his avowal of the fact that the Lord had hidden from him the cause of the woman's distress would explain to her why he had not gone to her aid. In ordinary circumstances, prophets and apostles were subject to all human limitations as to knowledge and power. Although there is no record of the fact, it would seem a reasonable supposition, and, from what follows, a probable supposition, that the Shunammite told the Prophet all that had befallen her, and, declaring her faith in his ability to restore her son to life, importuned him to return with her to her home. The two brief questions which have been recorded as addressed by her to the Prophet, would seem to be an explanation or enforcement of a statement or an entreaty previously made. "Did I desire a son of my lord? Did I not say, do not deceive me? In this seemingly reproachful language there is argument. She had not asked a son. She had even refused to believe it possible that the promise that she should have a son could be fulfilled. Like the disciples when they saw the risen Lord, she "believed not for joy." Notwithstanding this, the promise had been fulfilled, a son had been given her, that love which none but a mother can know had been kindled in her breast, only that she might be bereft a few years later and left more desolate than before this joy had come into her life. If the Prophet really meant to reward her for her kindness to him, not to vex and to punish her, he would now exert all his power to undo what death had done, and restore her loved one to her. The Shunammite's plea is not made in vain. At once the sympathy of the man of God is enlisted in her behalf, and to Gehazi he gives this direction, "Gird up thy loins, and take my staff in thine hand, and go thy way: if thou meet any man, salute him not; and if any salute thee, answer him not again: and lay my staff on the face of the child." What the purpose of this procedure was, what results the Prophet expected from it, is not evident from the narrative. That Gehazi expected the child to be restored to life, we gather from the statement that "there was neither voice nor hearing" when the staff was laid upon the child's face; and from the report which Gehazi makes to his master, "The child is not awaked." But it does not appear that Elisha shared in such expectations. There is no intimation that he was surprised or disappointed by the apparent failure of Gehazi's mission. It has been suggested that the Prophet sought in this way to test the faith of the Shunammite, but he certainly must have felt that he already had sufficient evidence of the genuineness and strength of her faith. Nor would such instructions as he gives to Gehazi, seem to be necessary, if this were the only design. Might it not be that the staff was thus employed simply to prevent decomposition of the body until such time as the Prophet could reach Shunem? Perhaps this may account in part for the action of the Shunammite in placing the dead child upon the Prophet's bed before starting upon her journey to Carmel. In a climate like that of Palestine, decomposition speedily follows death. Hence Gehazi who could probably travel more rapidly than his master, is directed to go with all possible haste, and lay the Prophet's staff upon the face of the dead. Whether this be a correct supposition or not, we must believe that the mission of Gehazi was not barren of good results, though he himself may have felt that such was the case. Doubtless the purpose of the Prophet in sending him, whatever that purpose may have been, was accomplished. It may be thus with us. As we look back over life, it may seem to have been a failure; but, if at the last, each one of us can say, "I have finished the work which thou gavest me to do," in God's sight life will be a glorious success. Persuaded that, even with the Prophet's staff in his hand, Gehazi must prove unequal to the task of wresting her loved one from the embrace of death, the Shunammite declares her fixed purpose not to return to her home until the Prophet should accompany her. "As the Lord liveth, and as thy soul liveth, I will not leave thee." Yielding to her importunities, Elisha "arose and followed her." It was perhaps the midnight hour ere the home in Shunem was reached, but without seeking rest, Elisha at once essayed the stupendous task to which he doubtless felt himself called of God.

Repairing to his room, where the body of the child lay upon the bed, he "shut the door upon them twain" and gave himself up to importunate prayer. The prayer has not been recorded, but since Elisha, in this instance, imitated so closely the actions of Elijah when the son of the widow of Zarephath was restored to life it is not improbable that his prayer was modeled after the prayer of his master upon that memorable occasion. "O Lord my God, hast thou also brought evil upon her," her who has shown such kindness to me, "by slaying her son?" O Lord, my God, I pray thee, let this child's soul come into him again." Taking up the Shunammite's own plea, he would urge that she had been content with her childless condition. That she had not desired a son when it had seemed to be the purpose of God that she should not be thus favored. He would tell God how lonely and desolate she was left; how much she needed this child to comfort and to sustain her; and how difficult it was for her to be reconciled to such a providence. Was it right that Elisha should thus plead that the life of this child should be restored? Did he know that it would be for the glory of God and the highest welfare of parents and child that it should be so? We are constrained to believe that such was the fact, else God would not have permitted him to offer such a prayer, much less, have granted the answer which he sought. Perhaps he saw with prophetic vision, a life of piety, usefulness, and honor before the child. With us it is different. The future is hidden from us.

"We know not what's before us,
What trials are to come."

Hence it does not become us to pray without qualification for the recovery of those who are sick or for any other material blessing. God alone knoweth what is best for us and for our loved ones, and it is for us to commend ourselves and ours to him, that he may do for us that which seemeth good in his sight. We cannot hope that those who have gone from us into the unseen world shall ever be restored to us in this life. We shall go to them, but they shall not return to us. Ought we to cherish for a moment the wish that it might be that they could come back to us? Is it not better that they should be with Christ? As we think of them in that bright and happy land where Jesus is, a land where there is no night, where weariness, sickness, and sorrow are unknown, where sin cannot enter, could we wish them to come back to us? Would we bring them back if we could? But the Prophet does not rest with the act of supplication, he adds works to prayer, uses the means to bring about an answer to prayer. It was doubtless by Divine direction, as well as in imitation of his Master, that he arose from the attitude of prayer and stretched himself upon the child, placing "his mouth upon his mouth, his eyes upon his eyes, and his hands upon his hands." "It is by no means improbable that the method Elisha thus adopted in bringing his own living body in contact with the dead child, had a natural adaptation to the end intended. Man can and does impart his disease to another by contact. There is nothing, therefore, absurd in the idea of his imparting life and health by contact." (Trench.) Elisha, however, must be taught, and must teach, the importance of perseverance in well-doing. As a result of his first prayer and first effort, "The flesh of the child waxed warm," simply. It was not until he had prayed a second time, doubtless, and a second time had stretched himself upon the motionless form, that the child lived. Who shall declare the joy of that mother as in obedience to the Prophet's summons she came and received her child alive. And yet, is there not cause for greater joy on the part of Christian parents, when the children whom God has given them are saved from the darkness and gloom of spiritual death?

This miracle was the reward of timely and persistent effort on the part of a mother in behalf of her child. Had the Shunammite remained at home and made no effort to reach the prophet with her appeal, or had she been content to send some one to him less interested than herself, a servant who might have loitered by the way and whose story might have failed to impress the Prophet as profoundly as the needs of the bereaved mother required, her child might never have been restored to her fond embrace. Many of us have friends and loved ones who are "dead in trespasses and sins." Are we willing that they shall be lost forever? We shall contribute to such a result if we simply neglect to put forth an earnest, persistent effort for their salvation; if we leave to other hands the work which God has given us to do in their behalf, a work which none other can do so well as we.

In this fragment of history may we not find some suggestions as to the methods to be pursued by those who seek the salvation of souls? Our Lord says, "No man can come to me, except the Father which hath sent me draw him." "Paul may plant, and Apollos may water, but God giveth the increase." The excellency of the power is of God. Hence, in all our efforts to save souls from death, we must have recourse to prayer. If, as parents, we would see our children brought to Christ, we must earnestly and persistently bear them up on the arms of a living faith, to a throne of grace. O that there were more earnest, believing, wrestling with God in behalf of the perishing. In a very real sense the turning of the nations unto God, waits on the prayer of God's people. But it is not the Divine purpose that prayer should stand alone, that we should dispense with the use of means. We show the sincerity of our prayer by the promptness and persistence of our effort.

Elisha prayed, but he had work to do as well, and the answer to his prayer, under God, depended upon the faithfulness with which that work was done. Means were to be employed. The result desired was not obtained until he had stretched himself upon the child. God has answered prayers without the use of means. "Elijah prayed fervently that it might not rain; and it rained not upon the earth for three years and six months." But the rule is that we are to use all proper and available means to answer our own prayers. "A diseased man may pray earnestly for health, yet he has no right to expect an answer to his prayer, if he neglect the Divine conditions upon which health is given. A poor man may pray to be rich, but ordinarily, wealth comes to the man who is diligent and sagacious in business." The wise man says, 'He becometh poor that dealeth with a slack hand: but the hand of the diligent maketh rich.' The sin-convicted man may pray to be delivered from the power and consequences of his sin, but until he believes on the Lord Jesus Christ, his sin remaineth. The God of order conducts his government both in the material and moral departments of his universe by certain laws, conditions or means; and these, as a rule, he will not interfere with, even in answer to the prayers of his own loyal and loving children. "Pray for your daily bread but take care and work for it.

Pray for health, but be careful to observe the conditions of health. Pray for the conversion of the world, but translate the Gospel into your life and preach it in your every deed." There is another suggestion for us. To be God's instruments in the salvation of men, we must come into personal contact with them. Our lives must touch the lives of those whom we would lead to the cross. Elisha must go in person to Shunem, he must even place his own living body in contact with the dead in order to vanquish death. He might send Gehazi with his staff; he might pray earnestly: but he himself must touch the dead child, if he would kindle again the spark of life. It is praiseworthy, so far as it goes, to give money for the support of the gospel at home and abroad. We ought likewise to pray for the success of the gospel, that the kingdom of God may come. But our duty does not end here. We ought to go out into the highways and hedges, and persuade men to come to him who taketh away the sin of the world. The friendly grasp of the hand, the kindly look and word contribute in no small measure to make the preaching of the word effective. We must show the spirit and act the part of a brother toward the man whom we would help to a higher life. The spirit of exclusiveness, of selfish and heartless indifference to the needs of men, which pervades many a congregation, produces a feeling of antipathy in the hearts of multitudes toward the church and the saving truths which she professes to teach. Too many there are, even in our very midst, who find just cause to say, "No man cared for my soul." Not that any man is warranted in neglecting his own soul, though such complaint be never so well founded; but we ought to show our brother in every way possible, that we do care for him, that we do desire his salvation. One more suggestion we may find in the story before us. We ought not to rest satisfied with partial success in winning a brother for Christ. We should not relinquish our effort in his behalf until he is "soundly converted to God," until he is thoroughly established in the faith. After Elisha had, for the first time, stretched himself upon the dead child, "the flesh of the child waxed warm." But the man of God was not satisfied with this result. After walking to and fro in the house, doubtless wrestling with God in prayer, "he went up and stretched himself upon him," a second time; and the soul of the child returned "into him."

No doubt Elisha would have repeated this act a score of times if it had been necessary. In too many cases we are satisfied with simply warming our brother's soul. We relax our effort in his behalf when we have succeeded in leading him to confess Christ, and to "join church." But if we go no further than this "the last state of that" brother "is worse than the first." "Better it is that thou shouldst not vow, than that thou shouldst vow and not pay." It may work incalculable harm to a soul, to labor for it, to care for it, until it is simply warm, and then abandon it before the Spirit of Life has come into it.

Marvelous indeed was this miracle of raising the dead. Once only in all the previous history of the race, had such a miracle been wrought. Great as Elisha had already shown himself to be, it seemed to tax to the utmost extent the mighty power which he possessed. It required earnest and persistent prayer, and exhaustive effort. In this respect Elisha appears in marked contrast with him who was declared to be the Son of God with power. Elisha spoke and acted in the name of another, for he was a servant. The power which he exercised was a delegated power. But Jesus Christ spoke by his own authority; and by a power which he ascribed to none other, and with no greater effort than the utterance of a brief command, the storm-tossed sea was calmed, the eyes of the blind were opened, the leper was cleansed, the dead raised to life. All power in heaven and in earth is given unto him. He hath power on earth to forgive sins. "O death, where is thy sting? O grave, where is thy victory? The strength of death is sin; and the strength of sin is the law. But thanks be to God who giveth us the victory through our Lord Jesus Christ."

## CHAPTER XV.

### THE SEQUEL OF A REMARKABLE HISTORY.

"What in me is dark,
Illumine; what is low, raise and support;
That to the height of this great argument
I may assert eternal providence,
And justify the ways of God to men."
(Milton.)

THE Psalmist says, "The secret of the Lord is with them that fear him." God was about to bring a protracted famine upon the land of Israel. But before judgment was thus inflicted upon a wicked nation Elisha was sent to apprise the good woman of Shunem of that which was to be, and to direct her to seek safety for herself and household by sojourning in some foreign land until the years of famine were ended. It has been inferred from the narrative that Gehazi was still retained at this time as the servant of Elisha. If this be a correct inference, it follows that the chronological order of events in the life of the Prophet has not been observed by the sacred historian, in this instance at least.

The events now considered must have preceded the cure of Naaman's leprosy, at which time, Gehazi was dismissed from the service of Elisha. But whatever the chronological order may be, we have, in the incidents here recorded, the sequel of a remarkable history. The warning given to the woman of Shunem was from the Lord. That the friendship which Elisha personally cherished for her was sufficient to enlist him in such a service in her behalf may not be doubted; but the manner in which he addresses her indicates that God had sent him. "Arise, and go thou and thy household, and sojourn wheresoever thou canst soujourn." Our safety from the evils which threaten our present and eternal welfare depends not upon the friendship or the enmity of man, but upon the love and favor of God. To him, as the ultimate source, we are to ascribe all the honor and the glory of our salvation. The song of the Psalmist is, "The angel of the Lord encampeth round about them that fear him, and delivereth them." And again, "He shall give his angels charge over thee to keep thee in all thy ways. They shall bear thee up in their hands, lest thou dash thy foot against a stone." The warning given to the woman of Shunem was timely. This fact is brought out more clearly by the Revised Version, "Now Elisha had spoken unto the woman." This indicates that between the time at which the Prophet's words of warning were uttered, and the actual prevalence of famine in the land, a considerable period of time must have intervened. Ample time was allowed the Shunammite to reach the place of her sojourn. God does not require us to do impossible things. He has warned us to flee from the wrath to come; and, while he insists that we are not to delay our flight, that to-day is the day of salvation, it is equally true that he gives us ample time to come to a decision as to what we shall do, and to set our house in order. No man can stand before the judgment throne of God and plead as an excuse for failure on his part to seek salvation, that he had not timely warning of his danger, that he had not sufficient opportunity to repent, to turn from the service of sin unto God. The plea most commonly put forth by those who allow themselves to be deceived by Satan is that "there is time enough yet." The fact that they have urged this as a reason for not accepting salvation when offered to them, will put to silence multitudes who shall hear with dismay the dread sentence, "Depart from me, ye cursed, into everlasting fire, prepared for the devil and his angels." The warning given to the Shunammite was based upon a good and sufficient reason, "For the Lord hath called for a famine." In all his dealings with men, God recognizes the fact that, a motive or reason is essential to intelligent action. The Prophet does not advise this woman to leave her comfortable home and all her possessions, and to remove to a foreign land, without telling her why she should do so. To the contrary, he tells her that her safety depends upon her doing as he directs. If she remains where she is, she must suffer the hardships of famine. On the other hand it is implied that if she goes to sojourn in some one of the surrounding countries, she will escape the evils which the Lord is about to bring upon her own land.

God warns the sinner to repent, and at the same time he tells him why he should do so. Sin produces soul famine, the lack of all that which conduces to spiritual life and growth. "The wages of sin is death, but the gift of God is eternal life through Jesus Christ our Lord." God sets before us life and death and urges upon us the choice of life. His words are, "Turn ye, turn ye from your evil ways; for why will ye die, O house of Israel?" It was a personal warning that was given to the Shunammite, and the duty which it imposed was likewise personal. She could employ no substitute, for no one could do for her what she was directed to do for herself. There may have been thousands more in Israel to whom a similar warning was given, but the Prophet was sent to speak directly to this woman. God's words of warning and of promise are addressed to all men. He says, "Look unto me, and be ye saved, all the ends of the earth."

"Hear this, all ye people, hear,
Earth's inhabitants give ear,
All of high and low estate,
Rich and poor together met."

But God warns men individually of the consequences of sin, and upon each one is laid the responsibility of accepting or rejecting salvation as it is offered in Jesus Christ. In giving her a son, and in restoring that son to life when smitten by death, God had rewarded the kindness which the Shunammite had shown to his servant, Elisha. But the timely warning now given her of impending calamity may be regarded as an additional reward for such kindness. "Truly may the Shunammite be reckoned among those who have exercised hospitality and entertained an angel unawares. She had no thought that the kindness she so cheerfully showed to Elisha would bring in so large returns." (Lowrie.)

God regards every act of kindness done to his servants as done to himself; and while he never forgets such kindness, he is not slack to reward it, not once only, but many times. In the great day of judgment, he to whom all judgment is given, shall say, "For as much as ye have done it unto one of the least of these my brethren, ye have done it unto me." The direction given to the Shunammite by the Prophet, may not have sounded so harshly in Oriental ears as it does in ours, but it is impossible to suppress the feeling that there is in it an apparent lack of sympathy and of consideration. Never was this woman in greater need of some one to advise her, to tell her just what to do, than at this moment, for she had never been confronted by so grave a problem. From the language of the narrative it would seem that she was now a widow; and yet the Prophet, to whom she had hitherto looked for counsel and assistance, can only say to her now, "Arise, and go thou and thine household, and sojourn wheresoever thou canst sojourn." Perhaps the expression, "wheresoever thou canst," is equivalent to wheresoever is most convenient for you, but even so, it must have been very perplexing to this woman to be told to abandon her princely estate, to turn her face from her comfortable home, and to seek a temporary residence in some strange land. How much it must have lightened the burden she was thus called upon to bear had the Prophet but told her where she should go! But he leaves her to exercise her own discretion in the matter, and to bear all the responsibility. Perhaps we have a sufficient explanation of the Prophet's failure to give more detailed directions to the Shunammite in that it would seem to be the Divine purpose to relieve man of no share of the responsibility which he is able to bear. God does not do for us that which he has made us able to do for ourselves. He holds us responsible for the proper exercise of the ability with which he has endowed us to think, to reason, to decide for ourselves. Yet it is equally true that God is ever ready to help the helpless, to give light to those who sit in darkness. How precious the words of the Prophet! "And he saw that there was no man, and wondered that there was no intercessor: therefore his own arm brought salvation unto him."

Speaking by the mouth of the Psalmist, God says, "I have laid help upon one that is mighty." Not only has God warned the siner to flee from wrath to come, but he has indicated to him, in language which "the wayfaring men though fools need not err" in understanding, the only place of safety, even in Jesus Christ. "For there is none other name under heaven, given among men, whereby we must be saved." It was a hard thing which the Shunammite was required to do, since it involved a great sacrifice on her part. Had she belonged to the poorer class whose habitations were humble, and the tenure even thereto indefinite as to time, who enjoyed but scant fare even in prosperous times, it would have been comparatively easy for her to do as she was directed. But she was wealthy, a fact which has led to the supposition that the warning given her was based upon other considerations than the simple lack of food which she might experience in consequence of the approaching famine. The plausibility of such a supposition is further evident from the king's command that the price of the products of her lands during her absence from home be restored to her. In addition to the material loss which she must sustain if she obeyed the Prophet's direction, she would have to forego the social amenities of the quiet life of Shunem, and the religious privileges of her own land, a loss whose greatness she could not estimate until she had experienced it fully. But the Shunammite had learned to have faith in Elisha. The record is that she "arose and did after the saying of the man of God; and she went with her household, and sojourned in the land of the Philistines seven years." Her obedience was unquestioning. She does not now reply to the prophet, as when the announcement was made to her that she should have a son, "Nay, my lord, thou man of God, do not lie unto thine handmaid."

Incredible as the Prophet's warning might have seemed to others, for as yet there was no indication of the famine predicted, she seems to have given it the fullest credence, and to have acted accordingly. "Perhaps the sublimest act in the life of the Shunammite was when in simple faith she obeyed the Prophet's direction. For as yet there was plenty in the land, nor any indication of approaching famine, except in the message of Elisha. To yield such absolute obedience in what involved such trial and renunciation of all her own, simply on the ground of the prophetic word, was no ordinary victory over the world. It was to give up certainty for uncertainty, and to act directly contrary to all that prudence or worldly wisdom would have suggested. But must not ours be, in measure, a similar faith: simple trust in the word of our Master, when, without further evidence than it, we forsake all things that we may follow him? And is not that life the happiest in which, like Abraham, we are willing to go, not knowing whither, so that we may go at his bidding?" (Edersheim.) The obedience of the Shunammite was as prompt as it was unquestioning. She might have reasoned that it would be safe, and in every way advantageous for her to remain in her comfortable home at least until the famine began to prevail. "Time enough yet," she might have said. Thus men reason when warned to prepare for death and the judgment. Our Lord has said, "Be ye also ready: for in such an hour as ye think not, the Son of Man cometh." And yet many say, "Where is the sign of his coming?" "It is time enough to prepare for death when we know it is at hand." "Let us enjoy the world while we may." Though God could have saved the Shunammite by other means than that which he appointed, we must believe that, had she delayed her departure unduly, or for any reason had refused to do as she was directed and had remained in the land of Israel "while the tempest of God's wrath swept across it," she would have experienced all the evils against which she was warned. If at the last we are to stand accepted before God; if our hearts are to thrill with those joy-imparting words, "Well done, good and faithful servant," we must yield to God's commandments an obedience as unquestioning and prompt as the obedience of the Shunammite to the Prophet's direction.

The obedience of the Shunammite was exact. She did neither less nor more than she had been directed to do. In the absence of explicit direction, she chose to sojourn in the land of the Philistines, probably being determined in her choice by the proximity of that land to her own, the fertility of its soil, and its comparative freedom from drought and consequent famine.

In this land she remained until the seven years of famine had elapsed. It is not difficult to imagine how strongly she would be tempted to return to the homeland before the days of sojourn appointed her were ended. How she would long to feast her eyes once more upon that home in whose stones and dust she took pleasure, to greet again the friends and neighbors whom she had left behind! How her soul, grieved by the idolatrous practices of those with whom she was obliged to sojourn, must have yearned for the privilege of revisiting Carmel at the return of each new moon and sabbath to be taught the way of life by the man of God! But not until God's time had fully come, did she seek the gratification of a desire so natural and worthy. Hers was the spirit of Job when he said, "All the days of my appointed time will wait, till my change come." On the other hand we may well believe that this woman was ready, when God gave permission, to return to her native land. Not a day, not an hour, longer than was necessary, would she tarry. We should be careful to do all that the Lord requires us to do; but we should be no less careful not to exceed his commands, not to tarry longer in Philistia than his purpose provides. What joy home-coming has for us! How we look forward to such an event, and count the months, then the weeks, then the days, then the hours which must elapse before the journey can be begun! It must have been with a glad heart that the Shunammite turned her face toward home when the years of her exile were ended. It was not an age of railway mail service in which she lived, of telegraph and telephone facilities. Perhaps she had heard not a word of all that had transpired in Israel, during her long residence abroad. Doubtless her friends had long since come to think of her as dead. What pleasant surprises, what happy reunions, what blessed relief from the cares and anxieties which she had known as a stranger in a strange land were now awaiting! Such may have been the thoughts of this good woman as her beloved Shunem appeared in the distance. But how sore the disappointment, which, in fact, was in store for her! When she arrived at her home, she found it in the possession of strangers who met her at her own door and refused her admittance. Her estate had reverted to the crown or had been seized by some rapacious neighbor. "It is still common for even petty shieks to confiscate the property of any person who is exiled for a time, or who moves away temporarily from his district. Especially is this true of widows and orphans, and small is the chance to such of having their property restored unless they can secure the mediation of some one more influential than themselves." (The Land and the Book.)

It may be that again, the Shunammite would be disposed to question the justice and goodness of God's dealings with her. She had been obedient to the Divine direction, yet what advantage had it been to her to spend seven long dreary years as an alien in an idolatrous land? Could her experience have been more deplorable had she remained at home, like her neighbors, to care for her estates and to defend her property rights? After all, had she not fared worse indeed than her neighbors? For while they may not have been called to endure any greater hardships than she, they were now in quiet possession of their homes, while she was left destitute.

"Surely we may argue the love of God to her must have been very great when he had dealt so closely with her. First she had passed through a long period of silent endurance till her heart's desire had been granted. Then came the death of her child; then the death of her husband; then her departure from Shunem; then years of poverty and trial; and now the loss of property and position. What a thorough weaning of all her affections from that which is seen, and what lessons of trustfulness and of dependence on that which is unseen! Whatever she had loved, she had first to give up, that again she might receive it from the Lord, and hold it of him and in him." (Edersheim).

It seems strange that the Shunammite did not at once seek to avail herself of Elisha's assistance in such trying circumstances, and yet our second thought must approve the course she pursued. It was her duty to do what she could for herself before appealing to the Prophet. "And she went forth and cried to the king for her house and for her land." She had no other recourse. If the king refused to do her justice, to right the wrong which had been done her, she could do no more.

As we see her who was introduced to us as "a great woman" going forth humbly to supplicate the king's favor, our thoughts revert to that scene in the guest-chamber, more than half a score of years ago perhaps, when she declined to have Elisha speak to the king for her, with the proud assertion, "I dwell among mine own people." As much as to say, I have no need of the king's good offices. Was there after all a proud spirit in this good woman which must needs be humbled?

It should require nothing more than the inspired narrative to convince us that God ordered the time and the circumstances of the Shunammite's appeal to the king. "And the king talked with Gehazi, the servant of the man of God, saying, Tell me, I pray thee, all the great things that Elisha hath done. And it came to pass as he was telling the king how he had restored a dead body to life, that, behold, the woman, whose son he had restored to life, cried to the king for her house and for her lands." It was God, without whose knowledge not a sparrow falleth to the ground, who put it into the heart of the king to seek this information concerning Elisha's deeds at this moment. And while it was perfectly natural that he should consult Gehazi rather than Elisha concerning the matter, God so ordered events that the king and Gehazi met at this particular time; and that, while Gehazi might have been telling one of a hundred other stories, he was in fact telling of the great miracle of raising from the dead the son of the Shunammite, at the very moment when she, accompanied by her son, appeared to make her appeal to the king. Remarkable coincidence, we are wont to exclaim, so indeed it was. It was a remarkable coincidence that on the very night when Haman's plot for the destruction of Mordecai and all his people was ripe, king Ahausuerus should be troubled with insomnia, that he should order the chonicles of the king to be read before him, that the tablet read should be the one which contained the record of how this same Mordecai who was to be put to death on the morrow, had saved the life of the king by revealing a conspiracy against him, and that the discovery of this fact should lead to the defeat of Haman's wicked purposes, the honoring of Mordecai, and the saving of the Jewish people from destruction. Yet all such coincidences are brought about by an overruling Providence which directs all things with infinite wisdom, goodness, and power.

"Behind the dim unknown,
Standeth God within the shadow keeping
Watch above his own."
(Lowell.)

"The king's heart is in the hand of the Lord as the rivers of waters; he turneth it whithersoever he will." Had the Shunammite delayed her return to the land of Israel but a day; had she appeared before the king but a few moments later, she might have appealed to him in vain. At any other time, perhaps, he would have been little moved by the story of the wrong which had been done her. But he was so deeply interested in the account of what Elisha had done for her that he listened to her grievance, and "appointed unto her a certain officer, saying, Restore all that was her's, and all the fruits of the field since the day that she left the land, even until now." As we study the history of the Shunammite, these words of inspiration come to mind frequently. "Be not forgetful to entertain strangers: for thereby some have entertained angels unawares." "Cast thy bread upon the waters: for thou shalt find it after many days." "For riches certainly make themselves wings; they fly away as an eagle toward heaven." "Lay not up for yourselves treasures upon earth, where moth and rust doth corrupt, and where thieves break through and steal: but lay up for yourselves treasures in heaven, where neither moth nor rust doth corrupt, and where thieves do not break through and steal." "Cast thy burden upon the Lord, and he shall sustain thee." "Have faith in God."

## CHAPTER XVI.

### WILD GOURDS IN THE POTTAGE.

"Fate steals along with silent tread,
Found oftenest in what least we dread;
Frowns in the storm with angry brow,
But in the sunshine strikes the blow."

(Cowper.)

THE sacred narrative leads us once more to Gilgal whence Elisha had accompanied his master to the place of his translation. Although its location is now a matter of speculation, Gilgal was associated with many important events in the earlier history of Israel. It was here that the first passover was observed in the land of promise; and for many years thereafter it seems to have been made the resting place of the tabernacle and to have become, in consequence, the center of the religious life of the people. Prior to the beginning of Elisha's ministry it became the seat of one of the schools of the prophets. The visit of Elisha at this time was probably one of many which, as the head of the prophetic order, he had made to Gilgal. The presumption is that his time was largely spent in these schools, each of them being visited at stated periods for the purpose of imparting instruction, and of exercising a general supervision of its affairs. It was a time of famine. Perhaps the same dreadful scourge of which the good Shunammite had been warned now rested upon the land. Parched and barren fields and the dry courses of streams whose waters had vanished by reason of long-continued drought, met the eye on every hand. Instead of the joyous shout of those who gathered the abundant harvest, there was heard the cry of multitudes who lacked bread to satisfy their hunger. Elisha found the sons of the prophets at Gilgal in very straitened circumstances, as we gather from the narrative. Their condition seems to have presented no exception to the universal distress which prevailed, a striking illustration of the oft-attested truth that God's people are not always exempted from the evils incident to the life in the flesh. "Indeed it not infrequently happens that the children of God suffer more severely than the children of the world, and that help comes to the latter much sooner than to the former." (Krummacher).

Such was the thought which came to the mind of the Psalmist. His words are, "But as for me, my feet were almost gone; my steps had well nigh slipped. For I was envious at the foolish, when I saw the prosperity of the wicked. For there are no bands in their death: but their strength is firm. They are not troubled as other men; neither are they plagued like other men. Their eyes stand out with fatness: they have more than heart could wish." And yet the advantage is ever on the side of the child of God, notwithstanding such seemingly inexplicable facts. The Psalmist was not permitted to remain in doubt and perplexity in reference to this subject, nor to leave others in a like state of mind.

He says, "When I sought to know this, it was too painful for me; until I went into the sanctuary of God; then understood I their end. Surely thou hast set them in slippery places: thou castest them down into destruction. How are they brought into desolation, as in a moment! They are utterly consumed with terrors." To the human eye it may seem that God makes no distinction between the righteous and the unrighteous.

It may even appear that he deals less bountifully with his own than with those who know him not.

But to the believer, afflictions are sanctified, so that they work in him the peaceable fruits of righteousness; while even the greatest material prosperity may serve only to render more complete the alienation of the unbelieving heart from God. Perhaps Elisha was Divinely directed to Gilgal at this particular crisis, that by that instruction which he, above all others, was competent to impart, he might dispel the clouds of doubt and unbelief which hid the Father's hand from the sons of the prophets.

Distressing as their outward circumstances were it would seem that the Prophet felt that their spiritual needs were still more pressing. The narrative indicates that his first service in their behalf was to minister to their spiritual necessities. "The sons of the prophets were sitting before him." According to Oriental custom, the sons of the prophets, who were his students or disciples, would sit in a semi-circle at his feet while receiving instruction. We are not informed as to the character of the instruction imparted upon this occasion. As before intimated, it may have been that, in answer to the pressing inquiries of those who sat before him, he sought to offer an explanation of the providence which had filled the land with the horrors of famine, which entailed hardship and suffering upon God's faithful servants as well as their idolatrous neighbors. What advantage, it may have been asked, is there in serving God, seeing he deals thus with us? Such a question would seem pertinent, if, as may have been the case, these sons of the prophets could point to some idolaters who, instead of sharing the sufferings of their neighbors, were really advantaged by the famine, being able to exact exorbitant prices for stores which they had laid by against such a time as this. Many times "the children of this world are in their generation wiser than the children of light." Having sought to satisfy the spiritual hunger of his disciples, Elisha addressed himself to the task of satisfying their physical hunger. Gehazi is directed to set on the great pot and to prepare pottage for them. At the same time one of the young men, to whose lot it probably fell to provide for that day, went out into the field to gather the herbs of which the pottage was to be made, in part at least.

We do not question the piety of this young man, nor the honesty of his intentions, but it would seem that his knowledge of botany was limited, at least it was not exact. In his search for nutritious herbs he "found a wild vine, and gathered thereof wild gourds his lap full, and came and shred them into the pot of pottage."

Critics have been unable to determine with any degree of certainty, what kind of fruit this was. Dr. Thompson, in The Land and the Book, asks the question, "Is there anything satisfactory known about it?" (that is the wild gourd gathered). To this question he replies "Not much more than what the prophet's son that gathered them knew. The Septuagint does not translate but gives the Hebrew, showing that those learned men did not know what it was; and if they could not determine the question, it is not likely that we can at this day. The

Latin Bible calls it wild colocynth. The English renders it by the vague word gourd. I can hardly believe it was colocynth, because this is so well known, so bitter, and so poisonous, that the most ignorant peasants never dream of making pottage of it. He must have been a very stupid son of a prophet indeed, to have filled his "lap" with them. Various other herbs have been selected by critics, as the cucumis prophetarum, a small prickly gourd, rarely met with in this country. The Hebrew root seems to point to some herb that bursts or splits open, and some have thought that it might be the Ecbalium elaterium, which is found in various parts of the country, and is poisonous. When green, it might be mistaken for an edible gourd, or cucumber."

The pottage prepared, "they poured out for the men to eat." Doubtless each one present partook of it, being wholly ignorant of its deadly character. Even Elisha knew nothing of this, and unsuspectingly eat with the rest of the company. Indeed he seems to have been slowest of all to realize that death lurked in the food which he was eating; another illustration of the fact, already noted, that the prophets were not omniscient.

It was not until those who ate with him cried out and said, "O, thou man of God, there is death in the pot," that he realized what had befallen them.

It was a criminal act on the part of this young man to assume the responsibility of putting these wild gourds into the pottage without, as seems to have been the case, endeavoring to learn their nature. He should have consulted with his associates, and, in case they had been unable to inform him, he should have sought the advice of Elisha before venturing to eat of them himself or to offer them as food to others. The path of duty may not always be plain to us, and when we are in doubt we should seek the advice of those whose character and experience warrant our confidence. It is no crime to be ignorant, provided we have made an honest effort to be enlightened and are unwilling to remain in ignorance. It would be a foolish and dangerous procedure to attempt to prove by practical experiment whether a plant or a fruit of which we were wholly ignorant were nutritious or poisonous. Nor is it less foolish and dangerous to attempt to arrive at the truth in morals by experiment. We should avail ourselves of the wisdom and experience of others; and, above all, we should yield ourselves to the constraining and directing influences of the Holy Spirit and to the word of God which "is profitable for doctrine, for reproof, for correction, for instruction in righteousness: that the man of God may be perfect, thoroughly furnished unto all good works."

It is sometimes said that the education of the ordinary minister of the Gospel is not symmetrical; that while his knowledge of books may be profound, there are truths to be learned outside of classic halls and libraries with which he is not sufficiently familiar. Whether or not the charge is just, it cannot be insisted upon too strongly, that those to whom the Lord's business is committed, those who are called to manage the affairs of the Church, should be men of broad and liberal education. It could not have impaired the efficiency of this young man, as a theologian, had he been sufficiently versed in the science of botany to recognize the fruit of this wild vine as poisonous. It is no discredit, it is no disadvantage, to him who is called to preach the word to know something about the world in which he lives, to be able to distinguish between the vine and the bramble-bush, between the wheat and the cheat. A knowledge of men and of business principles, will never harm a true Christian. Paul, the prince of theologians, knew how to make tents, and enough of the civil law under which he was born and lived to claim the privileges of a Roman citizen, when it was necessary and proper for him to do so.

When the apostles were convinced that they should not leave the word and serve tables, they directed that men full, not only of the Holy Spirit, but of wisdom, be chosen to attend to such business. It is an easy thing to be deceived by appearances, hence it is a thing of very common occurrence. In form, size, and color, the wild gourds gathered by this young man doubtless resembled some fruit which he knew to be healthful. In the moral and the spiritual it is possible thus to be deceived by appearances. "There is a way which seemeth right unto a man, but the end thereof are the ways of death." Things are not always what they may appear to us to be. Perhaps the most harmful of all untruths is a half-truth.

Many false doctrines are so skilfully blended with the truth as to deceive those who are careless and unsuspecting. Like a sugar-coated pill, the bitter and the repulsive are hidden beneath that which is pleasing to the taste. Our Lord's words are, "There shall arise false Christs, and false prophets, and shall show great signs and wonders; in so much that, if it were possible, they would deceive the very elect." We do well to give heed to the words of the beloved disciple, "Beloved, believe not every spirit, but try the spirits whether they are of God; because many false prophets are gone out into the world."

Ignorance on man's part does not effect the results of his actions. Doubtless the intentions of this young man in gathering these wild gourds, and shredding "them into the pot of pottage" were the very best. He may have considered himself very fortunate in finding such a quantity of fruit in a time of such scarcity. Nevertheless the gourds were poisonous, and, as a result of eating them, he and his companions were brought face to face with death. It is often said that it matters not what a man believes if he is only sincere in his belief. This is a most pernicious error. Elisha and the sons of the prophets with him had no other thought, we may believe, than that the pottage which was poured out for them was wholesome, as it was doubtless delicious to their taste, and a proper thing upon which to satisfy their hunger. Yet this honest conviction did not save them from the deadly effects of the poison which was contained in the pottage. Truth is no less important than sincerity, the two must go together. Though a man be never so sincere, if the moral and religious doctrines which he accepts be not true, he must suffer the consequences. Paul's words are eternally true, "Whatsoever a man soweth, that shall he also reap."

> "Immutable are nature's laws
> Regardless of our weal or woe,
> And though we scatter tares or wheat,
> We must all gather what we sow."
>
> (Barlow.)

There may have been many nutritious herbs in the mess of pottage which was prepared for the sons of the prophets upon this occasion, but the poisonous gourds rendered the whole mass poisonous. Soloman says, "Dead flies cause the ointment of the apothecary to send forth a stinking savor: so doth a little folly in him that is in reputation for wisdom and honor." One word spoken foolishly or unadvisedly, one wrong step taken, may cast a shadow upon an otherwise irreproachable character. To the young man who came to him with the question, "What shall I do that I may have eternal life?" our Lord said, "One thing thou lackest." But that one thing was sufficient, it would seem, at least for the time, to bar the gates of heaven against that young man: for our Lord, speaking to his disciples, said, as the young man went away sorrowful, "How hardly shall they that have riches enter into the kingdom of God." The Apostle James says, "Whosoever shall keep the whole law, and yet offend in one point, he is guilty of all." But one fatal error in a man's theology or ethics, vitiates the whole system.

It was wise for the sons of the prophets to cease from eating the pottage as soon as they discovered that it was poisonous. "And they could not eat thereof."

It would have been to tempt God, and to forfeit all right to expect deliverance from him, had they continued to eat of that which they knew was fatal to life. A man has no right to expect to enjoy physical health if he neglects, or violates, the laws of health, if he uses as food, or as a luxury, that which he knows to be injurious to health. It is our privilege and our duty to pray to be delivered from temptation, but, in so far as we are able, we are to answer our own prayer by keeping out of the way of temptation. To know that a certain course of life is wrong, that, "there is death in the pot," should be sufficient to induce us to abstain from it. In the wail of many a blighted, many a ruined life, we may hear this cry, a cry of warning to us, "O thou man, there is death in the pot." Every day men and women, some ignorantly others with a misdirected intelligence, are shredding, not lap fulls, but, car loads of wild gourds into our current literature, in the form of immoral and obscene books, papers, and pictures. How much time is squandered by the present generation upon trashy novels which give false and distorted ideas of life, and unfit the reader for the duties of life! How many of the real tragedies of life, how many of the crimes against society, how much of human suffering and wretchedness, is to be attributed to the poisonous gourds of literature!

Dr. Talmage says, "The greatest blessing that ever came to this country is that of an elevated literature, and the greatest scourge has been that of an unclean literature. This last has its victims in all occupations and departments. It has helped to fill insane asylums and penitentiaries and almshouses and dens of shame." If Christian men and women would be true to themselves and to God, they must refuse to eat such pottage or to permit it to be set before others. In the accounts of crimes, detection, disgrace and punishment, which fall under our notice almost daily, this same warning cry is heard, "O thou man, there is death in the pot." In the case of many the poisonous gourd in the pottage is the habit of speaking falsely. No one contributes more to render mutual confidence among men impossible, to undermine the very basis of human society and happiness, than he who will consent to speak untruthfully. "No sin cometh more directly from the devil who "is a liar, and the father thereof," or is more abominable in the sight of God, than that of lying. And when the habit has been acquired, it is a most difficult thing to be free from it. "After the tongue has once gotten into the knack of lying 'tis not to be imagined how impossible almost it is to reclaim it." (Montaigue.). But there are many who insist that it is permissible to tell what we politely term a white lie when no one can be injured by it, but such a case is not to be found. If the untruth spoken harms no one else, it harms him who utters it; for it robs him of some measure of self-respect, and of that veneration for the truth which is so necessary to the preservation of the truth.

Every untruth is a nail which helps to rivet upon its author the character of a liar, and no liar shall enter the kingdom of heaven. When Aristotle was once asked what a man could gain by uttering falsehoods, he replied, "Not to be believed when he shall tell the truth," a punishment which all must concede is by no means inconsiderable. Young man, young woman, hear the cry of warning, "There is death in the pot," as you consent to admit to the circle of your friends and companions, persons of questionable character, who seek to entice you from the sanctuary on the Lord's day, whose effort is to induce you to accompany them to places which your conscience cannot approve, it may be the dancing hall, the theater, the saloon. The words which Shakespeare puts into the mouth of Polonius are worthy of earnest consideration,

"Be thou familiar, but by no means vulgar,
Those friends thou hast, and their adoption tried,
Grapple them to thy soul with hoops of steel;
But do not dull thy palm with entertainment
Of each new-hatched, unfledged comrade."

"There is death in the pot" for a man when he begins to bet, to gamble, and to cultivate illicit friendships. Such a course almost invariably leads on to other crimes. In most cases the beginning of the end has come. By and by, such a man will be found appropriating his employer's or his partner's money in order to make up his losses, to speculate more heavily, or "to show his friends a good time." At first he takes but a small amount, fully intending to return it again, perhaps he does return it, but when he is again pressed for money he will resort to the same method of obtaining it. As he becomes more deeply involved his ability and willingness to replace his unlawful borrowings are correspondingly diminished.

At length he ceases to make effort to restore that which he has taken, trusting to his ability to conceal his crime by false entries. But the day of reckoning comes at last. There is a discovery of his crookedness, there is an arrest, a trial, a conviction, there is punishment, and permanent disgrace. "Look not thou upon the wine when it is red, when it giveth his color in the cup, when it moveth itself aright. At the last it biteth like a serpent, and stingeth like an adder." O thou man or woman that dareth to put to your lips the intoxicating cup, "that giveth" thy "neighbor drink, that addest thy venom thereto and makest him drunken also," hear the mighty cry which comes up from the great army of starving, rag-covered children who, in filthy hovels, swelter in summer and shiver in winter; from the myriads of abused, heart-broken, and despairing women who have suffered the loss of all that is held dear in this life; from that endless procession of diseased, maimed, bloated-faced, blear-eyed men and women who are staggering to a drunkard's grave and to an endless death beyond, "There is death in the pot."

Many persons insist that they can drink or abstain from drinking as they choose. This may be true of some; but for every one of whom it is true, there are scores of whom it is not true. Then, in a very important sense, every man is his brother's keeper. The influence which we exert, the example which we set, may prove the safety or the ruin of others. The very thought of being held responsible at the judgment bar of God for having contributed in any measure to make a brother a drunkard, is sufficient to appall the stoutest heart. In the spirit of Christ, Paul says, "If meat make my brother to offend, I will eat no flesh while the world standeth, lest I make my brother to offend." The safest rule for all concerned, in regard to strong drink, is, "Touch not; taste not; handle not." The conviction that they had partaken of a deadly poison seems to have filled the hearts of the sons of the prophets with terror. In the presence of death they were afraid, and their piteous cry, "O thou man of God, there is death in the pot," was an appeal for help. Was this fear of death unworthy of these who were heirs of heaven? Perhaps so. It is the blessed privilege of the Christian to recognize in death the messenger of God, sent to break the bands of his captivity, to open the door of his prison house, and to bear him above to the realms of endless light and glory. And yet frail nature shrinks from dissolution. The Christian, while he fears not the consequences of death, but rather rejoices in the contemplation thereof, may fear the act of dying. While the presence of the poisonous element in the pottage had not been revealed to Elisha, until after its deadly effect had been felt, he seems to have been Divinely directed in the choice of an antidote for the poison. With the calmness of perfect assurance, he replies to the appeal of his terror-stricken disciples, "Then bring meal." Having received the meal, he cast it without any display, into the pot, and immediately gave the direction, "Pour out for the people that they may eat." The narrative simply states that, as a result of this act, "There was no harm in the pot." How grand this simplicity of statement! The poisonous element in the pottage was counteracted by casting in that which was healthful. Like the mess of pottage, the human heart has been poisoned. Not ignorantly, as this student-prophet in gathering the wild gourds, but with cruel malice and cunning design, the prince of darkness shred into the hearts of the first of human kind the element of eternal death. "Sin entered into the world, and death by sin." In healing the pottage, the Prophet might have employed other remedies as effectively as the one chosen; but for sin there is one remedy only, "The blood of the crucified one." How great must have been the confidence which the sons of the prophets reposed in Elisha, when, with no further assurance that the poison had been removed from the pottage than his act of casting in the meal, they accepted of his invitation to partake of it again. May our confidence in God be as unquestioning.

# CHAPTER XVII

## A GIFT OF FIRST-FRUITS.

"And I will trust that he who needs
The life that hides in mead and wold,
And stains these mosses green and gold,
Will still, as he hath done, incline
His gracious care to me and mine."

(Whittier.)

THE seven years of famine which had desolated Israel, and driven many of the people into exile perhaps, were now almost completed. The land had enjoyed its sabbath, the showers had come again, and the sight of fields that were "white already to the harvest," made glad the heart of a nation which had been reduced to extreme need. The cheering task of securing the harvest had already been begun, but to the sons of the prophets at Gilgal the prospect of abundance in the near future brought no relief from present distress. The promise of provision for to-morrow does not fill the empty larder of to-day, does not appease the hunger which is felt at the present moment. God had provided for them hitherto, yet at no time, perhaps, in excess of their immediate needs. Past experience must have convinced them that they were the objects of God's loving care, and that he was as able as he was willing to provide for them. Hence, though they may have been distressed by hunger, they were not in despair; nor were they astonished when there came by the hand of one who may have been a stranger to them, this supply of food, "twenty loaves of barley, and full ears of corn in the husk thereof." It was nothing more than they had learned to expect. If any surprise were felt, it must have been due to the fact that the supply was so small.

The loaves were simply cakes one of which would no more than satisfy the appetite of a hungry man.

What, then, would twenty loaves be among a hundred men, and, perhaps, a larger number of women and children. Nothing is known concerning this generous donor further than that which is here recorded. His name has been withheld from us, and it may be doubted whether the place of his abode has been identified. Eusebius and Jerome describe Baal-shalisha as a city twelve or fifteen Roman miles north of Diospolis, and known in their day as Beth-shalisha. This has led to the supposition that the ruins of Khurbet Hatta mark the site of the city. The statement that the gift of this unknown man was "of the first-fruits" seems to indicate that he was more than a mere philanthropist; that the act of bringing of the first-fruits to the Prophet was a service of devotion to God as well as of love to man. Every Israelite was required by the law which was delivered to Moses, to dedicate to the Lord his firstborn, the firstlings of his herds and flocks, and the first-fruits of his land. The firstborn child was to be redeemed by the payment of money; but the firstlings of cattle and sheep, the first-fruits of corn, wine, and oil, and the first fleece of the sheep were to be devoted to God, and given to the priests for their support, since they were without inheritance.

But at the time to which this event belongs, Israel, following after the sin of Jeroboam, had renounced the law of Moses, banished the priests of the Aaronic order, and adopted Baal-worship as the national religion. With no Divinely appointed priests in the land, it would not seem an illogical conclusion that even those who were faithful in Israel were released from obedience to the law concerning first-fruits. Unless the love of God, and the heaven-inspired desire for the salvation of immortal souls constrain us, we are ready to avail ourselves of every pretext which may offer for withholding from the Lord that which is his. Those in Israel who at this time still adhered to the worship of Jehovah, could not contribute to the support of the priest of Baal. At the same time, as subjects of the Northern kingdom, they might question the propriety of contributing to the support of the religious institutions of the Southern kingdom.

In such circumstances many who professed to walk in the old paths would excuse themselves from giving any thing. There are those to-day who, while claiming to be the followers of Christ, yet refuse to give to the support of foreign missions, because there are so many unsaved persons in our own land. It is a lamentable fact that, while we are seeking to Christianize the heathen, we have millions at home who know not the way of salvation. At the same time, those who have most to say against foreign missions, who demand that the masses in our own land be Christianized before we attempt to send the Gospel to the heathen, are not always distinguished for their zeal in behalf of home missions. Whatever may have been the views of others, this man of Baal-shalisha felt that the first-fruits of his land belonged to God, and, although circumstances rendered it impossible for him to comply with the Mosaic law in the letter, he found no difficulty in discovering how it could be obeyed in the spirit. Elisha, though not a priest, was God's minister, in his official capacity acting by Divine authority, and standing as the representative of true religion in Israel. Hence it was to him that the first-fruits were brought. It has been suggested that the name of this devoted man has been withheld from us in order to teach us that we are not to make a show of our liberality. Perhaps this is a correct view. Our Lord said, "Take heed that ye do not your alms before men to be seen of them: but when thou doest alms, let not thy left hand know what thy right hand doeth."

The display of beneficent deeds is a folly and sin against which many men have need to be warned. When our giving is for our own glory, and not wholly for God's glory and the welfare of our fellow-men, without any thought of self in the matter God cannot reward it. Our Lord does not teach, however, that it is in every case wrong to make known the extent of our beneficence. The evil against which he warns, lies not in the act of publishing our good deeds, but in the spirit in which this is done, "to be seen of men," that they may honor us. If the knowledge of your liberality will redound to the glory of God by inspiring in other men a willingness to be more liberal, it becomes your duty to make known the amount of your contributions. We should at least guard as carefully against making the injunction of our Lord a cloak to cover up the smallness of our contributions as against the spirit of ostentation in giving. The man who out of his abundance casts a mutilated coin into the collection basket need not think that these words of the Master are designed for him, or that he has any special reason to remember them. They are designed for a different class of offenders. For such a man it would be more appropriate to remember those other words of Scripture, "Thou God seest me," or those words of the Apostle, "Upon the first day of the week let every one of you lay by him in store as God hath prospered him." The gift of this man from Baal-shalisha, though not sufficient to supply the needs of the hungry sons of the prophets, was by no means inconsiderable in the circumstances. It was the first-fruits after a famine of seven years. What proportion it bore to that part of the harvest which had already been secured, we have no means of knowing. He must have had very little of the first-fruits of his harvest for himself, after such a generous gift. Perhaps he would have to depend upon the harvest yet to be reaped, for the supply of his own needs. His gift may have been measured not by his ability at the time to give, but by the necessities of those to whom he gave. That is the true standard of Christian beneficence which the Apostle gives us. "As the Lord has prospered us." "As we have therefore opportunity, let us do good unto all men, especially unto them who are of the household of faith." This will involve the giving of the tenth in the case of some, while it may mean more or less than the tenth in the case of others. In certain circumstances the demands upon our liberality may be greater than in other circumstances. If a man have ten loaves of bread, and a number of starving men come to him to be fed, he has no warrant, in ordinary circumstances, to limit his giving to them to one loaf. If, of two men who receive the same salary, one has to pay house-rent and to support a large family while the other owns his house and has no one to support but himself, the latter owes more to the Lord's treasury than the former. "That can scarcely deserve the name of Christian liberality which is not proportioned to our means. Rare as such contribution is, and large as it may seem, even to give a tenth may not be a fair standard. There are those to whom a tenth may be more than a just contribution; for a man is to give of what he hath, not of that which he hath not. And there are considerations connected with the position which we may necessarily, and as appointed by God, have to occupy, which may involve the obligation to curtail our givings. This is indeed a principle capable of abuse; nor is it possible to lay down rules for its right application. Spiritually-minded Christians will rightly apply it; others will not, whatever be said or explained. On the other hand there are those in whose case a tenth would represent what is far below the right proportion of their giving, whether viewed by itself, or proportionately either to their other expenditure or their savings." (Edersheim.) Seven years of famine must have left this man of Baal-shalisha greatly impoverished. Doubtless he had need of all that the harvest would bring him. Debts may have been contracted during the years in which the land had produced no fruits. If so, he must now provide for their payment, while other unusual demands would be made upon him. Even feeling as he did that this contribution should be made, the arguments for postponing it to the end of the summer, or, at least, until the harvest had all been gathered, would have been cogent to many another mind. Yet this man seems to have felt that the

Lord's portion must be rendered to him at once, hence he brings to "the man of God, bread of the first-fruits." There are many Christian men and women who act differently, whatever be their convictions with reference to this subject. Instead of remembering the Lord with the first-fruits of the year, they give to him the last-fruits. Had this man from Baal-shalisha been less prompt in meeting the claims of God which he recognized as resting upon him, either the distress of Elisha and his friends must have been prolonged and intensified, or relief had been provided for them from some other source; in which case the honor and joy of being used as God's instrument in the accomplishment of his gracious purpose must have been denied this man. How many precious opportunities have been lost to the Church, how great the inconveniences, the material loss, and actual suffering entailed upon those who labor for the up-building of the walls of Zion, through the failure or delay of God's people to meet their obligations to him. Many there are who fail to recognize the truth that they are morally bound to give, as they are able, for the support of God's cause at home and abroad, and that a promise to pay money to the church is sacred and binding, involving our honor as truly as would a note of promise given to the bank. God's aid, while always timely, may not antedate our actual needs. It would seem that it was not until the prophets at Gilgal had come to feel the pangs of hunger, and, doubtless, had been led to cry to God, "Give us this day our daily bread," that this supply of bread, from an unexpected source, came to them. To those who are his, God gives wisdom and strength for service, and grace for every trial, but not always in advance of the actual need of such gifts. It was when Israel, with the sea before them and the hosts of Pharaoh in battle-array behind them, heard the command of Moses to go forward, that a way of escape from their pursuers was provided for them "through the midst of the sea."

To Jeremiah, protesting his inability to speak, pleading his youthfulness, the Lord said, as he put forth his hand and touched his lips, "Behold I have put my words in thy mouth." Dying grace is given to the believer when he comes to die, however much the thought of death may have terrified him beforehand. No one, perhaps, is born with the spirit of the martyr in him, yet multitudes have welcomed death in its most cruel and appalling forms, that they might witness for the truth, and win the martyr's crown. One feature of the gift of this man of Baal-shalisha is especially suggestive and touching. The record is that in addition to the "twenty loaves of barley," there were "full ears of corn in the husk thereof," or, as it is given in the Revised Version, "fresh ears of corn in his sack." The tender regard which the donor cherished for the Prophet, and the heartiness with which he gave to him, are attested by the fact that he was not satisfied with contributing the bare necessities of life, but felt that he must supplement this with that which he regarded as one of the choicest delicacies.

To give to one whom he esteemed so highly was to this devout man, a privilege as well as a duty. In the same spirit should our gifts be made to God. If our hearts are right with God; if we love him who first loved us; if we are like Christ in desiring the salvation of perishing souls: we shall esteem it a privilege to give of our means that the Gospel may be preached, and God's glory advanced. "God loveth a cheerful giver." This implies that he does not love him who gives grudgingly. Our Lord said, "It is more blessed to give than to receive." Such must have been the experience of this man from Baal-shalisha. The many tokens of gratitude which he must have received from those whose distress he came to relieve; the consciousness that his visit had proved a blessing to others, that sad hearts had been gladdened, would be to him many-fold more valuable than the offering which he brought. To be regarded by the destitute and famishing as God's messenger for their relief, must have filled his soul with a pure and holy delight.

O that all men might learn that the way to be truly happy, is to live to make others happy! The Divine plan is "That no man liveth to himself." The talents with which one man is endowed, the wealth which has been committed to his care, the influence which he possesses, all are to be employed, not simply to minister to his own comfort and aggrandizement, but to promote the good of others as well. Therefore, although this supply of food which the man of Baal-shalisha brought was presented to Elisha personally, the Prophet recognized it as sent of God to be used, not for his own personal comfort only, but also for the relief of the needy sons of the prophets among whom he dwelt for the time. Accordingly he promptly directs his servant to "Give unto the people that they may eat." He was not ignorant of the fact that a large company was present, a hundred men, and, perhaps, an equal or larger number of women and children; and that, in ordinary circumstances, the twenty loaves which he directs his servant to set before the people must prove utterly inadequate to satisfy their hunger.

It is evident that God had in some manner made known to him that the small supply at hand would prove sufficient to satisfy all. Upon one occasion our Lord said to his disciples, when they expressed amazement at what he taught them, "With God all things are possible." Thus Elisha felt, and in answer to his servant's incredulous question, he simply repeats his command, "Give the people, that they may eat," adding, "for thus saith the Lord, They shall eat, and shall leave thereof." So far as the inspired record goes, nothing further was said to Gehazi.

As to how the Prophet's words were to be fulfilled, he was not informed. Nor was it needful that he should be told. It was enough for him to be told what his duty was, and to obey, without concerning himself about results. It was God's part to care for the results. If the hungry people were not satisfied with bread after he had distributed that which was put into his hands, the fault would not be his. As the servants of Christ, we are called upon to distribute the bread of eternal life to those who must perish if they receive it not. The Master has said, "Go ye into all the world and preach the Gospel to every creature." In other words, he says to us, "Give the people, that they may eat." We may some times be disposed to question the possibility of saving the world by the Gospel, in view of abounding wickedness, the allegiance rendered on every hand to the prince of darkness. Our duty, however, is to obey the command which has been given us, rather than to contemplate the forces against which the gospel must contend. If we are faithful, God is responsible for the results of our labors. It is ours to cast in the seed, but God giveth the increase.

The inspired historian, leaving some things unsaid which we cannot but wish might have been said, closes his record of this event in the life of the Prophet with this brief statement, "So he set it before them, and they did eat, and left thereof, according to the word of the Lord." How the little which the Prophet possessed was made more than sufficient to satisfy the hunger of so many; to what extent the agency of the Prophet was employed in effecting this marvelous miracle, whether, as did our Lord, he invoked the Divine blessing upon the bread provided, or was employed simply to announce what Jehovah would do, we are not told. There are those who, without assigning any sufficient reason, assert that the miracle consisted, not in an increase of the bread which was set before the sons of the prophets, but in a lessening of the appetite, so that a small portion sufficed to satisfy each hungry recipient.

Such a view, however, has the appearance of being fanciful; while the similarity of this miracle to our Lord's miracles of feeding the multitudes, in which there was obviously an augmentation of the loaves and fishes which were made the basis of those miracles, naturally suggests that the Prophet's scanty supply was miraculously increased in quantity. "We have in this miracle all the elements of the miracle of feeding the five thousand. The two substances, one artficial, one natural, from which the many are fed." As here, the servitor is incredulous, and asks, "What, shall I set this before a hundred men?" so there the disciples say, "Shall we go and buy two hundred pennyworth of bread and give them to eat?" As there twelve baskets of fragments remained, so here "they did eat and left thereof. "When we endeavor to realize to ourselves the manner of the miracle, it evermore eludes our grasp. We seek in vain to follow it with our imaginations. For, indeed, how is it possible to realize to ourselves, to bring within forms of our conception, any act of creation, any becoming?

How is it possible for our thoughts to bridge over the gulf between not-being and being, which yet is bridged over in every creative act? And this being impossible, there is no force in the objection which one has made against the historical truth of this narrative" (the narrative of the feeding of the five thousand) "namely that there is no attempt at close description to make clear in its details the manner in which this wonderful bread was formed. It is true wisdom to leave the description of the indescribable undescribed, and with not so much as an attempt at the description." (Trench.)

After all, is this miracle of the multiplication of the loaves and fresh ears of corn to be regarded as any more wonderful than the great miracle of reproduction and multiplication which God is constantly performing in the realm of nature, than the production of handfuls of grain from a single kernel or the mighty oak from the acorn?

> "My heart is awed within me, when I think
> Of the great miracle that still goes on
> In silence round me; the perpetual work
> Of thy creation, finished, yet renewed
> Forever." (Bryant.)

May the study of this narrative inspire within our hearts faith in God. May we, as his children, honor him by trusting him at all times, in all circumstances, and for all things. Then shall we be able to say with the Psalmist,

"O taste and see that God is good;
Who trusts in him is blest.
Fear God, his saints, none that him fear
Shall be with want oppressed.

The lion's young may hungry be
And they may lack their food;
But they that truly seek the Lord
Shall not lack any good."

## CHAPTER XVIII.

### NAAMAN THE LEPER SEEKING TO BE HEALED

"With equal pace, impartial fate
Knocks at the palace as the cottage gate."
(Francis.)

On the banks of the river Abana, now called Barada, between fifty and sixty miles from the seaport of Beyrout, stands the city of Damascus, during the time of the Hebrew monarchy the capital city of Syria. It is perhaps the most ancient city in the world. Josephus ascribes its founding to Uz, the third in the descent from Noah. If we read aright Gen. 15:2, Damascus dates as far back, at least, as the time of Abraham. The city stands in the midst of a plain twenty-two hundred feet above the level of the sea, more than four thousand square miles in area, and of surpassing beauty and productivity. "The citron perfumes the air for many miles round the city; and the fig-trees are of vast size. The pomegranate and orange grow in thickets. There is the trickling of water on every hand." (Quoted by Irving in Mahomet and his Successors.) "From the edge of the mountain-range you look down on the plain of Damascus. It is here seen in its widest and fullest perfection, with the visible explanation of the whole secret of its great and enduring charm, that which it must have had when it was the solitary seat of civilization in Syria, and which it will have as long as the world lasts.

The river is visible at the bottom, with its green banks, rushing through the cleft; it bursts forth, and as if in a moment, scatters over the plain, through a circle of thirty miles, the same verdure which had hitherto been confined to its single channel. Far and wide in front extends the level plain, its horizon bare, its lines of surrounding hills bare, all bare far away on the road to Palmyra and Bagdad. In the midst of this plain lies at your feet the vast lake or island of deep verdure, walnuts and apricots waving above corn and grass below; and in the midst of this mass of foliage rises, striking out its white arms of streets hither and thither, and its white minarets above the trees which embosom them, the city of Damascus. On the right towers the snowy height of Hermon, overlooking the whole scene. Close behind are the sterile limestone mountains." (Stanley.)

Another writer says, "The appearance of the city from a distance is beautiful in the highest degree. The bright buildings, sparkling beneath a Syrian sun, rise out of a sea of various tinted foliage, while all around, save on the northwest, where stretches the long, bare, snow-white range of the Anti-Libanus, extend charming gardens, rich cornfields and blooming orchards, with the river Bahada (the Abana of Scripture) and its branches winding through."

Mahomet is said to have refused to enter the splendid city, exclaiming, as he gazed for the first time upon it, "There is but one paradise for man." At the time to which the events which we now consider belong, Benhadad II. was king of Syria. He was a martial prince.

War was his delight, and in many instances it was a necessity, being forced upon him by neighboring monarchs. In such circumstances he would naturally gather about him the most distinguished military men of his kingdom. Among these was one who was recognized as chief. He bore the name of Naaman, meaning the well-formed, the beautiful. By the grace and providence of God, this man was brought into peculiar relations with Elisha the Prophet. The two lives touch one another in circumstances at once interesting and instructive. Naaman was a heathen man. From infancy he had been subjected to the blighting influences of idolatry. Doubtless he had heard of the living and true God, for the land of Israel in which Jehovah had been worshiped, and in which even yet, perhaps, there were the seven thousand who had "not bowed the knee to Baal, nor kissed his image," bordered hard upon Syria, only a range of hills dividing the two kingdoms.

So great, however, was the national prejudice which Naaman shared, so intense was his hatred of the rival kingdom of Israel, that he would be disposed to reject the truth, if for no other reason, simply because it had been revealed first to his enemies. Our prejudices many times prove the greatest barrier to our enlightenment and progress. Wherever man exists some form or degree of ambition is found in him. He covets and seeks distinction in some respect. Every many ought to be ambitious in the right direction. To have a wrong ambition is, perhaps, better than to have no ambition.

Naaman, we may believe, was no exception in this respect, unless it was that his ambition was greater than that of ordinary men. That a desire for glory and renown burned in his soul is evident from the vast enterprises in which he engaged, and the success which he uniformly achieved. To a large extent his ambitious dreams had been realized. He had come to be regarded as a great man, as indeed he must have been. Vast wealth and patronage had fallen to him. Any favor which he might ask of the king would be granted. Those whom he chose to favor would be advanced to honor, while those toward whom he was unfavorably disposed would be denied recognition or degraded if already in positions of honor and trust. The highest honors of the realm had been heaped upon him. Promotion had succeeded promotion, until he was now captain or general-in-chief of the armies of the kingdom.

The king loved him, trusted him, and honored him. Nor was he unworthy of the honors he received, for, "By him the Lord had given deliverance unto Syria." There is a Jewish tradition which identifies him as the archer whose arrow, shot at a venture, smote Ahab, king of Israel, "between the joints of the harness," inflicting a mortal wound. It is probable, however, that it was in battle against the Assyrians that Naaman had rendered the most signal service to the king and to his country. Placing himself at the head of the army he had beaten back the invading hosts of Shalmaneser and thus prolonged Syria's independence.

Naaman was a brave man, "a mighty man of valor." The honors which he wore had been won by deeds of arms. The achievements of many whom the world honors are more apparent than real. Many a victory has been ascribed to the skill of the commanding general, which was due wholly to the intelligence and courage of his subordinates and of the men in the ranks. But Naaman had fought his own battles, had demonstrated his prowess in many a hand to hand conflict. Naaman was a proud and haughty man. He did not undervalue his services, nor his importance as "captain of the host of the king of Syria." He was ready to resent any real or supposed disrespect shown him. But after all Naaman was simply an instrument which God employed in accomplishing His purposes. There is deep significance in the statement that "by him the Lord had given deliverance unto Syria."

Incidentally this statement shows us that, in the Jewish conception, Jehovah was not a mere national deity, but that his providence extended to other nations as well, that his control was supreme. It was not Naaman, it was not Rimmon, who had given deliverance to Syria, but Jehovah. Though Naaman's achievements might be celebrated in song, and his name mentioned as an inspiration to noble deeds, he had nothing that was not given him. Unless the Lord had willed it, he could not have won success in battle. From one point of view, Naaman's was a happy lot. In his experience there were many elements of sweetness. He was a great man with his master, the king, who leaned on his arm when going into the house of Rimmon to worship. His was the station nearest the throne. Rank, glory, wealth, influence, friendship, and esteem, all were his. Had the record ended here it would seem that the happiness of Naaman must have been complete, judged by a worldly standard. There is, however, one little adversative clause which mars the beautiful picture and causes us to shudder as we contemplate it. "But he was a leper."

It is impossible, perhaps, to imagine the consternation which must have seized the court and people of Syria when the announcement was made that the general in whose victories all rejoiced, and upon whose leadership the hope of the nation rested, had been smitten with the dread disease. To many it would seem as though the mainstay of the kingdom had fallen. And how must the heart of Naaman, brave man though he was, have sunk within him, for, from the first appearance of those shining white spots upon his flesh, he knew that he was a doomed man, that no human power or skill could save him. The one fact that he was the victim of a most loathsome and mortal disease was sufficient to obscure all his greatness and glory, to blot out of memory all his past achievements, to blast all hopes for the future and to leave him, wretched and miserable, to await the hour of his dissolution. The acclamations of applause which greeted him as he rode a conquerer through the streets of fair Damascus are no longer heard. The multitudes which once exulted in his presence, now avoid the sight of him. The hero of yesterday creeps into his room that he may be saved from the distressing and humilating gaze of those in whose praise he formerly found so much delight. The man who yesterday would have been flattered by one glance of recognition on the part of the great captain, would to-day refuse a friendly grasp of his hand.

"But yesterday, the word of Caesar might
Have stood against the world; now lies he there
And none so poor to do him reverence."

(Shakespeare.)

Probably the whole of Syria envied the greatness and the prosperity and the exploits of Naaman, and yet, in that vast empire, not the lowest slave would have been found willing to have inherited his honors if his leprosy had been a part of the entail. Remarkably equal in every age have been the dispensations of Providence. "If we knew the whole of each man's lot, perhaps of all those whom we are now most inclined to envy, there is not one with whom he would be willing to exchange conditions." (Blunt.) "Life is full of compensations. There is no misery without alleviation; no low estate without some gleam of joy or hope to brighten and glorify it; and also no happiness without some concomitant annoyance or discomfort."

> "There comes
> For ever something between us and what
> We deem our happiness." (Byron.)

"Everywhere, where there is, or seems to be, something great and fortunate, there is also some discordant 'but,' which, like a false note in a melody, mars the perfection of the good fortune. A worm gnaws at the root of every thing pertaining to this world." (Menken.) In every cup of human bliss there is a drop of gall. In the record of every life this little word, but, appears to mar the beauty of the page. How happy we should be, but for something which we either lack or fain would be rid of; something which we have done or left undone; something which we are or are not. After all how unsatisfying are the things of this life!

"God moves in a mysterious way
His wonders to perform;
He plants his footsteps on the sea
And rides upon the storm.
Deep in unfathomable mines
Of never-failing skill,
He treasures up his bright designs,
And works his gracious will."

(Cowper.)

It was God's design to win Naaman to himself, that he might magnify his mercy in him. In accomplishing his gracious purpose, God dealt with the poor heathen, as he so often deals with his children. Naaman had failed to recognize God's hand in the success which had crowned his life efforts, in the honor and renown which had come to him; hence there is sent upon him this most loathsome and fatal disease, that in the dust to which he was humbled, he might learn to fear and to worship God. Sometimes lingering and painful sickness, sore bereavement, or pecuniary losses, when sanctified, prove more effective in leading the soul to God, than years of unsanctified prosperity and immunity from trials. We are ever ready to ascribe our afflictions, our losses, our calamities, our failures to God, while we credit whatever success we achieve to our own superior wisdom and ability.

By a mysterious providence, God had provided the instrument whereby he was to lead Naaman to take the first step toward the realization of true greatness and eternal glory. After the great and decisive battle of Ramoth-gilead, in which king Ahab was slain and his army discomfited and routed, the conflict between Israel and Syria had assumed the character of a predatory or guerrilla warfare. Marauding bands of Syrian soldiers, without any to oppose them effectively, were continually devastating the borders of Israel. In one of these forays a peaceful village had been attacked. The morning sun had smiled upon a happy and joyous people. Unconscious of danger the shepherds were leading forth their flocks, and merry reapers were seeking the fields "white already to the harvest," when suddenly the cry was heard, "The Syrians are coming; flee for your lives." A moment later, a troop of savage horsemen, with gleaming sword and spear, burst like a tornado upon the terrified and defenseless villagers. It was useless to cry for quarters. Those who were unable to find a place of concealment were put to the slaughter or reserved for the slave-pen. Ceasing from their terrible work only when there was no more that could be seized or destroyed, these murderers and plunderers departed, leaving behind them the mangled bodies of their victims, the smoking ruins of the happy homes of an hour ago, and the blackened fields where had stood the ripe grain waiting the reaper's sickle. With them they bore at least one to a fate which, in view of the treatment accorded captives in that age, might justly be regarded as worse than death itself; the little maid, spoken of in the narrative before us. If her parents survived the terrible calamity which had befallen their home, and, after searching for her among the living and the dead, found her not, and were forced to the conclusion that she had been carried away into slavery, doomed to a life of shame and unrequited toil, what wonder if the question rose in their hearts and to their lips, Why hath God thus dealt with us and our beloved one?

Would it have satisfied them had they been told that the Lord had need of their child? Would it have comforted their hearts had they been permitted to look into the future, and to discover what the Lord was to accomplish by her? We trust so. So may we, when in the dark hours of bereavement similar questions come to our lips, find sufficient answer in the blessed assurance that God doeth all things well, that he hath need of our loved ones, and that from the evil to come, he hath taken them. The little maid is carried to Damascus, where she is, perhaps, thrust into the slave-pen to await a purchaser. Who shall tell the many and cruel indignities to which she was subjected by those who sold and purchased slaves? It may have been the wife of Naaman who, seeking in person for a slave among the captives, was attracted to the little Hebrew maid, and, paying the price that was asked for her, had led her to her home. The station in which this little maid was placed, was of the most obscure and humble character. To her the future must have been cheerless indeed, because utterly hopeless. Yet God had not forsaken her. She was the object of his loving care, and by her he was to do great things. This consciousness that God had used her in accomplishing his beneficent purpose was to impart to her a joy such as she might never have known in that home from which she had been so ruthlessly torn.

> "He that of greatest works is finisher,
> Oft does them by the weakest minister."
> (Shakespeare.)

By some means informed of her master's great affliction, the little maid ventured to approach her mistress, and to tell her of one who had power to heal even the leper. Her simple words are, "Would God my lord were with the prophet that is in Samaria! for he would recover him of his leprosy." There is in these words of desire and assurance, the expression of an implicit faith in God. It was because this little maid had been taught to recognize Elisha as God's prophet that she felt assured he could do that which the skill of all the physicians in the Syrian realm could not effect. Though far from home, and placed in circumstances which were most unfavorable to the cultivation of true piety, she faltered not in her allegiance to the truth as it had been taught her by God-fearing parents. She did not forget that God was looking down upon her while she served in the palace of Naaman, just as truly as He did when she was under her father's humble roof. "No matter where we go, let us take our religion with us, as Joseph took his into Egypt, as Daniel took his into Babylon, as the little Hebrew maid took hers into Syria." (Rev. C. H. Irwin.)

We have in these words of this little maid the expression of a sympathizing and forgiving heart. The knowledge of her master's suffering moved the poor captive to pity him, and to desire his relief. As she thought upon the grievous wrongs which had been done her by the Syrians, of the happy home that had been destroyed, of the loved ones who, perhaps, had been slain before her eyes, and of the dreary hopeless life to which she had been doomed: what wonder if she had exulted in the afflictions of the great general who, more than any other it may be, was responsible for her sad condition? Would it have been more than human for her to have regarded the terrible calamity which had befallen Naaman, as the judgment of God upon him for the sins of which he had been guilty? And to have found satisfaction in the

14

thought that God thus vindicated her cause? Instead of this, however, her sympathy is evoked for the sufferer, and, forgetting for the moment, her own great sorrow and the wrongs which she had suffered, she hastens to tell of the wonderful power of "the prophet that is in Samaria." Slave though she was, and of tender years, she was in a position to render an inestimable service to her master, and to glorify God in so doing. It was a service which none other could have rendered. From a human point of view, had she failed to tell of Elisha, Naaman must have died a leper, and in heathen darkness. What she did "shall be told for a memorial of her" till time shall be no more.

As the disciples of Him who alone can recover the soul from the leprosy of sin, God has made us individually responsible for some special service in the name of the Master. Some one waits for the message of life from our lips and life, and must perish if he receive it not. No one can speak the message for us, and if this were possible, we could not afford to have it so. The greatest and most far-reaching consequences may sometimes attend the simplest statements which we make. But a word, uttered it may be thoughtlessly, may have an endless power for good or evil. This little maid had no thought, perhaps, that her words concerning the prophet would be repeated in the ear of her master, and that he would be moved by them to seek the prophet's aid; yet so it was. However faint may have been the hope inspired, Naaman consults the king, who advises him to go at once to Samaria. His words are, "Go to, go," literally, "Go, depart." Be off at once. Let no time be lost. The king further encourages him by engaging, without solicitation, to write a letter in his behalf to the king of Israel.

Acting upon the advice thus given, Naaman, after making such preparation as was deemed necessary, bid adieu to loved ones, and set his face towards Samaria. It must have been a solemn moment in the life of the great chieftain, for he knew not but that the last farewell had been spoken. With the expectation that he would be obliged to purchase his cure, if obtained at all, he carried with him a vast sum of money, ten talents of silver and six thousand pieces of gold, equal, perhaps, to about sixty thousand dollars. There are few things which men prize so highly as health, especially when it has once been lost. Money and time are freely spent, torture is heroically endured, that health may be regained, and life prolonged. And yet how prodigal we all are of health while we have it! With what amazing carelessness we permit our health to be underminded and destroyed! How readily we surrender to defiling habits, to base appetite and passion which are the recognized enemies of health and happiness! The custom of exchanging presents of clothing has obtained from earliest times among oriental peoples.

Naaman made ample provision for showing such courtesy to the king of Israel and the Prophet whose aid he sought. He took with him "ten changes of raiment." But perhaps that upon which Naaman most relied for the success of his mission was the passport or letter of introduction which he bore to the king of Israel. It ran thus: "Now when this letter is come unto thee, behold, I have sent Naaman my servant unto thee, that thou mayest recover him of his leprosy." The little maid had spoken of the prophet in Samaria, but this letter is addressed to the king of Israel, and without so much as a reference to Elisha. Perhaps the Syrian monarch intended no more by this, than to enlist the good offices of his royal brother in behalf of his afflicted servant. Notwithstanding the haughty and peremptory tone of his letter, he meant no more than simply to request that the king should use his influence with the Prophet, or, more probably, his authority over him, to such an extent that his miraculous power might be exerted in behalf of the wretched sufferer. But the king of Israel interpreted the letter in a wholly different light. Its reading filled him with indignation and alarm. Knowing that it was impossible for him to do the thing which, upon the face of the letter, he was required to do, he at once concluded that the king of Syria was seeking a pretext to make war upon him. Rending his royal robes, in token of his amazement and indignation, he exclaimed, "Am I God, to kill and to make alive, that this man does send unto me to recover a man of his leprosy?" Leprosy was regarded as equivalent to death, and the restoring of the dead to life as an act possible with God alone, hence the king's words. The last ray of hope must have fled from the breast of Naaman as he heard this confession of helplessness upon the part of the king; but it was another step in the Divine method of revealing to him the one, "able to save to the uttermost them that draw near unto God through him, seeing he ever liveth to make intercession for them."

## CHAPTER XIX.

### NAAMAN HEALED OF HIS LEPROSY.

"His overthrow heaped happiness upon him;
For then, and not till then, he felt himself,
And found the blessedness of being little."
(Shakespeare.)

MAN in his daily experiences somewhat resembles the ship which rides upon a storm-tossed sea. One moment the ship appears upon the crest of the wave only to disappear the next moment in the deep trough between waves. So do man's hopes and fears, his joys and sorrows, alternate. But yesterday, Naaman was cheered by the hope, however feeble it may have been, that he was to be cured of his loathsome disease; to-day all hope has fled, and he thinks only of returning to Damascus to die. But, "Man's extremity is God's opportunity." Sore disappointment had come to Naahan that he might be prepared for the blessing in store for him. Deliverance was at hand, though he knew it not. Elisha, the Prophet of God, has been apprised of Naaman's presence at the palace, the purpose of his coming, and of his shameful reception by the king. Filled with holy indignation because of the king's unworthy conduct in the case, of his failure to glorify God in the sight of the heathen, the Prophet had hastened to address to him, by his servant, this imperious question, "Wherefore hast thou rent thy clothes?" It is a peremptory challenge of the king's conduct, and must have brought the blush of shame to his cheek. The question is not asked for the purpose of obtaining information, but is designed to rebuke the king's impious and cowardly behavior.

Impliedly the Prophet says, Why have you behaved yourself in this silly and faithless manner? Instead of confessing that which everybody knows to be true, why did you not tell this man of the God of Israel, who alone has power to kill and to make alive? Instead of rending your clothes in craven fear, why did you not send the Syrian general to me? Have you so soon forgotten how God delivered you and your allies from the destruction which threatened you in the wilderness of Moab? How your enemies were delivered into your hands to be smitten by you and put to flight? The Prophet's searching question is accompanied by a request or command that the distinguished visitor who had occasioned the king such alarm should be sent to him. "Let him come now to me." That the king may the more readily and promptly comply with this direction, the Prophet makes the bold assertion, "and he shall know that there is a prophet in Israel." Falling from other lips than those of an Elisha, such words might justly be regarded as presumptuous.

The man of God declares himself ready to accomplish that for which the monarchs of two kingdoms with all their wealth and power were not sufficient. But it is no vainglorious boast which he makes. His purpose was not to proclaim his own power, but, through the cure which by Divine direction he was to effect, to convince Naaman, and all who might be made acquainted with the fact that he had been healed, that back of the prophet was a living, wonder-working God. This is the controlling motive of every Christian life. If we can say, "Whose I am, and whom I serve," we shall seek by every word and act to glorify, not ourselves but Christ before men. To his disciples our Lord says, "Ye are the light of the world." If we have found peace with God through faith in Jesus Christ, we may confidently say to the soul smitten with the leprosy of sin, and for whose relief human wisdom avails not, let him come to us. We are in possession of that of which the world knows not, which money cannot purchase, nor earthly power command. We can point the perishing to "the Lamb of God who taketh away the sin of the world," and who says, "Come unto me, all ye that labor and are heavy laden, and I will give you rest. Take my yoke upon you, and learn of me; for I am meek and lowly in heart: and ye shall find rest unto your souls."

The sacred historian tells us nothing of the spirit in which the king received this message of Elisha, nor of his conduct in reference thereto. Anxious, as he doubtless was, to be rid of his unwelcome visitor at any cost, he probably submitted tamely to the Prophet's censure, and without loss of time, did as he was directed. Whether he told Naaman or not, he could recall the fact, perhaps, now that it suited his selfish purpose, that God had wrought great things by the hand of this prophet. If this information were imparted by the king it would serve to refresh the memory of Naaman and to revive hope in his breast. Perhaps he would recall the fact which, up to this moment he seems to have overlooked or forgotten, that the little maid in his home, far away in Damascus, had spoken of a prophet and not at all of the king of Israel. With the shortest delay possible, we may believe, Naaman quitted the palace, and, at the head of his splendid cortage, presently "stood at the door of the house of Elisha." Once again, as in the case of the three kings, earthly greatness was obliged to do honor to Elisha. Humble though his abode must have been, the proud and distinguished Syrian must come to him to be healed. We may believe that ordinarily Elisha was ready to receive in the kindest and most affable manner those who came to him seeking help or instruction.

The woman of Shunem, hastening to him in the hour of her bereavement, meets with a most tender and sympathetic reception. He not only sends his servant to meet her while yet "afar off," and to greet her with anxious inquiry concerning herself and loved ones, but when she arrives at the place of his abode he comes forth to receive her and to hear her impassioned appeal for help. But although he had directed that Naaman should be sent to him, he had no word of welcome for him when he came. Contrarywise, he seems to have refused him even courteous treatment. Instead of hastening forth to meet him in a manner befitting his station, he remains in his house and refuses to see him at all. It would seem like studied insult, yet back of it there was the most praiseworthy purpose. There are certain diseases to which the flesh is heir, which, humanly speaking, naught but the surgeon's knife can cure. A grievous wound must be inflicted that health may be restored. Naaman was the victim of a disease infinitely more deplorable in its results than that which tortured and consumed his body. Soul-leprosy had poisoned the fountain of his spiritual being, and its dreadful effects were continually manifest. God willed to save him from going down to the pit of eternal despair, but only the most heroic treatment could avail. Preliminary to successful effort in his behalf, his pride must be subdued. The proud chieftain who felt that the honor and glory which he enjoyed were due solely to his own prowess in arms must be taught that he is wholly dependent upon God who "doeth according to his will in the army of heaven, and among the inhabitants of the earth." Naaman must learn "that God is no respecter of persons"; that the sacrifice which he will not despise is "a broken and a contrite heart"; that "simple faith and implicit obedience are the conditions alike of man's worship and of God's help." Hence the Prophet's apparently uncivil treatment. It was the sharp blade with which God wounded that he might heal, and Naaman afterwards blessed the hand that smote.

"Since I have felt the surgeon's knife,
And come to know its meaning,
With it I am no more at strife,
From it my members screening.
Cut deep, I say, I'm not afraid,
Cut deep, the canker reaching:
Cut deep, O faithful, searching blade!
This is my whole beseeching.

He holds another searching blade,
My Lord, my soul's physician:
Another consultation's made,
Another great decision:
And can I yield me silently
No struggle interposing?
I leave the whole, O Lord! to thee,
Be it of thy disposing."

(President J. E. Rankin, D.D., L.L. D.)

The letter of introduction which Naaman bore from his king, his own proud fame, the bags of silver and gold which were at his disposal, and the cases filled with rich and beautiful garments, served him no purpose whatever. With all the splendor and pomp of his retinue, Elisha would not see him. The only recognition which the Prophet accords him is to send forth to him a messenger with this direction, "Go and wash in Jordan seven times." It was a critical moment with the distinguished Syrian, the turning point in his life, and the angels of God, in whose presence there is joy over one sinner that repenteth, must have watched with deepest solicitude as his pride sought to assert its wonted power over him. Accustomed as he was to receive the deference and honor shown to those of his rank and merit, his indignation was aroused at being treated thus by one whom he doubtless regarded as an inferior. "Naaman was wroth, and went away, and said, Behold, I thought, he will surely come out to me."

"How unreasonable is pride in any one! And yet it is a common failing. There are very few of us without a little of it. What have any of us to be proud of? Has the sinner any reason to be proud? He is walking in the broadway that leadeth to destruction, not a journey, not a prospect, to be proud of, certainly! Has the saint any reason to be proud? It is by the grace of God he is what he is." (Rev. C. H. Irwin.)

The cure prescribed by Elisha, though simple in itself, yet imposed a burden of no small magnitude. The Jordan, at its nearest point, was twenty miles or more distant from Samaria. To a sufferer, such as Naaman must have been, the journey would involve great hardship. But there was the promise of a great reward, "Thy flesh shall come again to thee, and thou shalt be clean." To this hope of reward God ever appeals in dealing with his children. Though the Divine plan of salvation is simple, without works in that no merit can attach to any thing which man can do, it yet imposes certain hardships. There are certain things to be given up, sacrificed, there are certain things to be endured if we would be Christ's disciples. His words are, "If any man will come after me, let him deny himself, and take up his cross daily, and follow me." At the same time the reward of obedience is held up to view, the crown of glory, the inheritance incorruptible and undefiled that fadeth not away, the glory and blessedness of the heavenly home, and, above all, the Master's approving words, "Well done, good and faithful servant."

It would seem that in three respects at least the Prophet's direction proved disappointing to Naaman. In the first place it did not provide an immediate cure. Not at once, as he had expected, but after he had performed a laborious and painful journey, was he to be restored to health. Addressing God, the Psalmist says, "My times are in thy hand," meaning, doubtless, that every event of life and the time thereof, are appointed of God, and that the sweet singer rejoiced to have it thus. Patiently to wait upon the Lord, to know no time but that which he has decreed, to commit the way to God, assured that he will bring it to pass, is a grace which reflects the highest honor upon God, and which all must possess who would enjoy his favor.

Naaman must bow to the will of God in all things, hence he is called to bide God's time to heal. But the method or manner of healing was likewise disappointing to Naaman. He had made up his mind as to how he should be healed. Familiar with the methods of thaumaturgus and priest in his own land, he had been led to expect that his cure would be attended with great pomp and ceremony; that the Prophet, in recognition of his high rank, would come out to him, "and stand and call on the name of the Lord his God, and strike his hand over the place, and recover the leper." "He had perhaps thought of himself as the central figure in some such striking scene, the observed of all observers, the cynosure of all neighboring eyes." (Pulpit Commentary.) He may have imagined the thrill which would pass through his body as the potent word was spoken, and the magic movement was made. Many persons who know nothing experimentally of salvation, have pictured to themselves how a saved man ought to feel, and because they cannot experience just such a feeling as they have imagined, they will have nothing to do with Christianity. Such persons cannot understand that belief in Jesus Christ is not a feeling, but an act. Expecting such eclat in connection with his healing, it must have been very disappointing to Naaman to be told to journey away to the Jordan, and simply to wash himself seven times in its muddy waters with none, perhaps, save his immediate attendants to observe. He must have felt that the cure prescribed for him was exceedingly humiliating. It was such as might have been provided for the humblest slave.

Certainly such an one might have availed himself of its provisions. It required the payment of no money, while in itself it was most simple. A little child might wash in Jordan. There was nothing exclusive about this cure which would limit it to the great ones of earth. Any body, however lowly and obscure, might wash in Jordan. In fulfillment of the words of prophecy there is "a fountain opened to the house of David and to the inhabitants of Jerusalem for sin and for uncleanness." To this fountain all who will may come. By the prophet God says, "Ho, every one that thirsteth, come ye to the waters, and he that hath no money; come ye, buy and eat; yea, come, buy wine and milk without money and without price." And the words of our Lord are, "If any man thirst, let him come unto me and drink." There is no privileged class, no way of saving a king which is not opened to the humblest subject. Money cannot purchase, influence cannot secure the favor of God. Salvation is of grace, not of works.

> "There is a fountain filled with blood,
> Drawn from Immanual's veins;
> And sinners plunged beneath this flood,
> Lose all their guilty stains."

How vitally and lastingly we are sometimes affected by our preconceived opinions. Applying a wrong principle of interpretation to the words of prophecy concerning the Messiah, the Jewish people had been led to expect him as a national hero, a temporal prince, who should deliver the chosen race from Gentile rule, and reign with great power and glory. Consequently when the Messiah came as the prophets had foretold, they could not receive him, "For he grew up before him as a tender plant, and as a root out of a dry ground: he had no form nor comeliness: and when we see him. there is no beauty that we should desire him." The Jewish eye, longing to behold the regal form, and the stately stepping of the expected warrior prince, saw in the lowly Nazarene no splendid form, no majesty, no sightliness, such as to draw them to him, and cause them to find pleasure in him. Even up to the time of his crucifixion, the disciples of Jesus cherished the hope that the national expectation concerning the Mesisah would be realized in him. There is a refrain of sadness and disappointment in the words of Cleopas and his companion to the risen but unrecognized Lord, "But we trusted that it had been he which should have redeemed Israel."

Naaman "turned and went away in a rage" when told what he must do to be healed, because he thought that his cure must be effected in another way. "Behold I thought." "He does not stop and ask himself whether he had reason and right for his expectation," but "trusting to himself as possessing an infallible insight, he departs. How faithful and true the old picture is! How fresh and new it is, as if men of the day had sat for it! Ask thousands who are devoted to human pursuits with enthusiasm and zeal, and who leave what is holy and divine in contemptuous neglect, why they do so, and they will be able to give but this one answer: I thought that the Divine must speak and act, and will and work in a different way from this; I cannot reconcile it with my opinion; if I should accept this, I should have to throw away my opinion, and that of the public and the time. This, I thought, is the most mighty of all mighty things on earth, and even if it is not the most ruinous of all ruinous things, it is yet certainly the most unfortunate of all unfortunate ones. This, I thought, brought sin and misery and death into the world, and it prevents redemption from sin and death in the case of thousands.

These thousands, if they perish in their opinion, will begin the next life with, I thought." (Calwer Bible.)

O, the incredible hardihood of venturing out into a boundless eternity on the frail and deceitful plank of a human opinion! No prudent business man will hazard the whole of his earthly possessions on a mere supposition or hope that this or that speculation may prove a success; but to risk the salvation of the soul on a mere opinion is a small matter in the estimation of many.

The means of healing were likewise disappointing to Naaman. He doubtless felt them to be wholly inadequate. In all probability he had tried this cure at home without being benefited to any extent. His disease would not yield to such treatment. Something more effective than water must be found, or he must die a leper. It was likewise displeasing to Naaman to be told to wash in Jordan. Such direction would seem to him like slighting the splendid rivers of his own land. He may have reasoned after this manner, If I am to be cured by the application of water, why require me to go to the Jordan? Why not wash in Abana and Parphar, rivers of Damascus, "the golden streams." We naturally regard those things which belong to our own country or community or family as superior to all others. In Naaman's estimation, the waters of his own land were "better than all the waters of Israel." And from a human point of view he was correct. The cool crystal waters of the Abana and Parphar far surpass those of the muddy Jordan. But we are not to be guided always by outward appearances. "The point of the Prophet's direction lay not in the command to wash, but to wash in Jordan." (Edersheim.)

Though Naaman could not discover it by physical

sight or taste, God had specially blessed the waters of Jordan for his healing. Whether or not they possessed chemical properties which at other times they did not possess, and which the waters of other streams did not possess, God had appointed them to be a cure to Naaman, and to neglect to wash in Jordan would be to forfeit the cure for which he sought. There are those who insist that it matters not what a man believes so long as he is sincere in his belief. It is asserted that there is something good in all religions; that there are certain principles which all religions have in common. But what is to be gained even granting this to be true? This would not prove them of equal worth. The waters of the Jordan and those of the rivers of Damascus were precisely similar, in almost every respect, yet in the former only was there healing for Naaman. However much we may think ourselves competent to improve upon God's methods and means, the great fact remains that salvation is to be found in Jesus only. "Neither is there salvation in any other: for there is none other name under heaven given among men, whereby we must be saved."

"Was it not a foolish thing for Naaman, a poor miserable leper, with his life a burden to him, to be questioning the method and means of his cure? Is it not a foolish thing for any sinner, with death at any moment staring him in the face, and a dark and hopeless eternity yawning before him, to question God's plan of salvation?" (Rev. C. H. Irwin.)

"Naaman turned and went away in a rage," perhaps upbraiding himself for having come upon a fool's errand, and vowing vengeance upon the people whose king and prophet had trifled with him in his great affliction. In moody silence the homeward journey had been prosecuted until the Jordan had been reached. His wrath may have abated somewhat as he came to reflect that if he persisted in his determination to disregard the Prophet's direction, the future was absolutely without hope for him. At the right moment, when the inclination to relent and to do as he had been bidden had to some extent taken possession of his mind "his servants came near, and spake unto him and said, My father, if the prophet had bid thee do some great thing, wouldest thou not have done it? How much rather then, when he saith to thee, Wash and be clean?" These servants must have been true students of human nature. This is evident from the fact that they wisely waited until Naaman's rage had spent its force, before they ventured to remonstrate with him, and to show him the folly of pursuing such a course as he had resolved upon. In most instances it is like casting pearls before swine to attempt to reason with a man when he is angry, or, as we commonly say, mad, which expresses the truth, though we may not always employ the term intelligently. When the brain is on fire with anger, the man is mad, beside himself, and the voice of reason becomes inaudible. But these servants of Naaman proved themselves to be true students of human nature in that they discerned that the one thing which now prevented their master's cure, was his pride. Had the Prophet imposed some difficult task upon him; had he required him to make a long and painful journey; to afflict and torture his body; or to pay a large sum of money, he would have obeyed at once. But to wash in Jordan! the very simplicity of such a method of healing offended him. For the same reason multitudes reject salvation as it is offered in the gospel.

Men want to do something great in order to be saved, they want to pay for their salvation. When, therefore, they are told that in order to obtain eternal life, they must simply believe on the Lord Jesus Christ, they will not hear it.

"From the pillar monks of antiquity, who, to obtain the favor of God, stood for days and nights and years upon their columns, exposed to every change of temperature and season, down to the ascetic of the present hour, who hopes, at least in part, to win his way to heaven by the self-inflicted miseries and privations of earth; men have in all ages preferred the great things of their own invention to the simple remedy of God's revealing. The more appalling the difficulty, the more flattering to our proud spirits, its achievement." (Blunt.)

The one thing which, above all other things, Naaman at this time desired and sought, was to be healed of his leprosy. What mattered it to him, then, how the cure should be effected? Why should he be so deeply concerned as to the manner and method of cure? Had he wisely considered, the very fact that the cure was so simple and inexpensive, must have commended it to his acceptance. Even so the simplicity of the gospel plan of salvation, should commend it to the impoverished and helpless sinner. Instead of trying to devise some difficult and painful method of being saved, reason would urge that he accept God's offer, life, without money and without price, through faith in Jesus Christ.

Everything, so far as Naaman was concerned, depended upon his decision at this moment. If he refused to hearken to the earnest entreaty of his servants to do as the Prophet had directed, he must remain a leper, and, more dreadful to contemplate, a benighted heathen. Health for body and soul was near at hand, but he must accept the conditions upon which it was offered. To one of his questioners, our Lord said, "Thou art not far from the kingdom of God." There is unutterable sadness in the reflection that multitudes rest satisfied with the near approach, and never enter the kingdom. Some persons there are who have a greater dread of being inconsistent than of being unreasonable and stubborn. It is a hard matter to change their minds when they have once arrived at a conclusion. "Consistency is a jewel," but it is better to sacrifice it than to sacrifice the right. Thus Naaman must have thought. His mind now free from the rule of anger, he was open to conviction, and, perceiving that his servants had reasoned well, he yielded at once to their entreaty. "God has his instruments in readiness when he needs them, and often they are of the humblest character. Once more were salves to become the means of effecting their master's true freedom." (Edersheim.)

Alighting from his carriage, Naaman stood at the brink of the river. Strange thoughts must have held possession of his mind. "It was a decisive and important moment, the most important in his life." The last hope which he was permitted to cherish was about to be tested. Soon it was to be made manifest whether or not there was "a prophet in Israel." And now, according to the Prophet's direction, he washed the affected member or that portion of his body in which the disease was located, then staid his hand for a moment. Then again and again he repeated the ablution, each moment, we may believe, his anxiety becoming greater. Six times the water had been applied, but without apparent result. With hope almost extinguished, and it may have been with an inaudible prayer to the God of Israel, he essayed to make the seventh and final application of the water. This was no sooner done, than, lo, his mortal sore was healed; the poison of death disappeared from his veins; "and his flesh came again like unto the flesh of a little child, and he was clean." Even so are they made spiritually clean who wash in the precious blood "of the Lamb slain from the foundation of the world." "The blood of Jesus Christ his Son cleanseth us from all sin."

# CHAPTER XX.

## NAAMAN'S CONVERSION.

"O Savior, whose mercy, severe in its kindness,
  Hath chastened my wanderings and guided my way,
Adored be the power which hath pitied my blindness,
  And weaned me from phantoms that smiled to destroy.

Subdued and instructed at length to thy will,
  My hopes, and my wishes, my all I resign;
O give me a heart that can wait and be still,
  Nor know of a wish or a pleasure but thine."

(Grant.)

As ONE who receives an unexpected and unhoped-for pardon while standing upon the scaffold awaiting the fatal springing of the trap which is to send him into eternity, so Naaman must have felt when, after having washed the seventh time in Jordan, he found himself wholly cured of his leprosy. The sensation which he experienced must have been like that of one awaking from troubled dreams to find himself surrounded by loving friends, and for ever safe from the evils which had seemed to have come upon him. The darkness of despair had vanished, the clouds had lifted, and the sunshine of joy and peace filled his soul. He was now a converted man. With him old things had passed away, and all things had become new. Many persons regard conversion as a miraculous event which takes place according to a fixed rule, and which is followed by uniform results. To many minds a soul cannot be converted to God unless it has first been terrified by the thunderings of the law, and plunged into deepest anguish and despair.

This has been the experience of many in conversion, but it is not necessarily true of all who pass from death unto life. Men differ in environments and temperament, and because of this fact, God does not deal with any two persons, perhaps, in precisely the same manner in bringing them to repentance. No two persons are affected in precisely the same way and to the same extent, by the same event. Each of two mothers has been bereaved at the same time and in the same manner, of a darling child; the one is bathed in tears and is loud in her lamentation; while the other, though her sorrow may be more profound than that of her neighbor, turns away from the new-made grave without a tear, without a murmur. It is said that when the lofty palm of Zelian puts forth its flower, the sheath bursts with a report which shakes the forest; but there are thousands of other flowers which open to the kisses of the sun as noiselessly as the light falls. It is thus in the spiritual life. "There are differences of administrations, but the same Lord. And there are diversities of operations, but it is the same God which worketh all in all."

To effect the conversion of some men it seems necessary for God to employ the thunders of his wrath, to stretch forth his hand to afflict and chasten, while others who cannot hear God in the great and strong wind which rends the mountains and breaks in pieces the rocks, nor see him in the earthquake or in the fire, are won by the "still small voice." For a like reason, one man's conversion is sudden and radical. He can indicate the precise moment of his conversion, and the circumstances which led to it, the words spoken, the sermon preached, the affliction or bereavement sent; while in the case of another the change takes place gradually and almost imperceptibly. This will depend largely upon the character of the life previous to conversion, and upon the constitutional tendencies of the man. The openly profane and viciously wicked, if arrested by the spirit of God, are liable to experience a sudden and radical change; while those who, like Timothy, have from childhood "known the holy scriptures," have been brought up "in the nurture and admonition of the Lord," may be unable to say when they did not love the Lord, and yield to him the allegiance of the heart.

"God is sovereign; and he calls men as he pleases. Some he calls amid thunder and storm, some in a calm, some in winter, some in summer. Men come into the kingdom of God in as many different ways as plants come to flower. Some plants come right up out of the earth to blossom. Some come up and grow the whole summer, and then bloom. Some grow a year, and then blossom the second year. Some grow up like trees and do not blossom till they are three or four or five or six years old. Some put the leaves out first, and the blossom afterwards; and some put out the blossom first, and the leaves afterwards. Now when a man is converted, he blossoms; and some persons blossom almost from the cradle. I do not doubt that God's work begins in the hearts of children three or four years old, and of persons of every age beyond that period. As the wind bloweth where it listeth so God's Spirit worketh where he pleases.

He comes when he pleases, and as he pleases, and no man can tell beforehand how he will come, or when he will come." (H. W. Beecher.)

"It is the sheerest folly to attempt to force every religious experience into the same mould. It cannot be stereotyped. To give direction in each individual case respecting how a man must or must not feel is the least business of the preacher. If any person waits to have a religious experience exactly like that of some one else, he will wait forever without receiving it. There are no exact repetitions; if you find them, one is a counterfeit. Seize the hand of Christ in your own way; step forth: all will be well." (Townsend.)

Whatever be the circumstances attending conversion, the results are the same. There is begotten a love for God, and for that which is pure and holy and true; and there is a corresponding turning away from that which is impure, unholy, and untrue; and there is that irrepressible feeling of gratitude to God which finds expression in words and deeds of love. Naaman's conversion was sudden. It seems to have followed immediately the discovery that he had been healed of his loathsome disease. A moment's reflection leads him to recognize the hand of Jehovah in the marvelous cure which he had experienced. Naaman's conversion was radical. Without the aid of teaching or argument, his experience had produced a complete change in his views, had annihilated at once and forever the bulwark of false sociological and religious doctrines, and of intolerable prejudice with which he had been surrounded. As the light dawned upon him, his hatred of Israel and of Israel's God disappeared, and, with a heart overflowing with gratitude for the mercies vouchsafed unto him, he at once prepared to return to the man of God.

If hatred and anger had fired the soul of Naaman and lent impetuosity to his driving as he went from Samaria to the Jordan, love and gratitude now rendered him impatient to stand once more at the Prophet's gate. To gratify this desire involved a sacrifice, however, which was by no means inconsiderable. Naaman was now well on his way to Damascus. Perhaps a fourth part of the journey had been accomplished. A few more days, and he would be at home, in the midst of his friends and loved ones who would hail his coming with joy and be filled with delight by the good news which he had in store for them. To return to Samaria, meant to delay, by at least two days, his arrival at Damascus, and imposed upon him the necessity of making an additional journey of perhaps fifty miles. But Naaman felt that he must do this. He was too magnanimous of heart to receive such a blessing as had come to him, and make no acknowledgment of the same. He must go back and tell the Prophet of the great cure which he had experienced, the change which had been wrought in his heart, and, doubtless, apologize for the haughtiness and rudeness which had characterized his behavior toward him who had proved to be his greatest human benefactor. It was also in his purpose to recompense the Prophet to the extent of his ability for the inestimable service which he had rendered him.

How admirable the spirit of gratitude thus exhibited by Naaman! But, while we admire it, may not the conduct of this new-made convert to the true religion serve as a rebuke to many in Christian lands today? Manifold are the mercies which crown our lives. They are new unto us every moment. And yet how little of the sacrifice of gratitude do we render unto God, the author of all our mercies! How many there are who are content to receive the blessings which God graciously bestows, without acknowledging His kindness, without thanking Him for the same! What a touching and instructive story is that which Luke tells of the healing of the ten lepers who, standing afar off, lifted up their voices and cried to Jesus for mercy. As, in obedience to his command, they went to show themselves to the priests, they were cleansed! "And one of them, when he saw that he was healed, turned back, and with a loud voice glorified God, and fell down on his face at his feet, giving him thanks."

Luke adds this significant remark, "And he was a Samaritan." Most tender and loving are the words of assurance with which the Master dismisses this grateful man from his presence. "Arise, go thy way; thy faith hath made thee whole." But it is with an evident tone of sadness and disappointment that he notes the lack of gratitude on the part of the nine others who had been healed, and from whom he had a right to expect more than from the Samaritan, for, it would seem, they were Jews. "Were there not ten cleansed? but where are the nine? There are not found that return to give glory to God, save this stranger." Let us be persuaded that our heavenly Father takes knowledge of our ingratitude, and that according to the measure thereof, must his displeasure be incurred. Nor should we be indifferent to the fact that ingratitude robs us of the ability to enjoy, in the highest and noblest sense, the blessings which God bestows. Gratitude has been described as the sixth sense, since it heightens the power of enjoyment. No matter how much a man may call his own, no matter how much he may have to delight the various senses, if he be destitute of gratitude, he must still be denied the most delightful sensation. "Grateful thankfulness is allied to, nay, forms an ingredient in, the very chief of our deepest enjoyments, and purest springs of blessedness." (E. P. Hood.)

Very different from his first reception was that which was accorded Naaman as he appeared the second time at the home of Elisha. The Prophet at once granted him an audience, for there was no longer need that he should be treated otherwise. The lesson so essential to his welfare had been learned, and the once proud and haughty chieftain who had been so jealous of his honor and dignity, who had resented any lack of deference to himself, could now speak of himself as servant to the Prophet.

As one for whose salvation God had made him the instrument, Elisha welcomed Naaman to his abode, and with rapture of heart must have listened to the declaration of his faith in the God of Israel as the only true God. "Behold now I know that there is no god in all the earth, but in Israel." Some have chosen to criticise this statement, and have asserted that it does not express the truth with sufficient accuracy, for the God of Israel is, and was, not only in Israel, but in all the earth. But while the form of statement may be shown to be somewhat infelicitous, it seems evident from the context that the thought of Naaman was that there were no other gods in all the earth worthy to be recognized as such; that Jehovah, the God of Israel, was the only living and true God. Other nations might have their gods, so called, to whom ignorantly they offered worship, but,

"Their idols are silver and gold, the work of men's hands. They have mouths, but they speak not: eyes have they, but they see not: they have ears, but they hear not: noses have they, but they smell not: they have hands, but they handle not: feet have they, but they walk not: neither speak they through their throat."

The statement of Naaman appears most remarkable when we consider that it fell from the lips of a man who, but a few hours before, had been in heathen darkness. It was the belief of ancient heathen nations that every land and every community or locality had its own governing and protecting deity, and that every god possessed supreme power in the country or region over which he presided. This was the thought of Naaman, when, in disappointment, he said, "I thought he will surely come out to me, and stand, and call on the name of the Lord his God."

Naaman now took a position far in advance of his heathen contemporaries when he declared that there was "no god in all the earth, but in Israel," and that henceforth he would "offer neither burnt offering nor sacrifice unto other gods, but unto the Lord." He now, and finally, as we love to believe, renounced all faith in and allegiance to all gods, save Jehovah, "cast his idols of silver, and his idols of gold, to the moles and to the bats." We should not fail to note the perfect assurance with which Naaman speaks. "Now I know that there is no god in all the earth, but in Israel." In other words he says, "I am sure that Jehovah is not only a god, but the only true God." While we are disposed to look with little favor upon the dogmatist, it is always refreshing to hear a man of positive convictions speak. How the hearts of believers in every age have been cheered and encouraged by the Apostle's words of assurance, "For I know whom I have believed, and am persuaded that he is able to keep that which I have committed unto him against that day." "I am now ready to be offered, and the time of my departure is at hand. I have fought a good fight, I have finished my course, I have kept the faith: henceforth there is laid up for me a crown of righteousness, which the Lord, the righteous judge shall give me at that day: and not to me only, but unto all them also that love his appearing."

Many who profess to be Christians seem to be unable to determine where they stand, whether they are for God or against him. How many times we hear it said, "I hope" or "I trust that I am a Christian," "that I am saved." And yet our Lord has said, "He that believeth shall be saved." Why is it that any man who professes to be a Christian must say he "hopes" or he "trusts" he is saved? Does he doubt the Master's promise? or is it impossible for him to know his own mind, to determine whether he believes God's word or does not believe it? Naaman was at no loss to determine whether he believed or did not believe. "He knows that Jehovah lives; for he bears the seal of his truth in his purified body, and his cleansed and regenerate soul which is imbued with celestial peace. His knowledge is founded on his own consciousness and experience." (Krummacher.)

Naaman was not content to express his gratitude in mere words. In the most humble and earnest manner, but not, as it would seem, with the thought that material things could compensate for the blessing which he had received, he urged the Prophet to accept a present from him. "Now therefore I pray thee, take a blessing of thy servant." He begs that, as a favor to himself, the silver and the gold and the costly robes which he had brought with him, may be accepted as a substantial token of his gratitude. "Affection and gratitude are never dumb. They have a hundred ways of speaking. They always speak warmly; they always speak earnestly; and they always speak modestly. 'Behold Lord, the half of my goods I give to the poor; and if I have taken anything from any man by false accusation, I restore him fourfold.' The precious ointment in the alabaster box, the price of lands and possessions laid at the apostles' feet; the abounding liberality of some in the midst of their deep poverty, are all manifestations of the self-same spirit." (Edersheim.)

Although Naaman persistently urges the acceptance of the gift which he offers, Elisha as persistently declines it, upon what ground it is difficult to conjecture. Perhaps he felt that Naaman had need to learn more thoroughly the lesson that God's blessings, however great they may be, are graciously bestowed, and cannot be compensated for by the payment of any price. Indelibly the truth must be impressed upon the mind of this man, who was but a babe spiritually, that Jehovah was not like the gods of the heathen, and that his servants, the prophets, were wholly free from mercenary motives. Perhaps the Prophet regarded also the spiritual welfare of those associated with Naaman, and of those who in all subsequent ages should read the story of his miraculous cure. Perhaps in this manner Elisha may have sought also to disclaim any credit whatever for Naaman's cure; to teach him that all the glory and all the gratitude were due to Jehovah by whose power alone the cure had been effected.

Viewed in this light, Elisha's conduct challenges our highest admiration. In moral sublimity, in unselfish fidelity, and in self forgetting heroism, the history of the world furnishes few, if any, parallels to it. As we contemplate it, the words of the great forerunner of the Christ seem to fall upon our ears. "I am not the Christ." "I am the voice of one crying in the wilderness." "He must increase, but I must decrease." So too the words of the Apostle Peter when the lame man had been healed "at the gate of the temple which is called beautiful." "Why look ye so earnestly on us, as though by our own power or holiness we had made this man to walk?" "By the name of Jesus Christ of Nazareth * * * doth this man stand here before you whole."

How much self-renunciation and self-sacrifice were involved in the course which Elisha chose to pursue! How great the honor and the glory which he thus put aside! How much this generous gift which was offered the Prophet might have contributed to his comfort, and that of the prophet disciples who were his care! Ere this they had known what it was to lack bread to satisfy their hunger, and it may have been that even now they experienced such lack. Be it even so, the proffered gift must be declined, for God thus willed it. His gift finally refused, Naaman preferred this strange request. "Shall there not then, I pray thee, be given to thy servant two mules' burden of earth?" This request was remarkable, in that it was addressed to Elisha, who, perhaps possessed neither houses nor lands, rather than to the king who would have jurisdiction in such matters. But aside from this, the nature of the request was most remarkable. Naaman who had been affronted when directed to wash in the Jordan that he might be healed of his malady, now begs to be permitted to carry home with him a few bushels, perhaps, of earth from the land whose waters he had despised. For what purpose did he desire this? Doubtless Naaman made known his intentions to Elisha. That he asked such a favor, implies that he desired the Prophet's sanction of the purpose which he had in view. In the absence of any statement in the record as to what that purpose was, we can but surmise its character. Owing, probably, to the fact that Naaman seems to assign as a reason for his request his determination that he "will henceforth offer neither burnt-offering nor sacrifice unto other gods, but unto the Lord," it has been supposed that he purposed to build an altar with it.

In further support of such a view, it is urged that it was provided that altars erected for the worship of Jehovah should be composed of earth. But, as Dr. Kitto observes, "Naaman was not likely to know this; and Israel did not actually offer the example of any such altars. This moreover would have involved the grievous irregularity of the new convert performing a function reserved to the priests, the offering of sacrifice. If this had been his meaning, much harm might have ensued from Elisha's neglecting to correct the notions and purposes thus indicated, * * * and as we do not hear that he did so, we apprehend that something less dangerous, and which might be conceded to the weakness of a novice must be meant."

From the custom which is known to have obtained among the Jews in ancient times, and which may have been indulged by the people of other lands, of carrying portions of earth from one country to another for the purpose of worshipping upon it, the supposition being that the ground of one locality is more holy than that of another, it seems most probable that Naaman purposed to strew the portion of earth which he wished to carry home with him, upon the floor of a temple or enclosure to be dedicated by him to the worship of Jehovah. It is said that the Mohommedans consider sacred the soil of Mecca. "The man accounts himself happy who has in his possession the smallest portion of it for use in his devotions. He carries it about his person in a small bag; and in his prayers he deposits this before him upon the ground in such a manner that, in his frequent prostrations, the head comes down upon this morsel of sacred soil, so that in some sort he may be said to worship thereon." (Kitto.)

It is inferred that Elisha granted the request of Naaman, though it is not even intimated that he did so. If he did, it was not because he shared the view which prompted such a request, but rather because he chose to indulge a harmless superstition in one whose instruction was necessarily imperfect. More perplexing and serious than this request for earth, are the last recorded words of Naaman to Elisha. "In this thing the Lord pardon thy servant, that when my master goeth into the house of Rimmon to worship there, and he leaneth upon my hand, and I bow myself in the house of Rimmon; when I bow down myself in the house of Rimmon, the Lord pardon thy servant in this thing."

Was this a prayer for indulgence in that which conscience disapproved or was it simply an inquiry as to duty? In support of the former view, it has been suggested that upon second, sober thought, Naaman felt that he was not prepared to accept the consequences of renouncing wholly the idolatrous worship of his own land. He anticipated that upon his return to Damascus he should retain the high position which he had hitherto occupied, and that in an official character he would be required to accompany the king when he went in state to worship in the temple of Rimmon. To refuse to do so, and to prostrate himself before the image or altar of the national deity, might bring him into disfavor with the court, which, in turn, might lead to his dismissal from the service of the king, if, indeed, it did not cost him his life.

"Naaman was not prepared to be a martyr to his religion," and hence sought a compromise. It seems incredible, however, that a sane man, such as we suppose Naaman to have been, after having declared that he would "henceforth offer neither burnt-offering nor sacrifice unto other gods, but unto the Lord," should with the next breath recant, and beg to be indulged in doing the thing which, after hours of quiet deliberation, he had resolved never to do. Men do not usually act thus, especially men of such positive character as the chief of Syria's armies must have been. Besides, Naaman had already gone too far to adopt such a course of dissimulation as, according to this view, he is supposed to have contemplated. He had already burned the bridges behind him, and retreat was impossible. In the presence of his numerous attendants, he had renounced all the gods of the heathen world, and had declared his allegiance to Jehovah. However solicitous he might have been to conceal the fact, he could scarcely hope that it would not be divulged by some one.

No, we cannot believe that Naaman was seeking an easy way to serve the Lord, that he was seeking to compromise with his conscience. He simply sought light as to his duty in the very trying circumstances in which he soon should be placed. Had he been disposed to attempt to lead a double life religiously, is it reasonable to suppose that he would have sought the counsel of Elisha in the matter? What encouragement could he have expected from him? "The inquiry itself is perhaps one of the clearest proofs of the genuineness of Naaman's conversion. So tender was his conscience, that what might seem the appearance of evil, he felt to be intolerable. So decided was his religion, that from the first he clearly saw its bearing upon every department of life's work, and set himself to carry it out, not only in acts of devotion, but in every act of his private and public life. It was imposed upon him by his official position, as the king's nearest attendant, to be present in the house of Rimmon when the king worshipped, but even that passive attendance was dreaded by him, and its lawfulness submitted to the Lord, ere he would resume it." (Edersheim.)

Elisha's parting words to Naaman, "Go in peace," have been interpreted as an answer to his inquiry, a tacit permission to accompany his master during his devotions in the temple of Rimmon. Some have even found in the kindly wish that the peace of God might fill the soul of Naaman as he journeyed to his home, permission granted to unite with his master in the worship of the Syrian god. "Among Roman Catholics the passage has been used to justify the conduct of her missionaries who permit the newly-converted heathen to continue to observe pagan ceremonies." (Lange.)

But it is questionable whether in this word of farewell, we have any part of Elisha's reply to Naaman's inquiry, and it is much more questionable whether in these few words we have the whole of the Prophet's reply. We cannot believe that he would dismiss so serious and important a matter in such a manner. Surely he would not permit this earnest inquirer after truth to depart to his distant home, until he had been sufficiently instructed. Many earnest words of warning, admonition, and instruction, must have been spoken, of which no record has been left us, then came the parting, with the kindly good bye. Who shall say which was the happier, Naaman who had received so much, or Elisha who had been made God's instrument in giving so much? God had been very gracious to both.

## CHAPTER XXI.

### THE SIN AND PUNISHMENT OF GEHAZI.

"Mammon led them on,
Mammon, the least erected spirit that fell
From heaven; for even in heaven his looks and thoughts
Were always downward bent, admiring more
The riches of heaven's pavements, trodden gold,
Than aught divine or holy else enjoyed
In vision beatific." (Milton—Paradise Lost.)

COVETOUSNESS is not recognized by any human code as a crime; and yet the word of God represents it as a sin of the most heinous character. The Apostle Paul declares that covetousness is idolatry; that "the love of money is a root of all kinds of evil." Whether these words were original with the Apostle or were quoted by him from Diogenes, as Alford intimates, they were employed to express a truth which the Apostle was inspired to utter; to set forth the deadly character of covetousness. We have been taught to regard the act of eating the forbidden fruit as "the sin whereby our first parents fell from the estate wherein they were created." So far as the overt act of sin was concerned, this is true. But back of that act of disobedience, was the sinful desire to be possessed of that which God had been pleased to deny Adam and Eve. "When the woman saw that the tree was good for food, and that it was pleasant to the eye, and a tree to be desired to make one wise, she took the fruit thereof."

The sin which involved the race in ruin, was due to a spirit of covetousness on the part of the first two of human kind, a desire to have more than God had given them, to acquire knowledge which the Creator had withheld from them. Turn to the pages of the world's history, and we shall find that to the spirit of covetousness have been due, in large measure, those terrible conflicts which have drenched the earth with human blood, exposed the helpless and the innocent to insult and suffering, laid prosperous cities in ashes, desolated provinces, and dried up the fountains of man's prosperity and happiness. Covetousness makes a man a robber and a murderer. Back of those political corruptions which have resulted in the fall of nations, the subversion of dynasties and governments, and which are the menace of the social and political institutions of our day, is the insatiable greed for money and power which, with many, has proved to be more potent than the love of country, the desire to be just, or the sense of honor and self-respect. Covetousness or the love of money, has called into existence the barroom, the gambling table, and the dens of infamy and vice, the plague-spots of our present civilization.

We doubtless do Gehazi an injustice when we picture him as a man whose very countenance betrayed the avarice which lurked in his heart. It is incredible that the amiable Elisha should choose for his trusted and constant companion a man of such repulsive character as Gehazi has been represented to have been. It is not necessary to suppose that there was anything forbidding in the countenance of Gehazi, anything to suggest that avarice and deceit were predominant traits of his character. Outwardly the moral and religious life of this man must have been above reproach, for, it would seem, he was one of the sons of the prophets. And, while his sin is not to be palliated, it is but just to say that there is nothing in the record to warrant the assumption that he was a sinner above other men, that he was habitually dishonest and untruthful. The probabilities are that he was not a man of such sordid mind as we have been wont to regard him. Perhaps the temptation which came to him at this time had a peculiar power over him. Be this is at it may, there is need that we should constantly remember the words of the Apostle, "Let him that thinketh he standeth take heed lest he fall."

Elisha had persisted in his refusal to accept anything at the hand of Naaman, and had sent him away with all his gold, his silver and his changes of raiment. In the estimation of Gehazi, such generosity toward the Syrian was uncalled for and unwise. He may not have known the amount of wealth which Naaman had with him, but he coveted it. He thought of the costly garments which he might wear, of the olive-yards, the vineyards, the sheep and oxen, and the menservants and maidservants which might be his, if he had only a part of what Naaman was carrying back with him. The more he thought on these things, the more earnestly did he covet the money with which he might make them his own.

Here was an opportunity to acquire wealth easily, an opportunity which, if not instantly improved, would doubtless be lost forever. Without knowing, and perhaps without caring to know, the ground upon which his master had refused to accept that which so much excited his desire, he resolved upon this bold measure. "As the

Lord liveth, I will run after him, and take some thing of him." In answer to Naaman's entreaty that he would take a blessing at his hand, Elisha had said, "As the Lord liveth, I will receive none."

Gehazi, with equal earnestness but without any reverence, says, "As the Lord liveth, I will take some thing." As employed by Elisha, the strong asservation, "as the Lord liveth," was doubtless justifiable, for it was uttered reverently, and with the sole purpose of glorifying God. But as employed by Gehazi, who was determined to do that which he evidently felt to be wrong, it was simply profanity. How prevalent is such irreverent and sinful use of God's names and attributes among those even who profess to love and to serve him! The most trivial conversation abounds in such vehement assertions as that of Gehazi; in such ejaculations as "mercy," "goodness," "gracious," attributes which in the fullest sense belong to God alone. We may attach no importance to such expressions, but in reality it is but a form of profanity. How flippantly the name of God is pronounced in our courts of justice, and elsewhere, in connection with the administering and taking of oaths. It has come to pass in our day that in the most trivial transactions, an oath of confirmation is imposed.

"Sworn on every slight pretence,
Till perjuries are common as bad pence,
While thousands, careless of the damning sin,
Kiss the book's outside, who ne'er look'd within."

"When I remember the tremendous sweep of an oath, the extreme frequency with which it is administered, and in connection with the most trivial occasions, the flippant, almost merry volubility with which it is administered, the perfect nonchalance with which the most profane men take it, I shudder at the blasphemy which is practically perpetrated under forms of law." (Boardman.)

"How many a man shall find hereafter, that the horrible oath, the thoughtless imprecation 'the swearer's prayer,' so continually heard in our streets, has been heard also by the God whom it insults, and 'as the Lord liveth,' it shall have its full accomplishment upon the souls of the speakers." (Blunt.)

Gehazi seeks to justify the perfidious course to which his avarice tempts him, by depreciatory words concerning his master's refusal to accept the gift of Naaman, to whom, in the spirit of intolerant prejudice, he sneeringly refers as "this Syrian." He seems to have labored under the conviction that because Naaman was a Syrian, he deserved no consideration at the hands of an Israelite; that it was proper to take from him as much as possible. How readily we invent excuses, and discover justifying reasons for doing the things we wish to do! More carefully should we guard against persuading ourselves to do the things which conscience, enlightened by the word of God, tells us are wrong.

Naaman must have proceeded but a short distance upon his homeward journey, when Gehazi, stealing away from his master's presence, started to overtake him. No sooner did the unsuspecting Naaman recognize his pursuer than the onward movement of his chariot wheels was stayed, and "he lighted down from his chariot to meet him." "Descent from a vehicle is, in the East, a sign of respect from the inferior to the superior." Naaman sought to honor Elisha by thus honoring his servant.

He was willing to descend from his chariot to greet the Prophet's servant, although once unwilling to show such honor to the Prophet in person. Beholding Gehazi's great haste and the wild gestures by which he doubtless sought to attract attention, the fears of Naaman for the safety and welfare of the Prophet were aroused, and with unfeigned solicitude, he hastened to ask, "Is all well?" Gehazi's answer, "All is well," in so far as it related to his master, if, indeed, we may suppose he had his master in mind at all and assumed to speak for him, was strictly true.

All was well with Elisha though he had declined the wealth which had been pressed upon his acceptance, and must, in consequence, expect to continue to share a life of poverty with his disciples, the sons of the prophets. With self-sacrificing fidelity, he had sought, in all he had had to do with Naaman, to glorify God, and his heart was filled with that joy and peace which flow from the consciousness of Divine approval, and the assurance that, in God's care, all things needful shall be provided in due season. And Gehazi may have felt that, so far as he himself was concerned, his answer was true. It was well that his master had not seen him leave the tower; it was well that he was received thus courteously, and had so fair a hope that he should cheat this Syrian, and grow rich at his expense, and escape detection. And so the sinner says, All is well, while hiding his guilty practices from those around him. But could Gehazi have seen the leprosy which even then was hanging over his devoted head, could the hardened sinner view the gulf which even now is yawning at his feet, we doubt if either of them would so readily reply, "All is well."

"No! all may doubtless be well in the prospect, and often in the committal of sin, but all will not be well when in the day of righteous judgment, God shall smite the sinner until he destroys him. The mill of God grinds late, but grinds to powder." (Blunt.)

Gehazi had but little time to reflect as to what he should say to Naaman. He was obliged to act promptly with but a few moments to form his plans. Perhaps it was as he ran after the rapidly disappearing chariot that he invented his plausible story. "My master hath sent me, saying, Behold even now there be come to me from mount Ephraim, two young men of the sons of the prophets: give them, I pray thee, a talent of silver, and two changes of garments."

It has been suggested that there may have been some foundation in fact for this statement, that at the very time of Naaman's final departure from the Prophet's abode, there actually appeared two young men of the sons of the prophets, seeking aid from Elisha. The fact, however, that Gehazi does not mention this in the first instance as a reason for his determination to "take some thing of" the Syrian, would seem to indicate that the story was wholly a fabrication. This base falsehood of Gehazi would naturally tend to discredit his master in the estimation of Naaman and his companions, in that it would make him appear to be a fickle minded man; governed, not by high and holy principle in all that he did, but by mere caprice. But a few moments had elapsed since he had positively refused the princely gift a part of which he now, in craven spirit, begs. Not only so, but thus to discredit the Prophet, must necessarily bring reproach upon the religion of which he was the highest living exponent. Doubtless Naaman had been made to understand that Elisha in declining his gift, had obeyed Divine direction, that regard for the honor and glory of God, required such a course. But how could he reconcile with this understanding the request now made for a talent of silver and two changes of garments. The natural, and, in the circumstances, almost inevitable conclusion would be that the God of Israel was mutable as men are mutable, that his knowledge was limited, at least to the extent that future events were not known to him.

But intent only upon gratifying his selfish greed, Gehazi considered not how crushing might be the blow which he thus dealt to the faith of Naaman, and of men of all subsequent ages. Every patriotic consideration, and all care for his master's reputation, and for God's honor, he pushed aside for a piece of silver and a bundle of clothes. We may be ready to cry, Shame upon Gehazi! And truly such ingratitude to friends, to country, and to God, is worthy the severest condemnation; but it becomes us to "let him who is righteous cast the first stone." Do we at all times act with an eye single to God's glory and to the welfare of our fellowmen? Are we sure that our lives are of such a character as to commend to those who know us, the gospel which bringeth salvation? We believe the statement of the Westminister Shorter Catechism to be true, "Some sins in themselves, and by reason of several aggravations, are more heinous in the sight of God than others."

Had Gehazi's religious education been neglected, some apology might be found for his sin. But his advantages in this respect must have been superior to those of any of his contemporaries. For years, perhaps, he had been the trusted friend and the constant companion of the man of God. His days were spent in the light of a high and holy example. Of the childlike faith of the Prophet, he had been a constant witness. With every detail of that life so wholly devoted to the service of God, he was familiar. In addition to this he must have enjoyed the personal instruction of Elisha. Privilege is the measure of responsibility. Our Lord's words are, "Unto whomsoever much is given, of him shall much be required."

Measured by the Divine standard, Gehazi's conduct was reprehensible to the last degree. He "knew his lord's will," but, "prepared not himself, neither did according to his will." He was therefore worthy to "be beaten with many stripes." It well becomes us who live in the light of the gospel dispensation to consider our privileges that we may know the measure of our responsibilities. "He that despised Moses' law, died without mercy under two or three witnesses: of how much sorer punishment, suppose ye, shall he be thought worthy, who hath trodden under foot the Son of God, and hath counted the blood of the covenant, wherewith he was sanctified, an unholy thing, and hath done despite unto the spirit of grace."

In striking contrast with the craftiness, greed, and falseness of Gehazi; were the childlike credence, the noble generosity, and perfect candor of Naaman. The grateful Syrian, with no suspicion, as it would seem, of the deception that was practiced upon him, and doubtless rejoicing in the thought that he could be of some service to his benefactor, insisted that Gehazi should take two talents instead of one, "Be content, take two talents." Avarice was abashed in the presence of such generosity.

With feigned modesty, Gehazi seems to have hesitated for a time to accept so large a sum. Perhaps he made a show of declining to receive more than he claimed to have been authorized to ask for. But Naaman had received freely, and he was disposed to give freely. "He urged him," and having succeeded in overcoming the objections which Gehazi doubtless offered, he "bound two talents of silver in two bags, with two changes of garments, and laid them upon two of his servants: and they bare them before him."

The conduct of Naaman was as courteous as it was kind and generous. He would not suffer the servant of the Prophet to bear back to him this princely gift, the weight of which, exclusive of the clothing, must have exceeded a hundred pounds. He placed it upon the shoulders of two of his servants, doubtless with the direction and expectation, that they would lay it at the feet of the Prophet. This, however, was prevented by the duplicity of Gehazi who, as a precaution against detection, when they had reached a point in the way designated as the tower, more properly the hill, as in the revised version, referring to some eminence, doubtless, near the Damascus gate, "took them," that is the bags of silver and the two changes of raiment, "and bestowed them in the house," probably not the house in which Elisha resided, "and let the men go, and they departed."

Naaman probably never knew how heartlessly he had been deceived, how cruelly he had been sinned against. "The dangerous point of Gehazi's impious act broke upon the childlikeness of the man. He had acquired too high an idea of the members of the schools of the prophets, to permit him to imagine there could be anything but the purest truth in the message which Gehazi delivered." (Krummacher.)

So far as the inspired record shows, Elisha made no effort to right the wrong which his servant had done, to correct the falsehood which he had uttered, or to disabuse the mind of the Syrian of any incorrect impressions produced thereby. Perhaps the Prophet acted upon the principle which, in many instances, we would do well to observe, "the least said, the easiest mended." Undue zeal on the part of the pastor or other church officer, in precipitating church trials, in investigating every story of the gossip-monger, has brought about the disruption of many a congregation, and the complete alienation of many a soul from the fellowship of God's people, and may be, sad to think, from the fellowship of the redeemed in heaven.

Perhaps the Prophet feared that, to expose the perfidy of Gehazi would prove disastrous to the faith of Naaman. Be it as it may, Naaman was permitted to continue his homeward journey, "no doubt all the more joyfully for the service which he had been permitted to render. The reward of what we may do for the Lord shall not be lost, because of the misapplication and deception of any Gehazi to whom we may entrust our offerings. If we have offered our gifts unto the Lord, he will own and receive them." (Edersheim.)

Naaman now disappears from sacred history. The curtain drops as he lays the bags of silver upon the shoulders of his stalwart servants that they may bear them to the Prophet as a token of his love and gratitude. It has been said of some men that they died at the right time, when the zenith of their popularity had been reached. Thus their fame was rendered imperishable As we take our last glimpse of Naaman, he appears at his best, humble, devout, generous, and candid. Whether he remained steadfast in his purpose to worship Jehovah alone, or yielded at length to the tremendous influence which would draw him to the worship of Rimmon, we can but surmise. The very silence which prevails concerning him after his return to Damascus is perhaps to be considered as in his favor. "We read soon again of Syria and of Syrian wars with Israel, but this officer of the king, this great man with his master, this general of their armies, is heard of no more. Hazael is the captain of the king's hosts." (Lowrie.)

The inference is that Naaman had been dismissed from the king's service. If this inference be correct, we can scarcely attribute such treatment to any lack of ability on the part of Naaman. Physically and mentally, he must have been as well qualified to lead the armies of Syria as he had ever been. Perhaps he was unwilling to fight against Israel, and had resigned his command rather than do so. But more probably, his religious views and practices were no longer in accord with those of the court, and, hence, he was superseded by Hazael.

Our Lord's single reference to Naaman, while obviously primarily designed to illustrate God's sovereignty in saving whom he will, is at the same time an indirect testimony to the faith of Naaman, and serves to strengthen the hope that to the last he was faithful. Profound must have been the joy that was felt in Damascus, though no note of it has come to us, when the great captain of the king's armies returned, and it was found that he had been healed of his leprosy. With tears of joy and ejaculations of gratitude he would be welcomed and caressed by a devoted wife and admiring children. Perhaps the king would show his delight by decreeing a holiday to be devoted to feasting and dancing. Cheers and patriotic songs would be heard on every hand, banners and trophies of victory would adorn temples and palaces, and congratulations would be heaped upon the great chieftain by high and low.

But there was one whose joy, though it may have been subdued, and unnoticed by the shouting multitudes, must have been more profound than that of any other in Damascus that day. Our Lord has said, "It is more blessed to give than to receive." Do we do violence to the meaning of his words, if we interpret giving to include serving, and read, "It is more blessed to serve than to be served"? The little maid who had been the chosen instrument in leading Naaman to seek the Prophet's aid, must have felt so, at least. But there would be a still higher source of joy to the little maid; for, in her master's marvelous cure, she would find a mighty confirmation of her faith in Jehovah. Like the people who on mount Carmel beheld the fire of the Lord fall upon the sacrifice of Elijah and consume it, she would be constrained to cry out in joyful ecstasy, "The Lord, he is the God; the Lord, he is the God."

Like her master, the little maid disappears from history. The writer of the sacred story leaves her a captive. But we must be permitted to cherish the assurance that Naaman, who had shown such high appreciation of what the Prophet had done for him, would not forget to reward her. That he would perhaps return her to her sorrowing parents, and endow her with ample fortune.

Or, if her parents had been massacred at the time of her capture, and there were none left to care for her, that he would adopt her as his own child and lavish upon her the affection of a parent, and all the comforts of his princely home.

Having carefully and successfully secreted, as he supposed, the bags of silver and the garments which he had taken from Naaman, and no doubt congratulating himself upon the complete success with which his undertaking had been crowned, Gehazi hastened and "went in and stood before his master," lest his absence should arouse suspicion, and lead to his detection. His elation, however, was to be of very short duration, for he had no sooner entered the Prophet's apartment than he was met with the searching and startling question, "Whence comest thou, Gehazi?" One sin frequently leads to another. Covetousness had led Gehazi to lie to Naaman, and practically to rob him; and now, to conceal his guilt, he must lie to his master. In the most unconcerned manner possible for him, but surely with a throbbing heart and with tingling cheeks, he made answer, "Thy servant went no whither." Already Gehazi must have come to realize that to be rich is not all of life.

> "Can wealth give happiness? look round and see
> What gay distress! what splendid misery!
> Whatever fortune lavishly can pour,
> The mind annihilates, and calls for more."
>
> (Young.)

Falsehood could not deceive him in whom was the Spirit of prophecy. With righteous indignation Elisha declared to his servant that he had full knowledge of his impious conduct. Sternly he said to him, "Went not mine heart with thee, when the man turned again from his chariot to meet thee?" He went further than this, and showed Gehazi that he was acquainted with his very thoughts; that his dreams of the future had been revealed to him; his plans as to what he should purchase with the money which he had gotten so fraudulently.

"Is it a time," he reprovingly asked, "to receive money, and to receive garments, and olive-yards, and vineyards, and sheep, and oxen, and menservants, and maidservants?" But the Prophet has not yet done. Appalled and confounded, Gehazi hears these words of doom, "The leprosy therefore of Naaman shall cleave unto thee, and unto thy seed forever." There was no suspension of the execution of this dread sentence. Immediately the poison entered the veins of Gehazi, "And he went out from his presence a leper as white as snow."

"There is not, perhaps, throughout the whole of the eventful history which we are reviewing, a more awakening or a more instructive fact than that which led to the detection and punishment of Gehazi. His indignant master's eye had seen, and his heart had accompanied him through all the tortuous road of his dishonesty and falsehood. If the Prophet had the power thus to follow his servant into his most secret retirements and to be witness of his most concealed and guilty actions, what must be the power of that Being who could communicate such a supernatural gift to Elisha?" (Blunt.)

God is omnipresent and omniscient. "His eyes are upon the ways of man and he seeth all his goings." "The eyes of the Lord are in every place, beholding the evil and the good." It is impossible to hide our acts or our thoughts from God. The Psalmist says, "If I ascend up into heaven, thou art there; if I make my bed in hell, behold thou art there. If I take the wings of the morning, and dwell in the uttermost parts of the sea; even there shall thy hand lead me, and thy right hand shall hold me."

While this thought of God is suited to produce alarm in the breast of the sinner, it brings comfort to the humble believer, to whom the promise is given, "I will instruct thee and teach thee in the way which thou shalt go: I will counsel thee with mine eye upon thee." Gehazi went out from the presence of Elisha. There was of necessity a separation. The healed Naaman had quitted the Prophet's presence, a living monument of Divine mercy; but Gehazi goes forth a monument of Divine wrath. "Wherever he went in all Israel he must preach the Divine law, a solemn warning that God is just." (Lowrie.)

Let us hope that Gehazi's punishment was limited to time, that for his great sin he sought and found repentance and forgiveness. In such case death, at least, would bring him deliverance from the sore judgment visited upon him. How terrible the state of those who are living without God; for whom death has naught but terror, because they have no hope beyond, and who must be banished forever from the presence of God and the society of his people. Surely our Lord has left no more terrible words than these, "And these shall go away into everlasting punishment." "Oh, Lord God of Elisha, have mercy on us!"

## CHAPTER XXII.

### NATURE'S LAW OVERCOME.

"How blest the sacred tie that binds
In union sweet according minds!
How swift the heavenly course they run
Whose hearts, whose faith, whose hopes are one."

THAT ambition which seems inherent in man to possess authority and to exercise it, has proved a great barrier to the advance of Christianity. Kingly powers have been assumed by those who have claimed to be the ministers of the meek and lowly Jesus, though he himself declared that his kingdom was not of this world. In consequence of this unholy desire for position and power, the energies of those who have professed allegiance to Christ have been expended largely in intrigues to accomplish ambitious, selfish, designs, or in resisting such designs on the part of others. In every way, the result has proved disastrous to vital piety. Men have come to regard obedience to their superiors as paramount to all other duties; and the spirit of pride and arrogancy has taken possession of those who have claimed the right to be lords over God's heritage. They have come to regard their brethren as inferiors, and to feel a corresponding contempt for them, while fear, not love, has been their recompense.

How different from all this must have been those homes of the prophets in the time of Elisha! Between him and the members of these communities or schools, the most tender and loving relations seem to have subsisted. Though the Divinely appointed leader, there was no disposition on the part of the Prophet to magnify his office unduly or to exact any treatment from those about him which would indicate that they were not his equals. At the same time, he seems to have enjoyed the love and respect of the sons of the prophets, and without any compulsion, save that of love, to have been accorded the most courteous and reverent treatment.

The preponderance of opinion favors Jericho and its vicinity as the scene of the incidents described in the narrative which we now consider. This opinion is probably correct, yet it cannot be proven to be so, since there is no direct information upon the subject. Wherever this particular school of the prophets may have been located, a new building had become a necessity with them. "And the sons of the prophets said unto Elisha, Behold, now the place where we dwell with thee is too strait for us." The marginal reading is, "the place where we sit before thee," referring to a meeting place or house. A new church was needed. The number of those who sought to receive instruction from the Prophet had increased to such an extent that the building hitherto occupied had become too small. What the character of the growth had been, whether gradual or sudden, it is impossible for us to determine.

Perhaps the cure of Naaman's leprosy, and especially the judgment which had been visited upon Gehazi, had contributed in some measure to produce a revival of true religion in the hearts of the people. It is recorded that after the punishment of Ananias and Sapphira, "Great fear came upon all the church, and upon as many as heard these things." And in the very next paragraph we read, "And believers were the more added to the Lord, multitudes both of men and women." God sometimes employs his fierce judgments to rouse men to a sense of duty, and to a willingness to perform duty. Augustine has said, "Every judgment of God is a real sermon of reformation and repentance, every judgment hath a voice." Afflictions, when sanctified, serve to bring us nearer to God. The Psalmist says, "It is good for me that I have been afflicted; that I might learn thy statutes."

The story is familiar of the two painters who were employed in frescoing the walls of a great cathedral. They stood upon a rude scaffold, constructed for their purpose, and at a considerable distance from the floor. One of them, so absorbed with his work as to forget where he was, in surveying critically the creation of his brush, had stepped backward slowly until he had reached the edge of the plank upon which he stood. His companion, perceiving his danger, seized a wet brush and threw it against the wall, spattering the picture with unsightly blotches of coloring. The painter flew forward and most bitterly upbraided his companion, until told of the perilous position in which he had stood; then, with tears of gratitude, he blessed the hand that had saved him.

We sometimes become so absorbed with the pictures of the life which now is, as to be insensible to the perils to which we are exposed; and then God in his mercy dashes out the beautiful images, that he may draw us into his outstretched arms. But more largely, doubtless, than to any other agency, the growth of this school of the prophets was due to the blessing of God upon the earnest, faithful ministry of Elisha. He seems not to have been an eloquent preacher, but rather a man of few words, and of a retiring disposition. But he was faithful to the trust committed to him. He neglected no duty, however arduous, shunned not to declare unto his generation "all the counsel of God." At the same time his life was a living epistle, known and read of all men. He taught by example, as well as by precept, for, as before observed, he lived the religion which he preached to others.

Like the great Apostle of the Gentiles, Elisha might have said, as he came to the close of his long and eventful ministry, "I have fought a good fight, I have finished my course, I have kept the faith." Such a ministry as was his, cannot fail to bear an abundant harvest to the honor and glory of God. Though such an one as he "goeth forth and weepeth, bearing precious seed" he "shall doubtless come again with rejoicing, bringing his sheaves with him."

But Elisha was not alone in his efforts to serve the Lord. The prosperous condition of this school of the prophets was doubtless due, in no small measure, to the loyal support which was given the Prophet by those among whom he labored. We may well believe that they were consecrated men and women, much given to prayer, and filled with the desire that God might be glorified in the prevalence of his truth, and, as a consequent of this, the salvation of souls. Surely they were earnest workers in that church, no drones, no stay-at-homes; none who were more faithful in attending the services of other churches than they were in attending the services of the church to which they belonged and to the support of which, in every way possible, they were in honor bound. There were none to make slighting, ungenerous, unkind, untrue remarks concerning the Prophet and his work; none to draw invidious comparisons between him and his predecessor. None to insist that if they had some other man for prophet, a greater work might be accomplished.

There were no tattlers in that community; no busybodies, seeking to attend to everybody's business but their own; no faultfinders, laboring to undermine and to tear down as fast as all others could build up; ready to criticize and to oppose everything that was undertaken, yet never ready to do anything themselves. There were none in that congregation, we must believe, who were more anxious to "get even" with some brother, to spite somebody, than they were to have the Lord's cause prosper. To the contrary, these sons of the prophets were doubtless active in disseminating the truth as it was taught them by the Prophet. Every member of that school doubtless became a missionary. Wherever he went, he doubtless sought to interest and to enlist men in the cause of truth. To their friends and neighbors, these sons of the prophets were ever ready to say, "Come thou with us and we will do thee good." As they labored, they prayed; prayed for Elisha that he might be endued ever more richly with "power from on high," that he might be sustained and directed in his efforts to maintain the cause of truth.

How much the minister needs the prayers of those to whom he ministers! The Apostle Paul constantly sought the prayers of those to whom he spoke the word of life. "Brethren, pray for us." "Finally, brethren, pray for us, that the word of the Lord may have free course and be glorified." The very fact that the minister of the gospel is called to handle the word, in some sense, as a business renders his position a dangerous one. Is it to be wondered at that with such a pastor and people working together thus, in humble dependence upon the Lord, they should find the place where they worshipped "too strait" for them?

Much as the sons of the prophets felt that they needed a larger place, such was their respect for Elisha that they would do nothing toward securing it, until they had consulted with him concerning the matter, and had obtained his approval of their project. "Let us go, we pray thee, unto Jordan, and take thence every man a beam, and let us make a place there, where we may dwell." This was not only a mark of respect for Elisha on the part of these young men but a recognition of his authority as the Divinely appointed head of the school. "Order," it has been said, "is heaven's first law." The welfare of mankind demands that governments should exist, and that the authority of rulers should be respected. Hence the Apostle's words, "Let every soul be subject unto the higher powers. For there is no power but of God: the powers that be are ordained of God." "God is not the author of confusion, but of peace." "Let all things be done decently and in order."

The spirit of lawlessness, the lack of respect for authority, is all too prevalent in our day. In their zeal for democratic principles, men too frequently mistake license of liberty and are consequently intolerant of all restraint. Both in church and state this tendency is becoming more pronounced. That this state of affairs is due, in part at least, to home training, or, more properly speaking, to the lack of proper home training, can scarcely be questioned. Parental authority is not only less rigid, but less real than in former times. If we are to have law-abiding citizens and church members, we must have obedient children in the homes. The child must be taught to respect the authority of the parent, if he is to "honor the king." He should be encouraged to seek the counsel of the parent in all affairs of his life. How many fathers, especially, are blame worthy in this respect! "The father occupies a place in the family that can be filled by no other person. He is the head of the family, he is the priest, and is charged with the proper training of the children in holy things. But how many fathers there are who refuse to trouble themselves with such duties! How many leave all such things to the mothers while they devote themselves to the material things of life! The father withdraws more and more from his place, leaves early, stays late, returns jaded and fretted, not able to bear long the restlessness and noise of the children. He is in no mood to sit down and read with his boy, to look over his examples, or ask where he goes nights; to get acquainted with his daughter's companions and young gentlemen friends.

The household must be managed without him. For attention to its real bodily, mental, and spiritual welfare, he has little time or thought. If anything goes amiss with the lad, if he cries, 'my head, my head!' or a teacher warns to look out for his soul, like the man with the reapers, the father says, 'carry him to his mother.' And perhaps that is all that can be done now. The man has lost the gracious touch of tender ministering, has failed to cherish the frank, childish, confession of his little ones, and grown out of their confidence with their years. They do not feel that he understands them. A vague separation, which would be resented if clearly stated, has cut off the father from the heart life of his home. These children are his own flesh and blood; but the neighbors, whose children play with his, the teacher who hears their lessons, knows, perhaps, more of their inmost thought and character and real promise than he does.

Poor man! to find not merely his own life cheated out of the softening and purifying influences which the dear ones of his heart could give, but to see himself powerless in the crisis of character! And for what? To get them a living. Say, rather, an existence. Living is not food and clothing and furniture. Living is good morals and gentle manners, cultivated intellect, purified conscience and glowing heart. Home life is a wife's bright smile and little children's arms about the neck, and soft cheeks against his, and waiting kisses; long talks with growing sons, and halfplayful gallantries with blooming daughters. Home is a realm where father and mother should be king and queen, enthroned together on the fond delight and unbidden reverence of well-trained youth." (Rev. C. M. Southgate.)

These sons of the prophets were wholly practical in their purposes. "Let us make a place where we may dwell." They were not prompted to undertake this work by any desire for vain show. There was need for such a building as they proposed to erect. Frequently this is not true of churches erected in our day. "Churches and chapels are often built from ignorant zeal and from a spirit of rivalry." In most communities, the churches we now have are more than sufficient to accommodate all who attend Divine service. The problem which confronts the church in our day is not so much how we shall increase the size and number of our church edifices, as how we shall fill with earnest worshippers the churches we now have. "On all sides empty churches and chapels abound, millions of money contributed for religious purposes lie as the one talent wrapped in a napkin, unused." Full more than a board of church erection we need in every community, in every congregation, a board or committee of church filling. The policy of our time is to locate churches in such places as will make it convenient for the largest number of people to attend them. There is certainly wisdom in this.

But the plan proposed to Elisha seems to have contemplated the removal of this school of the prophets from the place where it was then located, probably, as we have said, the populous city of Jericho; at least the additional building required was to be erected in some new locality. "Let us make us a place there." It was probably only their lack of facilities for transporting the materials for the new building any considerable distance that suggested the thought of building where the materials would be at hand. It was simply an expedient. Each one of these sons of the prophets was to assist in the carrying out of this church-erection project. "Let us go unto Jordan and take thence every man a beam." In such circumstances, how surely and speedily the work would be accomplished; all joining in it heartily, each one doing what he could.

These young men recognized the principle that God helps those who are willing to help themselves. They were in need of a larger place, but they did not expect God to provide it for them in some miraculous manner. They did not pray and then sit still and wait for some rich man to assist them. They did not send begging letters to the king and to Naaman, and to other distinguished persons of their own land and of foreign lands, asking them to furnish memorial windows, or to make a donation, in recognition of some real or fancied claim which they had upon their generosity. Neither did they propose to go beyond their means, to build a great edifice, while they had no money to pay for it.

It has been insisted that these were unskillful workmen, but this can scarcely have been true of them, since every Jewish father was required to teach his son some trade.

In the Talmud it is asked, "What is commanded of a father towards his son?" And the answer is, "To circumcise him, to teach him the law, and to teach him a trade." Surely the latter is a wise regulation. No matter what calling a man may choose the mastery of some trade whereby, if necessary, he may be able to earn an honest living will prove no disadvantage, while it may be of inestimable value to him.

Paul, who sat at the feet of Gamaliel, and was one of the greatest thinkers the race has produced, was a tentmaker. Every young man and every young woman of the land, no matter what the social and financial standing may be, should know how to work.

Assured, doubtless, that the Lord had put it into the hearts of his disciples to undertake this work, Elisha unhesitatingly gave his consent to it. "And he answered, Go ye." Not content with the mere permission to do as they had proposed, one of the prophets entreated Elisha to accompany them to the Jordan. "Be content, I pray thee, and go with thy servants." We are reminded by these words of entreaty of the prayer of Moses as he contemplated the arduous task of leading the people of Israel after that the Lord had refused to go with them "because they made the calf, which Aaron made." "If thy presence go not with me, carry us not up hence." Great as was the zeal of these sons of the prophets for the object sought, and confident as they were of success, they yet felt the need of Elisha's presence with them. With him to counsel and to direct them the work, however arduous, would be lightly borne, and the time would pass swiftly and pleasantly.

How sweet and comforting to the believer is the precious assurance of the Lord, "Lo, I am with you always, even unto the end of the world." How it lightens our toil and makes heavy burdens easy to be borne, to know that Jesus, our Lord, is with us; that his eye is continually upon us; that "He leadeth" us "in the paths of righteousness for his name's sake;" that, though we "walk through the valley of the shadow of death," his "rod and staff they comfort" us!

Perhaps Elisha only waited to be invited to accompany these would-be builders. However it may have been, he at once made answer, "I will go." Cheered by the presence of Elisha in their midst, the company of prophets had proceeded to the banks of the Jordan, and were busily engaged in felling the timbers to be used in the construction of the new building. The ring of many an ax kept time to the exultant songs which were heard on every hand. But presently the harmony is marred by a cry of distress. The cry came from one who was felling a tree which probably grew near the bank of the river. In a moment least expected, the ax head flew from the handle or helve and was lost to sight in the deep murky waters. Elisha quickly reached the scene of the mishap, and the story of the man's distress was told him. We have the story epitomized, doubtless, in these words, "Alas, master! for it was borrowed." The fact that the lost ax was the property of another, added to this man's distress. He had borrowed it that he might assist in the work undertaken, and now it was beyond recovery. Perhaps the peculiar circumstances justified his borrowing, but, in ordinary circumstances, borrowing is a poor policy. It is better, so far as possible, that we should be independent of our neighbors; that each workman should own the implements which he employs in labor; then, if loss occur, he has the satisfaction of knowing, at least, that he himself is the only sufferer. Those are wise words which Shakespeare puts into the mouth of Polonius.

> "Neither a borrower nor a lender be;
> For loan oft loses both itself and friend,
> And borrowing dulls the edge of husbandry."

It seems probable that this was a poor man, and that he was unable, in consequence, to make good to his neighbor the loss of the ax. The fact that he was a borrower would seem to indicate that he was not able to own an ax. It may be questioned whether, in such circumstances, he was required to assist in this work in which the prophets were engaged, especially in felling trees. Whatever the correct view may be, Elisha did not upbraid him. so far as the narrative shows. Recognizing in the man's lament an appeal for help, the Prophet at once proceeded to recover the lost property. His method was characteristic. There was no unnecessary display, no "flourish of trumpets." We have no record that the Prophet even called upon God, yet it cannot be doubted that he was Divinely directed in what he did. He simply "cut down a stick," perhaps a branch from a tree, or a small shrub, or bush, "and cast it in thither," that is into the water, "and the iron did swim."

Two suppositions have been offered to explain away the miraculous nature of this event. Von Gerlach suggests that Elisha simply "passed a piece of wood underneath the ax head which he saw lying at the bottom of the river, and then lifted it up to the surface." While Thenius insists that Elisha must have "thrust a stick or bar of wood through the hole in the ax head, made to receive the haft, and so pulled it out." But if this were possible for Elisha, why not for the student prophet? Why should he make so much ado about the falling of the ax into the water, if it were possible to recover it by such ordinary means? Not only so, but why should Elisha do the work for him, and not rather direct him how he might help himself, if such a simple method of recovery were possible? Against such explanation as that to which we have referred, it is urged that "the Jordan is at Jericho so deep and rapid that there was a thousand chances to one against the stick falling into the hole of the ax head" (Jamieson, Fausset, and Brown). Not only so, but such an explanation as either of those suggested does violence to the text. The word *shalak* means to cast or throw. Elisha took the stick which he had cut and cast it from him into the stream where it would naturally float. He did not thrust it into the water, retaining hold of one end as would seem necessary, if it were to pass under the ax head or to enter the hole made for the handle. Furthermore, had either of the suppositions referred to been true, "we may be sure the occurrence would not have been recorded. The sacred writers are not concerned to put on record mere acts of manual dexterity." (Pulpit Commentary.)

Let us be content to take God's word for it that "the iron did swim." We are not called upon to attempt to explain how it was made to do so, but simply to accept the statement of the fact. In two other places only does the word which is here translated, swim, occur in the Scriptures, and in both these instances the translation is to flow over or overflow. In Deut. 11:4, we read, "He made the water of the Red Sea to overflow them as they pursued after you." And in Lam. 3:54, "Waters flowed over mine head."

How God caused the iron ax head "to flow" from the bottom of the river to the surface, we are not able to explain, and, happily, as we have said, we are not required to do so. We must necessarily believe many things which fall under our observation and experience which it would be utterly impossible for us to explain. So far as we can perceive, there was no necessary connection between the casting of the stick into the water and the overflowing of the ax head. "But the question as to our belief of the fact," that the iron did swim, "cannot be discussed separately from that of our belief of the Scriptures as a whole. If on rational and sufficient grounds we believe the truth of the Scriptures, we shall, of course, believe the reality of this event." (Edersheim.)

Only so far as was necessary was the Divine power exerted in recovering the lost ax. As far as possible, human agency was employed. Strange as it seems, it was not divinely revealed to Elisha where the ax lay hidden beneath the waves. The man who lost it was required to indicate the spot; and when the ax appeared upon the surface of the water, he was directed to "take it up."

God's "might and goodness are revealed in the smallest detail as well as in the greatest combination. He helps in what are apparently the smallest interests of the individual person, as well as in the greatest affairs of entire nations, and he rules with his grace especially over those who keep his covenant, and turn to him in all the necessities of life. That is the great truth which this little story proclaims, and just for the sake of this truth, it was thought worthy to be inserted in the history of the theocracy." (Hess.)

# CHAPTER XXIII.

## THEY THAT BE WITH US.

"The angel of the Lord encamps,
And he encompasseth
All those who do him truly fear,
And them delivereth."

"From troubles that surround me
Thou shalt my soul keep free;
With songs of thy salvation
Thou shalt encompass me."

IT has been said that the gratitude of kings is short-lived. While it may be questioned whether those invested with kingly prerogatives are sinners above others in this respect, the conduct of Ben-hadad in making war upon Israel at this time certainly does not contribute to disprove the charge. But a few years, at most, had elapsed since Naaman, the renowned field-marshal of Syria, had been healed of a loathsome and fatal disease through the instrumentality of Israel's great prophet; yet the king of Syria now "warred against Israel." Although war was "the normal relation between the two countries," the record seems to indicate that, in this instance, the Syrian monarch was the aggressor. Without provocation, he devastated the borders of Israel, pillaging and burning, putting the inhabitants to the sword or carrying them off to the slave-pens of Damascus. His hostile activities seem to have been confined for the time to a succession of forays, having for their primary object the capture or destruction of the king of Israel, as is inferred from the statement that by attending to the warnings given him, the king "saved himself there, not once nor twice." The probability of the correctness of this view is strengthened, perhaps, by the statement of Josephus that, "Elisha sent a hasty message to Joram, and exhorted him to take care of that place, for that therein were some Syrians lying in ambush to kill him. So the king did as the prophet exhorted him, and avoided his going a hunting." "Man proposes, but God disposes."

> "The best-laid schemes o'mice and men,
> Gang aft a-gley,
> An' lea'e us nought but grief and pain
> For promised joy." (Burns.)

With deepest cunning and wisdom, and with the profoundest secrecy, as seems to be intimated, the king of Syria planned his campaign against Israel. After consulting with his most competent and trusted officers, and availing himself of all the information to be obtained, he determined that his camp should be fixed at certain times at certain places. His words are, "In such and such a place shall be my camp." So far as human wisdom could foresee, doubtless, every contingency had been provided for. But Ben-hadad fell into the error which has characterized many an otherwise well-laid plan in subsequent times. He did not reckon upon the part which God was to take in the campaign. It may be that by the method of warfare which he had adopted, he hoped to eliminate God from the conflict. He may have thought that "while the God of Israel would not fail them in ordinary warfare, he might be able in petty engagements, by means of ambushes and surprises, to snatch an occasional victory." (Pulpit Com.) But the plans whispered to his advisers behind closed doors in the inner chamber of the palace, it may be, indeed, in his bedchamber, could not be hidden from God. His eye noted those secret conferences, his ear heard those whispered sentences, and by his omniscience the very thoughts of those wicked hearts were discovered. To Elisha, in far-off Samaria, was revealed all that transpired in that secret council-room.

In the spirit of the true patriot, the prophet, forgetting all his personal grievances against the king of Israel, thinking only of his welfare and of the people over whom he ruled, hastened to give timely warning of the danger which threatened. "And the king of Israel sent to the place which the man of God told him and warned him of, and saved himself there, not once nor twice."

O, that all who profess to be of God's spiritual Israel were thus devoted, ready to overlook all real or imagined slights and wrongs, to forget self, when necessary, that Zion's welfare might be conserved, and God's glory advanced. But, alas, how many there are in the church in whose eyes a personal slight, a real or an imaginary injury, is a bigger thing than the success of God's cause in their community or in the world. How many there are of those who profess to love and to serve the Lord Jesus, who would rather resent some petty wrong done them or gratify a grudge which the prince of darkness has begotten in the heart, than labor to build and strengthen the things that are of God. "When tribulation or persecution ariseth because of the word, by and by" they are "offended", and the fact is made manifest by their abandoned pew, by their neglect of duty. O, that, like Elisha, all might be led to recognize fidelity to God as paramount to every other consideration.

How comforting to the heart of the believer is the assurance that God knoweth all things, even from the beginning: that "whatever plans the enemies of God and his people may make, they are known to our Prophet. Whether the attack be on the truthfulness and inspiration of the Scriptures, or consists in defiance or scorn of his church, or be directed against the character and well-being of his people, the Lord can easily provide means of safety. He knoweth their thoughts afar off, and, He that sitteth in the heavens shall laugh; the Lord shall have them in derision." (Edersheim.) Not only does God know the character, purposes, and plans of his and our enemies, but he has warned us of the perilous places, the ambuscades, the toils and snares by which Satan seeks to accomplish our destruction. God's words are, "Enter not into the path of the wicked, and go not in the way of evil men. Avoid it, pass not by it, turn from it and pass away. For they sleep not except they have done mischief; and their sleep is taken away, unless they cause some to fall." "All scripture is given by inspiration of God, and is profitable for doctrine, for reproof, for correction, for instruction in righteousness: that the man of God may be perfect, thoroughly funished unto all good works."

Had the king of Israel disregarded the warning of the Prophet, he must have fallen a victim to the cunning strategy of his relentless enemy. In such a case, his blood would have been upon his own head. If we, having the word of God in our hands, suffer ourselves to be "taken captive by" the devil "at his will," we alone are responsible for our ruin. God warns us, not simply that we may save ourselves from the perils which surround us, but that, like Elisha, we may warn others of their danger, that they with us may find safety. "Son of man, I have made thee a watchman unto the house of Israel: therefore hear the word of my mouth, and give them warning from me. When I say unto the wicked, thou shalt surely die; and thou givest him not warning, nor speakest to warn the wicked from his evil ways, to save his life; the same wicked man shall die in his iniquity; but his blood will I require at thine hand." To have been warned of God, to have had revealed unto us the will of God for our salvation, and of all the lost and perishing of earth, perchance to have been made a watchman upon the towers of Zion, imposes a mighty responsibility, in presence of which even Paul was constrained to cry, "Who is sufficient for these things?" "As they that must give account," let us watch for souls. "We must know and tell where the Syrians lie in ambush" or souls must go down to death.

The king of Syria was greatly disturbed by his repeated failures to accomplish his designs against the king of Israel. The record is that, "the heart of the king of Syria was sore troubled for this thing." "The original verb is very graphic. It is the same that in Isaiah 54:11, is rendered "tossed with tempest"; and in Jonah 1:11, 13, is used to describe the raging of the sea." (Green.) Not unnaturally Ben-hadad attributed the thwarting of his purposes to treachery on the part of some one of his servants. First of all, perhaps, he would suspicion Naaman whose friendship for Israel would doubtless be open and avowed. Calling his servants about him, he thus addressed them, "Will you not show me which of us is for the king of Israel?" Very different from that which he expected, must have been the answer which he received. "And one of his servants said, None, my lord, O king: but Elisha the prophet that is in Israel, telleth the king of Israel the words that thou speakest in thy bedchamber."

Whether he who thus made answer to the king, spoke from information, or expressed a conviction, or simply made a shrewd guess, it is impossible for us to determine. It is a significant fact, however, that it was left for an unknown heathen man to bear this remarkable testimony to the prophetic power of Elisha. So far as the record shows, he never received such testimony from any of his fellow-countrymen. Our Lord sadly said upon one occasion, "A prophet is not without honor, save in his own country, and in his own house." That a man at so great a distance should read the thoughts of another was truly a marvelous thing. Yet Elisha's power was derived, and, at best, was but a faint adumbration of God's omniscience from which nothing is hidden. "There is, perhaps, no characteristic of the Almighty so absolutely necessary to our right conception of God, yet so difficult to understand, and at the same time so powerfully influential when justly apprehended, as his omniscience." (Blunt.)

Could we fully realize that all our thoughts, words, and deeds are registered in heaven, what a mighty deterrent from evil it must prove! "The eye of a child would have prevented many a deed of which our hearts and consciences are ashamed." (Blunt.) How much more should the knowledge that the eye of the infinite God is upon us even in the most secret places; that he sees all, hears all, and knows all, restrain us from the commission of those sins which so largely characterize our lives. O, that all might be thoroughly impressed with the truth of these words, "God shall bring every work into judgment, with every secret thing, whether it be good, or whether it be evil." On the other hand, should not the knowledge of God's omniscience prove a constant and powerful incentive to right living? To know that no matter how inconsiderable may be the act of service rendered, it is known and approved in heaven, ought to comfort and encourage the believer. Our Lord's words are, "Whosoever shall give to drink unto one of these little ones, a cup of cold water only in the name of a disciple, verily, I say unto you, he shall in no wise lose his reward." And at that last, great day, "The King shall say unto them on his right hand, Come ye blessed of my Father, inherit the kingdom prepared for you from the foundation of the world: for I was an hungered, and ye gave me meat: I was thirsty, and ye gave me drink: I was a stranger, and ye took me in: naked, and ye clothed me: I was sick, and ye visited me: I was in prison, and ye came unto me." And when, in humility, they shall disclaim having rendered such service. "The king shall answer and say unto them, "Verily I say unto you, inasmuch as ye have done it unto one of the least of these my brethren, ye have done it unto me." There is a divine record made of every act of kindness done in loving loyalty to Jesus, our Lord, to the end that it may be proclaimed before an assembled world and the heavenly hosts, and rewarded with the joys and the blessedness of the kingdom of heaven.

It seems a remarkable thing that Ben-hadad, heathen though he was, should not perceive the hopelessness of a contest with the prophet of God. With the cure of Naaman still fresh in memory, he could not be ignorant of the fact that it was given to Elisha to exercise divine power. This he practically conceded when he accepted the statement of his servant that the words which he spoke in his bedchamber were told by the Prophet to the king of Israel. Strange that it should not occur to him that if Elisha knew all the plans which were formed against the king of Israel, he would certainly be aware of the plans against himself, and be able to bring them to naught. Opposition to God is not only always unreasonable, but many times unreasoning. Considering not the power that must inevitably oppose him, and prove superior to him, the Syrian king conceived the design of making Elisha his prisoner, hoping thereby, at least, to deprive the king of Israel of his powerful support, if not, indeed, to make him his own ally. "Go and see where he is, that I may send and fetch him," are the self-confident words of the king. And when in the course of a few days, perhaps, he was informed that the Prophet was in Dothan, "he sent thither horses, and chariots, and a great host." Dothan was a small town, about twelve miles north of Samaria. A few ruins and a well are supposed to mark the site. It was situated upon a hill at a narrow pass in the mountains, on the caravan route from Gilead to Egypt. From its position, it became the key to the great plain of Esdraelon, and hence, to Palestine itself. It was the scene of some of the great events of history. Here Joseph found his brethren, and was by them imprisoned in the empty pit, and afterwards sold to the Ishmaelites, "those sailors of the desert in all ages." From that summit, Gideon and his chosen band rushed to the destruction of the hosts of Midian. "A remarkable place this, which might have taught Ben-hadad the hopelessness of his attempt," had he been familiar with its history. "In tropical and sub-tropical parts of the east, ordinary traveling is generally done by night; and in all parts of the east, the sudden raids which are so characteristic of Oriental warfare, generally take place at night." It was in perfect accord with oriental custom that the force sent to apprehend Elisha "came by night, and compassed the city about." The Hebrew words which are here translated "a great host" are employed with some degree of latitude. Sometimes the expression is used to designate a vast army. At other times, as doubtless in this instance, it simply means a strong force, a few hundred or a few thousand at most. From a human point of view, the odds were greatly against Elisha. He was alone, and at this time, perhaps, was "well-stricken in years;" yet this strong force, composed, doubtless, of the very flower of the Syrian army, was sent against him. Not only so, but while the life of the Prophet was characterized by the utmost publicity, his going and coming and the place of his abode being known to all who chose to know, his enemies resorted to secrecy and strategy. But "one with God is a majority," and secrecy and strategy are of no avail in contending against God. It is sometimes a pleasure to be surprised. The unlooked for return of a loved one, long absent from home, fills the soul with ecstatic joy. There may be unhappy surprises, however, which occasion grief and dismay. The morning had dawned brightly upon Dothan and, as the sun rose over the hills of Samaria, the servant of Elisha, who seems to have been another than Gehazi, having "risen and gone forth," beheld a scene which filled his heart with terror, and caused him to haste back to his master with the despairing cry, "Alas, my master! how shall we do?" On every hand the flashing arms, helmets, and shields of Syrian soldiers were visible, for, "behold, an host compassed the city both with horses and chariots." Death or captivity, which meant slavery, seemed inevitable. How often this cry of despair is heard in this sin-cursed world of ours. "How shall we do?" Blessed be God, we have an all-sufficient answer to this anxious inquiry in such words as these: "Cast thy burden upon the Lord, and he shall sustain thee: he shall never suffer the righteous to be moved." "Come unto me, all ye that labor and are heavy laden, and I will give you rest. Take my yoke upon you, and learn of me; for I am meek and lowly in heart: and ye shall find rest unto your souls. For my yoke is easy, and my burden is light." The danger to which Elisha's servant was exposed was as real before he became aware of it as it was at any time afterwards. Perhaps those armor-clad warriors whose presence, when discovered, inspired such terror, had been in position to attack for hours before he awoke. One of the poets has said,

"Where ignorance is bliss
'Tis folly to be wise." (Gray.)

But ignorance of danger or indifference thereto does not render it less formidable. The realization of his peril robbed the servant of Elisha of that peace of mind, that sense of security, which he had before enjoyed, and filled his breast with alarm, but in a very real sense, he could not discover the helpers that were at hand until he came to realize his danger. There is reason for hope when the sinner is led to cry, "What must I do to be saved?" Only in such circumstances can he hear with profit the words of the Apostle, "Believe on the Lord Jesus Christ, and thou shalt be saved." Did Elisha have knowledge of the designs of the Syrians against him, and yet calmly remain at Dothan awaiting their coming? So some have insisted. But, while we may neither affirm nor deny the correctness of such a view, in the absence of any direct information upon the subject, it seems probable that had Elisha been warned of his danger, he would have regarded it as a Divine direction to escape, and, consequently, would have withdrawn from Dothan as secretly as the Syrians approached. Perhaps this attempt against his liberty, or his life, was hidden from him that it might prove a trial of his faith. But whatever may have been the facts with reference to this, Elisha was unmoved by the intelligence which his servant brought to him. With a calmness begotten of perfect confidence, he replies to the terror-stricken young man, "Fear not: for they that be with us are more than they that be with them." Evidently Elisha perceived that his assuring words were not sufficient to allay the fears of his servant. The young man saw but too plainly the grim visages of the Syrian soldiers, but he could see no one to defend his master and himself. "The dim vision of the unseen helper and the unrecognized ministration, was not sufficient to dispel his fears." Hence, Elisha prayed, and said, Lord, I pray thee, open his eyes that he may see." "The Prophet's servant, in his experience, is our brother man. No doubt it was a weakness in him that he could not trust God without seeing; but it was a weakness for which the Prophet did not chide him, and of which he needed not to be ashamed. We share it with him. We all have moments of want and weakness, when the supreme need is an open eye to see the unseen helpers." Who has not been impressed as he has studied the prayer of the Prophet upon this occasion, first of all, how brief it is, "Lord, I pray thee, open his eyes that he may see." But eleven words, the longest of which contains but four letters. In this respect it was typical. Most of the prayers recorded in the Bible are remarkable for their brevity. When Peter was sinking beneath the waves upon which he would have walked to the Master, he had time to utter but the three words, "Lord, save me." Yet they were sufficient to evoke the Lord's aid. The publican, who went up to the temple to pray, could but cry, "God be merciful to me a sinner." Yet he went down to his house justified. We too often forget that "a man is not heard for his much speaking;" that the thing to be sought for in prayer is not a multiplicity of words, but power. Some one has called attention to the fact that the prayers of the saints are preserved in vials, golden vials, not in hogsheads or bins, indicating not only that they are precious, but that, like many another precious thing, they are contained in small compass. The prayer of the Prophet was likewise simple and explicit. He had a definite desire in his heart, and he made it known to God without any circumlocution. And how unselfish was this prayer. The Prophet asked nothing for himself. He saw the angelic defenders, and felt no fear, but he prayed that the vision might be granted to his servant, that he, too, might be comforted. Then, again, how fully God's sovereignty and infinite power are recognized by the Prophet. Much as he desired the blessing asked for his servant, he felt that he had no power to bestow it himself, that God alone had the right and the power. "Lord, I pray thee, open his eyes."

How important that we should remember that, while Paul may plant, and Apollos may water, God giveth the increase. Nor should we fail to note that the prayer of the Prophet prevailed with God. "And the Lord opened the eyes of the young man; and he saw; and, behold, the mountain was full of horses and chariots of fire round about Elisha." "The opening of the eyes signifies elevation into an ecstatic state in which the soul sees things which the bodily eye never can see." (Lange.)

"If, in the early morning, you stand in the vale of Chamounix and look up where you know Mount Blanc ought to be, there is nothing visible but a thick veil of mist that hangs so low as to seem to envelop you. But the sun rises and pours a flood of rays upon the thick bank of cloud, and presently it vanishes into invisible vapor, and, like the great white throne, there stands before you the unseen and eternal." (Dr. W. Adams.) If the mists that hide from our vision the unseen, were dissolved; if the scales were but removed from our eyes, what an amazing view we should have of the agents and agencies that work God's will in the silent and transparent atmosphere of life! "What a sight this trembling young man beheld, when his eyes were opened! Where he had seen only barren rocks or sparse vegetation, he now saw that same fiery host that had attended Elijah in his translation, now enclosing the unarmed Prophet and himself within a flaming ring. The manifestation, not the presence of the angel guard, was the miracle. It was a momentary unveiling of what always was, and would be after the curtain was drawn. The young man simply saw what had been before, the mountain full of horses and chariots of fire. The helpers, which to that moment had been unseen by him, were no more real, and no stronger, than before he beheld them." (Dr. Alexander McLaren.)

It would seem that the supernatural power of vision which was granted to this young man was of a physical character, rather than spiritual. He simply saw with bodily eye objects which before, and after, were invisible to him. "The outer world is to us according to our five senses. Had we fewer, it would be less than it is; or if more, it would be greater. There are probably properties in the material system which we have at present no sense to discover; or peradventure there may be senses, closed up within, that will one day be developed, and make this old world a new thing to us." (Dr. D. Thomas.)

There is a strange theory on which thoughtful men have speculated much, and concerning which considerable has been written, by which the attempt is made to account for those supernatural appearances of which we find record in the word of God. It is the theory of "Higher Space," or the "Fourth Dimension of Space," as it is usually expressed. This space is invisible to us, not because it is at an infinite distance from us, for it lies

19

close to us on every side, is in perfect contact with every point of our space in its whole extent: but "because we do not know in which direction to look for it, and because our senses are adapted for use in our own space."

There is absolutely no distance between us and the boundary line of the Higher Space, yet we cannot look into it. The telescope brings it no nearer to us, because we do not know where to turn our eyes, or how to turn our eyes. According to this theory, the ability to see, as Elisha and his servant saw; as Stephen saw when he beheld the heavens opened, and the Son of Man standing on the right hand of God; as Paul, on the way to Damascus, beheld the Lord, though the vision was denied those who journeyed with him; as John saw, when in the spirit he was permitted to be a witness of the worship of heaven: is simply the ability to gaze into this Fourth Dimension of space.

Those horses and chariots of fire are round about us to-day, and we should behold them, if our eyes were opened, if the limitations of our vision were removed. But enough for the theory. "The truest vision is the vision of faith," and the prayer of each one of us should be, Lord help my unbelief; increase my faith that I may see. "We so constantly look at the things seen, that we have no sight for the unseen." How much needless worry and anxiety we would be spared, could we but believe that, "they that be with us are more than they that be with them;" that, "when the enemy shall come in like a flood, the Spirit of the Lord shall lift up a standard against him;" could we but see with the eye of faith, "the horses and chariots of fire" which constantly surround us, as we strive to do the Lord's service.

For but a moment, perhaps, was the servant of Elisha permitted to look upon that resplendent host which encompassed his master and himself. Already the trumpets of the Syrians were sounding, and, like a lion springing upon his prey, those fierce soldiers rushed toward the gates of the city. But their onward movement was suddenly arrested, for "Elisha prayed unto the Lord, and said, Smite this people, I pray thee, with blindness. And he smote them with blindness, according to the word of Elisha." "God did according to the word of Elisha, a wonderful inversion of the ordinary formula. But that was because Elisha was doing according to the word of the Lord." (Dr. Alexander McLaren.)

God never fails to hear the cry of his servants. And how easy a thing it is for him to save; how mighty he is to deliver! Alexander Peden, one of the Scotch Covenanter ministers, and a few companions, were upon one occasion pursued by a band of the enemy. "At last, getting some little height between him and the enemy, he stood still and said, 'Lord, it is thy enemy's day, hour, and power. They may not be idle. But hast thou no other work for them but to send them after us? Send them after them to whom thou wilt give strength to flee, for our strength is gone. Twine them about the hill, Lord, and cast the lap of thy cloak over old Sandy, and thir poor things, and save us this one time; and we will keep it in remembrance, and tell it to the commendation of thy goodness, pity, and compassion, what thou didst for us at such a time.' And in this he was heard; for a cloud of mist intervened immediately between them; and in the meantime a post came to the enemy, to go in quest of Mr. Renwick, and a great company with him."

"Two Americans who were crossing the Atlantic met one Sabbath night to sing hymns in the cabin. As they sang the hymn, "Jesus, Lover of my Soul," one of them heard an exceedingly rich and beautiful voice behind him. He looked around, and although he did not know the face, he thought he recognized the voice. So when the music ceased, he turned around and asked the man if he had not been in the Civil war. The man replied that he had been a Confederate soldier. 'Were you at such a place on such a night?' asked the first. 'Yes,' he said, 'and a curious thing happened that night; this hymn recalled it to my mind. I was on sentry duty on the edge of a wood. It was a dark night, and very cold, and I was a little frightened, because the enemy were supposed to be very near at hand. I felt very homesick and miserable, and about midnight, when everything was very still, I was beginning to feel very weary and thought that I would comfort myself by praying and singing a hymn. I remember I sang this hymn,

'All my trust on thee is stayed,
All my help from thee I bring,
Cover my defenceless head
With the shadow of thy wing.'

After I had sung those words, a strange peace came down upon me, and through the long night I remember having felt no more fear.' 'Now,' said the other man, 'listen to my story. I was a Union soldier, and was in the wood that night with a party of scouts. I saw you standing up, although I did not see your face, and my men had their rifles focused upon you, waiting the word to fire, but when you sang out,

'Cover my defenceless head
With the shadow of thy wing,'

I said, Boys put down your rifles, we will go home. I couldn't kill you after that.'" (Dr. Henry Drummond.)

It seems evident that the Syrians did not suffer the loss of sight, for if so, they could not have followed Elisha to Samaria. A strange hallucination seized them, an aberration of mind, and they were unable to perceive things as they really were. Taking advantage of this, Elisha approached them without being recognized by them, and said unto them, "This is not the way, neither is this the city: follow me, and I will bring you to the man whom ye seek. But he led them to Samaria."

In speaking thus to his would-be captors, Elisha was not guilty of falsehood, as some have insisted. He simply said to them, This is not the way to find the one whom ye seek; neither is this the city in which ye shall see him. And in promising to bring them to the man whom they sought, he undertook no more than he performed. Having conducted the Syrians into Samaria, Elisha again prayed, and said, "Lord, open the eyes of these men." Again he was heard, "their eyes were opened, and they saw; and, behold, they were in the midst of Samaria." On all sides of them, doubtless, stood the solid phalanxes of Israel, waiting the command to cut them down. What terror must have seized them, as they realized their situation!

There is a day coming when the eyes of finally impenitent sinners shall be opened to behold a scene infinitely more appalling. They shall behold the great white throne of judgment, and for very fear, shall be constrained to say to the mountains and rocks, "Fall on us, and hide us from the face of him that sitteth on the throne, and from the wrath of the Lamb." O, that all might be wise, and, in the Divinely appointed way, prepare for that great and terrible day of the Lord.

The king of Israel eagerly entreated that he might smite the Syrians. But to have done so would have defeated the purpose of the great miracle that had been wrought. Elisha indignantly refuses to permit such cold-blooded murder; and, instead, directs that the captives be hospitably entertained, and then permitted to return to their master. It was done, and, as a result of this generous treatment, "The bands of Syria came no more into the land of Israel," at least for a time. Kindness and mercy had conquered; evil had been overcome with good.

"O weary ones! ye may not see
Your helpers in their downward flight;
Nor hear the sound of silver wings
Slow beating through the hush of night.

"But not the less gray Dothan shone,
With sunbright watchers bending low,
That Fear's dim eye beheld alone
The spear-heads of the Syrian foe.

"There are, who, like the Seer of old,
Can see the helpers God has sent,
And how life's rugged mountain-side
Is white with many an angel tent.

—Whittier.

## CHAPTER XXIV.

### JUDGMENT AND MERCY.

"His holiness remember
Ye saints give thanks and praise;
A moment lasts his anger
His favor crowns our days.
For sorrow, like a pilgrim,
May sojourn for a night,
But joy the heart shall gladden,
When dawns the morning light."

"Thy mercy, Lord, is in the heavens;
Thy truth doth reach the clouds;
Thy justice is like mountains great;
Thy judgments deep as floods."

JEHOVAH had not yet given over the effort to reclaim apostate Israel. He was yet unwilling to say, "Ephriam is joined to his idols, let him alone." Again his judgments were falling upon the people that they might be brought to see the error of their ways, and led to turn from them. After a short cessation of hostilities, which had been purchased by the generous treatment of the Syrian forces which had been sent to make Elisha a prisoner, but which had been delivered by him into the hands of the king of Israel, the king of Syria was permitted again to invade the land, and to lay siege to Samaria, the capital. Forgetting the gracious kindness which the king of Israel had shown him, "Ben-hadad, king of Syria, gathered all his host, and went up and besieged Samaria." Against the people who had requited his cruel designs with mercy; against the city wherein such generous treatment had been accorded his helpless subjects, he now hurled the whole force of his kingdom. To a less sanctified mind than that of Elisha, there might have come feelings of regret that such kindness had been shown to the Syrians whom the Lord had delivered into his hands. Seeing that no lasting impression had been made upon the mind of the king of Syria by the kindness of which he had been made the recipient; that the same men, perhaps, whose lives had been spared, and who had been permitted to return to their master, were now fighting against Israel, some would be ready to pronounce such kindness unwise, if not, indeed, criminal.

Thus do we often reason when our generosity has been imposed upon. Yet such regrets are not praiseworthy, for the good effects of an act of kindness may not be lost to us, though he to whom it is done should prove to be unworthy; and the world is the better for every such act. Though you should find the beggar whom you have assisted, wallowing in the mire in drunken stupor, the fact cannot rob you of the blessed consciousness that you tried to help him.

It would seem that the king of Syria, despairing, perhaps of success by the methods of warfare which he had employed heretofore, had determined upon more aggressive measures. Instead of sending forth guerrilla bands whose operations were doubtless largely confined to the borders of Israel, he now mobilized the entire military force of his kingdom, and carried the war to the gates of Samaria. Josephus states that when the men sent to apprehend Elisha had returned, "and had shown Ben-hadad how strange an accident had befallen and what an appearance and power they had experienced of the God of Israel, he wondered at it, as also at the prophet with whom God was so evidently present; so he determined to make no more secret attempts upon the king of Israel, out of fear of Elisha, but resolved to make open war with them, as supposing he could be too hard for his enemies by the multitude of his army and power. So he made an expedition with a great army against Joram, who not thinking himself a match for him, shut himself up in Samaria, and depended upon the strength of its walls."

With a persistence worthy of a better cause, Ben-hadad prosecuted his warlike designs against Israel. Repeatedly his forces had been repulsed, and his deep-laid schemes brought to nought; and yet, persuaded as he must have been, that all this was from the God of Israel, he retired, when defeated, only to prepare to make a new attack. Unwarned by past defeats, he had now come with all his host to renew the conflict. But, although in the first stages of the campaign he had been successful, he was destined to suffer defeat again, and to be driven home in confusion and shame.

Such, ultimately, must be the experience of all who fight against God. "The kings of the earth set themselves, and the rulers take counsel together, against the Lord and against his anointed, saying, Let us break their bands asunder, and cast away their cords from us. He that sits in the heavens shall laugh: the Lord shall have them in derision." Every impenitent sinner is the adversary of God. In persisting in the attempt to live without God, to live unmindful of God's revealed will, the sinner declares that he is in a state of rebellion against God. For a time such an one may seem to have everything his own way, but let him not flatter himself that it shall be always thus. His feet stand "in slippery places," and ultimately he must bow the knee. God is slow to anger and plenteous in mercy, yet he has said, "My spirit shall not always strive with man." In the end the persistent sinner must be driven away in shame and confusion, into everlasting darkness. Let us take heed unto ourselves, "lest haply" we "be found even to be fighting against God."

How long the siege of Samaria was continued, we have no means of knowing. It is evident, however, that during its continuance, all means of ingress and egress would be cut off. No provisions could be received from any source. As a result, the people were finally reduced to such a degree of destitution, that the most exorbitant prices were paid for food which, in happier circumstances, would have been despised as unclean and unfit for human food. The record is that "an ass's head was sold for fourscore pieces of silver, $25.20, according to one computation, $36.64, according to another; and the fourth part of a cab of dove's dung for five pieces of silver, equal to $1.57, as Keil estimates, or $2.41, according to Thenius. Various explanations have been offered of this statement. By some it has been urged that an ass's head signifies the whole animal, as when it is said that certain domestic animals are bought and sold for so much per head. But the fact that the head of an ass, which was considered an unclean animal, was sold for fourscore pieces of silver, is adduced as evidence of the extreme scarcity of food in Samaria. Such a condition, however, could scarcely be supposed to exist, if the whole carcass of an ass could be purchased for such a sum of money. It has been suggested that dove's dung was the name by which a certain kind of plant or vegetable was known. Others think that the reference is to the seed of a leguminous plant resembling the bean or pea. But why not understand the term literally? Such a view is not out of harmony with the facts which history records, while the evident design of the sacred writer to exhibit the terrible distress which prevailed in Samaria would seem to require it.

The statement of Josephus that "the Hebrews bought a sextary of dove's dung instead of salt," if it is to be considered as possessed of any historical value, would favor a literal interpretation of the term, since it shows the use that was made of the article in question.

We are at all times dependent upon God for the food which nourishes our bodies, but how often, when the full cup of Divine blessing is poured out to us, do we partake without any appreciation of God's goodness, without thought of gratitude to him who openeth his hand and satisfieth all our needs! Do we not sometimes need the chastisements of God's hand to teach us to appreciate the blessings which he bestows?

There were doubtless many poor in Samaria whose hunger was intense, but who had no money to purchase even such provisions as are here mentioned. "Hunger is one of the most commanding of appetites. In every land, and in every age, the first and the most interesting problem which the majority of men have to solve, practically, is, How are we to get bread?" (Orr.)

In their dire extremity the suffering poor of Samaria became dead to natural affection, and the shocking spectacle is presented, unparalleled, as Lange asserts, in the history of any other people, of mothers slaying and devouring their own children. Josephus states that "Joram was in fear lest somebody should betray the city to the enemy, by reason of the famine, and went every day round the walls and the guards to see whether any such were concealed among them." It was doubtless while thus visiting the guards and inspecting the defenses that this cry of a woman greeted him. "Help, my lord, O king." Very naturally supposing that the woman cried to him for food, the king, without waiting, as it would seem, to hear her story, replied with all the bitterness of despair, "If the Lord do not help thee, whence shall I help thee; out of the barn-floor or out of the wine-press?" This was not a brutal imprecation of God's curse upon the woman, as some have supposed, but a confession of the consciousness of utter helplessness on the part of the king to relieve the distress of his subjects.

It was a frank confession that the supply of food was now exhausted, and also an avowal of the king's conviction that the only hope left was in the interposition of God. It would seem that, when this impassioned statement of the king had been made, and the woman was permitted to speak again, she explained that it was not bread she sought, but justice. With surprise, and some degree of impatience too, perhaps, as though the procuring of food were the only thing which should claim attention, the king again interrupted her and demanded to know the cause of her complaint. "What aileth thee?" he asked. In answer he was told this story, one of the most horrifying in all history.

"This woman," doubtless pointing to the person against whom she complained, "said unto me, Give thy son, that we may eat him to-day, and we will eat my son to-morrow. So we boiled my son, and did eat him: and I said unto her on the next day, Give thy son that we may eat him: and she hath hid her son."

We may believe that this was not the only instance of such appalling conduct on the part of the beleaguered inhabitants of Samaria. Centuries before this, God, by his servant Moses, had warned Israel that if she should prove disobedient, and serve not the Lord her God "with joyfulness, and with gladness of heart," the horrors of siege should be visited upon her when parents should eat the flesh of their children, when a man's eye should "be evil toward his brother, and toward the wife of his bosom," and when the eye of the wife should "be evil toward the husband of her bosom." Signally was this prophecy fulfilled in the siege of Samaria by Ben-hadad; again in the siege of Jerusalem by Nebuchadnezzar; and finally in the siege of Jerusalem by the Romans under Titus. Astounded by the atrocity of the deed which the woman confessed, and horror-stricken by the state of affairs which the story revealed, the king rent his clothes. By this act he unintentionally disclosed the fact "that he had sackcloth within upon his flesh," a token of penitence for sin, and of humiliation before God. And yet his subsequent conduct would seem to forbid the belief that he was in any sense truly penitent and humble. He does not seem to have realized that the startling events transpiring in his capital were the fulfillment of prophetic utterance, that the calamities which had come upon him and his subjects were sent of God in punishment of sin. Much less does he seem to have felt that he himself was responsible above any other for all this.

So far as the record shows, there was no confession of sin, doubtless because there was no proper consciousness of sin. Perhaps, in wearing the sackcloth, he was simply "doing penance" as do the superstitious adherents of the Roman Catholic Church, with the belief that by torturing the flesh he might appease the wrath of Jehovah, and turn away his judgments from him. "What a small circumstance will often turn the current of popular feeling. What a little thing will in times of despair suffice to carry comfort and hope. The sight of king Joram in sackcloth almost blotted out the tale of horrors. For the moment it was a more joyous surprise to the people than tidings of approaching relief would have been. Yet after all what was it?

In seasons of sorrow, in times of calamity, even a man destitute of religion wears his sackcloth. He becomes more grave and earnest; he attends more to the outward duties of religion; he feels more deeply; he gives up certain sins; he forms certain resolutions. But this is not repentance. Tested by its results, it is sorrow which worketh death. There is no element of life in it. It passes away with the occasion, as the morning cloud and as the dew, and leaves the soul as before in its relation to God." (Edersheim.)

The fact that the innocent must sometimes suffer with the guilty, is one of the perplexing and distressing features of sin. If the drunkard alone suffered the consequences of his excesses, we should have abundant reason to regard his course with feelings of horror. The thought of spending money for that which is worse than naught; of wasting the precious moments of life in the indulgence of a habit which destroys both body and soul; of being chargeable at the last with the crime of self-destruction is certainly appalling. But the drunkard's sin entails the most intolerable hardships and sufferings upon those who are in no measure responsible for it. It involves the disgrace and the ruin, in many cases, of those who are nearest and dearest to him.

With Ben-hadad as a scourge in his hand, God was now punishing idolatrous Israel and more particularly the wicked house of Ahab; but even Elisha, the man of God, was not exempt from the terrible sufferings which prevailed in Samaria. Day after day, through many weary months, doubtless, he had experienced afflictions for which he was in no way responsible. He had striven to avert the calamities which all alike now suffered, by calling the people to repentance, and to turn unto the Lord. Marvelously he had delivered others when in distress, when oppressed by inexorable need, yet now he was helpless to deliver himself from the pangs of hunger, and the still sorer pangs of heart which he suffered because of God's displeasure against his people. In addition to the trials which he was thus called to endure, Elisha suddenly became the object of the king's vindictive fury.

Joram's first emotion, after hearing the tragic story of the woman who had slain and devoured her son, was that of horror. But as he contemplated this new and startling evidence of the extreme destitution of his people, horror gave way to violent anger, and he registered an oath that he would destroy the life of Elisha. "God do so and more also to me, if the head of Elisha, the son of Shaphat, shall stand on him this day." Very similar are these words to those of Jezebel, the mother of Jehoram, addressed to Elijah. "But Jezebel's threat had apparently more reason for it than Jehoram's." That Elisha was innocent of having anything to do with bringing about the wretched state of affairs existing in Samaria, the king doubtless very well knew. The impulse which found expression in this rash threat was probably due to the feeling that Elisha, while in no sense responsible for the calamities which the people suffered, had done nothing to remove these calamities.

Josephus says, "This story mightily grieved Joram when he heard it; so he rent his garment, and cried out with a loud voice, and conceived great wrath against Elisha the prophet, and set himself eagerly to have him slain, because he did not pray God to provide them some exit and way of escape out of the miseries with which they were surrounded." It has been surmised by some that Elisha had encouraged the king to persist in his defense of the city, by the promise that God would ultimately send deliverance. There is no direct intimation, however, that such was the case, and it would seem reasonable to believe that, had such assurance been given, the effect would have been to frustrate God's design in permitting the Syrians to invade Israel. It seems more probable that Joram's wrath was due to the erroneous belief that the Prophet could work miracles at his will; to ignorance of the fact that, save when the Spirit of

God was upon him, Elisha was subject to all the limitations of an ordinary man. In the same manner, doubtless, in which he had been apprised of the designs of the king of Syria against the king of Israel, Elisha was now apprised of the designs of the latter against himself.

As he sat in his house, surrounded by "the elders" who may have come to inquire of the Lord, through him, he seems to have heard, by some supernatural power given him, the king's command to the executioner. In vision he beheld the messenger hastening to his murderous task, with the king closely following to stay the execution of the sentence which he had pronounced but a moment before. Elisha was not terrified by the revelation made to him. He made no attempt to flee or to conceal himself. To the contrary, he boldly denounced the king in language which betrayed supreme contempt and intense indignation, and calmly awaited his coming. "See ye how this son of a murderer hath sent to take away mine head?"

Severe as this language may seem, it was in perfect harmony with the facts as known to those whom the Prophet addressed. But Elisha does not needlessly expose himself to danger, nor neglect the means of safety afforded him. While he would not flee from the danger which threatened, he directs that the door should be shut and the executioner kept at bay until the king should arrive. How very commonplace this procedure! There was no attempt at miracle; no striking of the king's messenger with blindness. The prophet simply directed that the door be shut. Any man could have done as much; no man perhaps would have done less. But there was no need that a miracle should be wrought, and God does not work miracles when by ordinary means his purposes may be accomplished. "The narrative is very compressed and elliptical. The reader is expected to supply missing links, and to understand that all happened as Elisha had predicted and enjoined, that the messenger came, that the elders shut the door and held him fast, and that the king shortly arrived." (Pulpit Commentary.)

It was the king who, having arrived, now spoke. "And he said, Behold, this evil is of the Lord; what should I wait for the Lord any longer?" This utterance is not to be understood as the statement of a reason why the king's command concerning the Prophet should not be executed, as some have insisted, but rather as an acknowledgment, which he had hitherto refused to make, that God was chastening Israel. Up to this time, perhaps, he had cherished the hope that the Divine wrath might be appeased, and that deliverance would come. But now all hope was gone. He was convinced that the city must ultimately fall into the hands of the Syrians Then why wait for the Lord any longer? Why not give over the unequal and hopeless contest, surrender the city at once, and thus end the terrible suffering which prevailed?

As our Lord sent forth his apostles to preach the kingdom of heaven, he made known to them that they should encounter the opposition and experience the cruel persecution of men. "But," said he, "when they deliver you up, take no thought how or what ye shall speak: for it shall be given you in that same hour what ye shall speak. For it is not ye that speak, but the Spirit of your Father which speaketh in you."

There is no record that such formal promise had been

given to Elisha, yet he was not left without Divine aid in this supreme moment when his life was trembling in the balance. It required heavenly wisdom to answer the king's question, and at the right moment such wisdom was given. Up to this hour, perhaps, Elisha had been permitted to speak no word of comfort or encouragement to the distressed king and people. However much they might have pressed to know the purpose of God concerning the result of the siege, no revelation was given them. They had forsaken God, and refused his counsel, and he had turned his face from them. Now, at length, the lips of the Prophet were unsealed, and he makes this remarkable prediction. "Thus saith the Lord, to-morrow about this time shall a measure of fine flour be sold for a shekel, and two measures of barley for a shekel, in the gate of Samaria."

From a human point of view the fulfillment of such a prediction would seem an utter impossibility. Not in the most plenteous season, perhaps, could such provisions be procured at a lower price. But at this time there was, perhaps, no such thing as wheat or barley to be found within the walls of Samaria; and the most exorbitant prices were paid for the most repulsive food. With the city surrounded by a powerful and vigilant enemy, from whence could come such a supply as would reduce present prices to such a rate? Even were the besieging army to withdraw, a most improbable thing, and the gates of the city to be thrown open to receive all the supplies that might come from the surrounding country, it would seem impossible to supply the needs of the starving multitudes by such a time, and to such an extent as indicated by the words of the Prophet.

Had the harvest been ever so abundant, and the means of transporting supplies been equal to those of the present time, the thing promised could scarcely have been accomplished. But the conditions were far from being so favorable. The resources of the country for miles in every direction had doubtless been consumed by the invading army, while the facilities for transportation were of the most primitive sort, and even these had been greatly impaired by the prevailing famine.

But those things which are impossible with man are possible with God, for with him all things are possible. Elisha was wholly ignorant, perhaps, as to how this abundant supply of food was to be provided, but he had God's word for it and doubted not. There is no intimation that the king failed to give full credence to the words of the Prophet; but "the captain on whose arm the king leaned, answered the man of God, and said, If the Lord should make windows in heaven might this thing be?" As a courtier, this high officer sought and expected the approbation of the king in what he said. But it was Elisha who answered his question, and his words must have been far from reassuring to the proud courtier. "Behold thou shalt see it with thine eyes, but shalt not eat thereof."

Doubtless this officer of the king thought that reason justified his statement; that the thing promised by the Prophet could not be. "But reason is no test of possibility. Many things which one generation has deemed impossible, have been proved to be possible by the next generation." Many of the greatest labor-saving and time-saving inventions employed to-day, methods of rapid transit, and almost instantaneous communication, were not thought of a century ago. The mere suggestion of their possibility would doubtless have been met with ridicule. It is scarce three hundred years since Galileo was condemned to a dungeon for asserting that the earth moved round the sun.

Like a flash the intelligence of the Prophet's announcement would spread over the city of Samaria. Emaciated men would come forth from their wretched abodes to learn the news, discuss the situation, and speculate as to how the promise of deliverance could have its fulfillment. All sorts of rumors would soon be afloat, and intense excitement would prevail. But hour after hour passed, the light finally faded from the western sky, and darkness brooded over the city. Again the camp-fires of the Syrians gleamed, and their martial notes were heard on every hand; still deliverance came not. It was probably in the second watch of the night that a company of four leprous men, who may have been obliged to remain without the city, drew near, and hailing the sentinel upon the wall, spoke thus: "We came to the camp of the Syrians, and, behold, there was no man there, neither voice of man, but horses tied, and asses tied, and the tents as they were."

There is a Jewish tradition that these four lepers were Gehazi and his three sons. Driven to desperation by the pangs of hunger, they had resolved, as a last resort, to cast themselves upon the mercy of the Syrians, reasoning that, though they should be killed, their fate could be no worse than to enter into the city or to remain where they were. "And they rose up in the twilight, to go unto the camp of the Syrians: and when they were come to the uttermost part of the camp of Syria, behold there was no man there." Entering into one of the deserted tents and finding the evening meal, perhaps, of its recent occupants untouched, "they did eat and drink" until satisfied. Perchance it was the tent of some prince or general which they had entered, and besides abundance to eat and to drink, they found silver and gold, and raiment. These things they carried away and hid; and returning, they entered another tent and spoiled it in like manner. Thus for a time they reveled in riches, scarcely able, perhaps, to persuade themselves that it was not all a dream.

At length, however, the thought of the suffering multitudes within the city came to them. "Then they said one to another, We do not well: this day is a day of good tidings, and we hold our peace: if we tarry till the morning light, some mischief will come upon us: now therefore come, that we may go and tell the king's household."

"The judgment of these leprous men that they did wickedly in keeping to themselves the good tidings that were so needed in the distressed city, expresses the just feeling which should dwell in every ingenuous mind. If the providence of God has freely given us his bounties, and there are others within our reach who stand in pressing need, our very abundance in contrast with their poverty is a call upon us to impart to them if we would have the Divine blessing upon what we enjoy. It is not in the selfish use of anything that we can find its best advantages. 'Freely ye have received, freely give.' If God has given us the gospel and its precious teachings, it is not for our exclusive use. We, poor lepers, have been mercifully led to find food and healing, and can we keep to ourselves the good things of God's grace when the necessities of a race lying in the darkness and misery of paganism are known to us, when these precious teachings can disperse their gloom and fill them with everlasting joy, and when indeed we have received these great blessings accompanied by the command to send them forth to others in all the earth?" (Lowrie.)

The tidings communicated by the lepers were immediately transmitted to the king, but he received them with suspicion. To his advisers who probably had been hastily summoned into his presence, he said, "I will now show you what the Syrians have done to us. They know that we be hungry; therefore are they gone out of the camp to hide themselves in the field, saying, When they come out of the city, we shall catch them alive, and get into the city." Perhaps king Jehoram has been unduly censured for entertaining such distrustful and desponding views. It has been urged that he should have perceived that the intelligence brought by these four men was in accord with the prediction of Elisha. But it must be remembered that the king had not been informed as to how the words of the Prophet were to be fulfilled; that although the promise that fine flour and barley should be sold in the gates of Samaria necessarily implied that the siege should be raised, it was not an unnatural thing that the king should overlook that fact; besides, such a stratagem as he suspected had been resorted to frequently before his day. Let us not be too harsh in our condemnation of the conduct of the king upon this occasion. Perhaps most of us, if placed in similar circumstances, would be as suspicious as he, and as slow to recognize in transpiring events the fulfillment of a prophet's words.

True, as has been suggested, Jehoram should have expected the occurence of some thing extraordinary, that the Prophet's words might have their fulfillment. "He should have been on the lookout for some strange intelligence." But is not this equally true of us? Among many other unfulfilled prophecies there is left to us the promise of our Lord's second coming. "This same Jesus which is taken up from you into heaven, shall so come in like manner as ye have seen him go into heaven." Are we constantly looking for the fulfillment of this promise? Were it told us to-day that our Lord had come, that he was now upon the earth, would we be able to receive him, if his coming had been in any respect radically different from our expectation?

It was at the suggestion of one of his servants or officers, that the king sent to learn the true state of affairs. "They took therefore two chariot horses; and the king sent after the host of Syrians, saying, Go and see. And they went after them unto Jordan; and, lo, all the way was full of garments and vessels which the Syrians had cast away in their haste. And the messengers returned, and told the king. And the people went out, and spoiled the tents of the Syrians. So a measure of fine flour was sold for a shekel, and two measures of barley for a shekel, according to the word of the Lord."

The explanation of the unexpected and precipitate flight of the Syrians is given in these words. "For the Lord had made the Syrians to hear a noise of chariots, and a noise of horses, even the noise of a great host;

and they said one to another, Lo, the king of Israel hath hired against us the kings of the Hittites, and the kings of the Egyptians, to come upon us. Wherefore they arose and fled in the twilight, and left their tents, and their horses, and their asses, even the camp as it was, and fled for their lives." The story of the panic of the Syrians may have been told by some stragglers who may have fallen into the hands of the Israelites, or the facts may have been revealed to Elisha. How the noise which occasioned the flight of this great army was produced, is not known.

That it was supernatural seems evident from the statement that "the Lord made the host of Syria to hear" it, and from the apparent fact that it was audible to the Syrians only. Perhaps they simply imagined that they heard such a noise. Be this as it may, there is no intimation that the vigilant watchmen upon the walls of Samaria heard any unusual noise at this time.

"How easy a thing it is for God to fulfill his purposes! With God nothing is impossible. Nothing is even hard for him. He has a thousand resources. He can send forth his angel into a camp at nightfall, and in the morning they shall be 'all dead men.' He can make brothers-in-arms to fall out, and turn their swords one against another. He can send a groundless panic upon the largest and best-appointed host, and cause them to flee away and disappear 'like the chaff of the summer threshing-floor.' He can make two men, like Jonathan and his armour-bearer, victorious over a multitude. A thousand shall flee at the rebuke of one, if God so wills it. Panic he can cause in a hundred ways. It is only necessary that in the darkness a wind should blow, or that water should splash in free course, or that an echo should resound from the mountains, or that the wind should rustle the dry leaves, to terrify the godless, so that they flee as if pursued by a sword, and fall though no one pursues them." (Pulpit Commentary.)

Those who have sought to destroy the authority of the Bible by asserting that errors are found in it, once pointed to the statement that the Syrians suspected that the king of Israel had hired against them the kings of the Hittites. It was triumphantly assered that no such nation as the Hittites existed at that time. "But the Assyrian records of the ninth and eighth centuries before Christ, make it evident that not only did the Hittite nation then exist, but that they were among the most powerful enemies of the Ninevite kings. It is also evident that they did not form a centralized monarchy, but were governed by a number of chiefs or kings." (G. Smith.)

The expression "kings of the Egyptians" has also been pointed to as an error, upon the supposition that Egypt was under the rule of one sovereign. "But Egyptian history shows us that about this time Egypt was becoming disintegrated, and that two or three distinct dynasties were sometimes ruling at the same time in different parts of the country." One by one the arguments against the inerrancy of the Bible have been refuted by the light of history and science, and the facts of human experience.

Wholly forgetful, it would seem, in the excitement of the hour, of what the Prophet had said to him but the day before; failing to perceive a fulfillment, in part, of the Prophet's words, in the now established fact that the Syrians had fled, leaving behind them vast stores of all that could minister to the material needs of his starving subjects; and equally oblivious of the fact that part of the prediction yet remained to be fulfilled, "The king appointed the lord, on whose hand he leaned, to have charge of the gate." Thoughtless of the words which the Prophet had uttered concerning him, and which should have rung in his ears as a solemn call to repentance, the proud courtier accepted the position assigned to him, doubtless highly gratified with the honor shown him.

"If we had been asked, how it would be possible most effectually to traverse the designs of the Almighty respecting this unbeliever, and to counteract the fulfillment of the prophecy, we should, perhaps, have selected the very means for its ovrthrow, which God appointed for its fulfillment. We should have said, Place the unbeliever at the gate, his rank and office will secure respect, and he shall not only see, but he shall partake of the very first load of provisions which arrives. The Almighty also says, Place him at the gate, where he shall see the plenty in which he disbelieved, but no grain of which shall ever pass his lips." (Blunt.)

It was probably while attempting to preserve order and to exact the king's tribute from those who bore the spoils of the Syrian camp into the city, that this lord was caught between the out-going and the in-coming tide of humanity and, borne down in the press, was trampled to death. Was this an accident? So we, perhaps, would have pronounced. But mark the words of the sacred historian, "And he died, as the man of God had said." To emphasize the truth of this statement, and thus impress it more firmly upon the mind of the reader, the

Prophet's prediction and the account of the circumstances which led to its utterance are repeated. "And it came to pass as the man of God had spoken to the king, saying, Two measures of barley for a shekel, and a measure of fine flour for a shekel, shall be to-morrow about this time in the gate of Samaria: and the lord answered the man of God, and said, Now, behold, if the Lord should make windows in heaven, might such a thing be? And he said, behold, thou shalt see it with thine eyes, but shall not eat thereof. And so it fell out unto him: for the people trod upon him in the gate, and he died."

How comprehensive is the providence of God! Every event of our lives, even to the most minute and unimportant, falls out according to the purpose of him without whose knowledge not even a sparrow falleth to the ground. The incidents we have just been considering furnish a striking illustration of the certainty with which God's gracious promises and righteous threatenings shall be fulfilled. Men may doubt, and scoff, and oppose, but God's word abideth. As he hath said, so shall it fall out for good or evil, blessing or judgment to the sons of men. For, "God is not a man, that he should lie; neither the son of man that he should repent: hath he said, and shall he not do it, or hath he spoken, and shall he not make it good?"

## CHAPTER XXV.

### ELISHA'S INTERVIEW WITH HAZAEL.

"But what will not ambition and revenge
Descend to! who aspires must down as low
As high he soar'd; obnoxious first or last
To basest things." (Milton.)

"How like a mountain devil in the heart
Rules this unreined ambition! Let it once
But play the monarch, and its haughty brow
Glows with a beauty that bewilders thought
And unthrones peace forever. Putting on
The very pomp of Lucifer, it turns
The heart to ashes, and with not a spring
Left in the desert for the spirit's lip,
We look upon our splendor, and forget
The thirst of which we perish." (Willis.)

The Bible is not a history, save in so far as the record of events serves to illustrate God's dealings with individual men, and with nations. Accordingly we find that the inspired writers omit many details which would be of interest from a historical point of view. The inspired record of Elisha's visit to Damascus illustrates this characteristic. "And Elisha came to Damascus." This statement seems to have no connection with that which precedes it, and no word of explanation follows. For what purpose did the Prophet make this visit? By whom was the fact of his presence in Damascus, or in its vicinity, communicated to the king of Syria? It would be gratifying to find in the record an answer to these questions, and others which occur to the mind as the record before us is studied, but this is denied us.

Whatever may have been the Prophet's errand, we may be sure that he went to Damascus because he was Divinely directed to do so. It was not a vacation or pleasure trip. God sent him on some special errand. Most Bible-students, perhaps, have associated this visit of Elisha to the Syrian capital, with the command given to Elijah at Horeb, to anoint Hazael to be king over Syria, Jehu to be king of Israel, and Elisha to be prophet in his room. To this view it is objected that Elijah was not authorized to delegate his successor to execute any part of this commission; that there is no intimation of his having done so; neither does it appear that Elisha did anoint Hazael.

All this may be true, the record shows nothing to the contrary, yet we read that Elisha sent "one of the children of the prophets" to anoint Jehu king over Israel, which clearly indicates that Elijah had not personally executed the command given him so far, at least, as it concerned Jehu, but had devolved it upon Elisha, who, in turn, had commissioned another to act for him in the matter. If this was true in the case of Jehu, it is not improbable that it was true in the case of Hazael. That Elisha's mission to Damascus at this time had to do with the throne of Syria, seems evident from the fact that, aside from the delivery of this message to Hazael, he performed no other service in Damascus, so far the narrative shows.

Elisha could not have been insensible to the danger attending this journey to Damascus. Not many years had passed since the king, who still reigned over Syria, had sent an army to make him a prisoner or to destroy him because he had baffled him in his designs against the king of Israel. So far as is shown, Elisha had no reason to expect that the attitude of the Syrian king was any more friendly toward him at this time than it had been in the past, yet he seems to have felt no fear. No effort was made by him to conceal his movements.

At the time of Elisha's visit to Damascus, Ben-hadad, the implacable enemy of Israel, the haughty and redoubtable king of Syria, was prostrated by a malignant disease, perhaps a fever of some sort. "And it was told him, saying, The man of God is come hither." The high esteem in which Elisha was now held in the heathen land of Syria is worthy of note. So great was the importance attached to his visit that the king must be informed of it, and in terms, too, which recognize the holiness of his character, as well as the sacredness of his office. "The man of God is come."

Not in any city of Israel, so far as we have record, was Elisha accorded such recognition. No sooner was the king thus informed than he "said unto Hazael, Take a present in thine hand, and go, meet the man of God, and enquire of the Lord by him, saying, Shall I recover of this disease?" It would seem that the king was convinced that his sickness was of a serious character, that his recovery was doubtful, hence this anxious inquiry.

Our anxiety concerning our spiritual condition and our solicitude for salvation, will be in proportion to our consciousness of danger. It is when the sinner is convinced of his sin, and consequent danger, that he is led to cry, "What must I do to be saved?"

There is, perhaps, an implied prayer to be healed, in this question which Ben-hadad addressed to Elisha. He remembered now, it may be, the marvelous cure of Naaman, and, with the hope that as much might be done for him, he thus greeted Elisha. In many instances sickness produces the most salutary effect in those upon whom it is sent. If our thoughts are ever serious, if our spirits are ever humbled, it is when we are prostrated by a serious sickness. Mr. Spurgeon was wont to say, "Sickness is the best doctor of Divinity in the world." Men may forget God, and forsake him, when they are in health, but when sickness and trouble come upon them, they will remember him, and seek his help. At such times the thoughts of the careless and godless may undergo a radical change.

The proud, imperious Ben-hadad had all his lifetime been the enemy of God. He had warred against the people whose God was Jehovah; he had plotted against the Prophet who spoke and acted in the name of Jehovah; but now, when laid upon a bed of sickness, he is told that "the man of God is come," he sends his trusted officer to inquire humbly as to whether he shall recover. It is to be feared that he was concerned about his physical condition only. "Strange that it should be so strong a feature in the human mind, to desire to be informed of that which would profit us little if known, and be indifferent to the only knowledge which 'is life eternal!' Lord, wilt thou at this time restore the kingdom of Israel? Lord, are there few that be saved? were questions from which even the apostles themselves could not refrain. How many at all times would like to indulge in similar inquiries! How few who desire to ask with the same sincerity and earnestness, Lord what shall I do to be saved? And yet the most explicit answer to the former could only gratify a fruitless curiosity; while upon the latter an eternity, yes, absolutely an eternity, of weal or woe depends." (Blunt.)

Ben-hadad was anxious to receive a favorable response from "the man of God," hence he sent a valuable present by the hand of Hazael, "even of every good thing of Damascus, forty camels' burden." "A camel-load is reckoned at from five hundred to eight hundred pounds, but it would be wrong to reckon the weight of these gifts accordingly at twenty thousand to thirty-two thousand pounds." (Dereser.)

"It is not to be understood that each camel was burdened with as much as it could carry; for it is and always has been usual in the East, especially in gifts to or from kings, to render honor both to the giver and the receiver by distributing the articles among a number of human or animal bearers, greatly disproportionate to what they are able to carry, ten or more men, camels, or horses being employed to carry what would be but a light burden for one. It is a piece of state; and as such has a parallel in the state custom among ourselves of six or eight strong horses being employed to draw carriages which one or two might pull with ease." (Kitto.)

Making proper allowance, however, for Oriental display in the conveying of this present to Elisha, we must conclude that it was of great value. Perhaps Ben-hadad hoped that by the munificence of his gifts the Prophet might be induced to exert his miraculous powers in his behalf. But money cannot purchase the favor of God. Doubtless, as upon a former occasion, Elisha refused to accept the present sent him. This seems the more probable, in view of the fact that he had no favor to bestow in return. There is food for meditation in the contrast between the conduct of Ahaziah, king of Israel, and of Ben-hadad, king of Syria, in circumstances somewhat similar. The former, when injured by a fall, forgetting the living and true God, "sent messengers, and said unto them, Go, and enquire of Baal-zebub, the god of Ekron, whether I shall recover of this disease." While the latter, though a worshiper of Rimmon, sends his servant with the same inquiry to the Lord's Prophet.

It is a sad thing, and yet it is sometimes true, that the conduct of professing Christians compares unfavorably with the conduct of the careless and unbelieving; that the man who is a member of the church is less honest and truthful, less worthy of confidence and favorable esteem, than his neighbor who claims to have no religious convictions. Elisha was not of those who bring reproach upon the truth. Even in Damascus he was known as "the man of God." Oh, to live in such directness of confession and consistency of conduct as to be every where known by a similar designation!

"Let us ask ourselves: What is most marked about us? Of what will men in their daily intercourse with us, have most occasion to take notice, as constantly appearing in our dealings with them, in all circumstances, and at all times? However much we may seek to shut our minds against the fact, mostly all of us carry the great characteristics of our history quite on the outside, intelligible to all who have knowledge of such matters, just like those great mansions all shrouded in silence that hang out the armorial bearings of their dead. By what will we be chiefly known and remembered in this generation and in the next, in this world and the other? Will it be as inheriting all the beatitudes, as good and holy men who love and do the work of God?" (Edersheim.)

How humble the tone of Ben-hadad's message to Elisha! "Thy son, Ben-hadad, king of Syria, hath sent me to thee, saying, Shall I recover of this disease?" There is here none of the insolence of conscious strength; no half-implied command such as characterized the message sent by Naaman to the king of Israel but a few years before. The mighty monarch who, after the fashion of the rulers of his day, had doubtless held human life in light esteem; who, in the wars which he had waged, had ruthlessly caused the death of thousands of his fellow-beings to whom life was as dear as it was to himself, now indirectly entreats the Prophet, and by a present seeks to bribe him, to stay the hand of death in his case. Anxiously he must have awaited the return of his servant with the Prophet's answer to his inquiry.

Well had it been for Ben-hadad had he been as fully sensible of the soul disease from which he suffered, as he was of his bodily disease! Well had it been for him, had he been as anxious to be healed spiritually as he was to be healed physically! Would that men to-day were as solicitous for the welfare of their souls as they are for the welfare of their bodies!

In all probability, "the serious thoughts and the anxious applications of the king of Syria had really little influence upon his general character. In time of trouble he asked for help when he thought he could secure it, but he had no more true drawing to Elisha's principles at one time than another. And men may live all their lives, convinced that they need the blessing which religion alone can bestow, and sometimes half-persuaded to seek for the offered mercies of the gospel, and yet they may pass through the world and die at last as truly separated from the people of God as the king of Syria was separated from the kingdom of Israel with which he so often warred." (Lowrie.)

Hazael, the bearer of Ben-hadad's message, is first mentioned in connection with the commission given to Elijah at Horeb to anoint him to be king over Syria. It is probable that even at that time he was one of the chief men at the Syrian court. The supposition is that Naaman, a short time after he had been healed of his leprosy, had been degraded, if not dismissed from the king's service, because of his friendly feeling toward Israel, and his persistence in worshiping Jehovah only; and that Hazael had succeeded him as general-in-chief of the army. Whether this supposition be correct or not, Hazael seems at this time to have occupied a position near to the throne. The sequel shows him to have been a bold, ambitious, cruel, and thoroughly unscrupulous man; incapable of gratitude, fertile in resources, treacherous in the highest degree, and pitiless as death. "Altogether, Hazael is perhaps one of the most repulsive characters presented in Scripture." (Edersheim.)

Our Lord said, "A man's foes shall be they of his own household." So it proved in the case of Ben-hadad. The one person who, above all others, perhaps, he had admitted into closest friendship; in whose integrity he reposed the greatest degree of confidence; and upon whom he had bestowed the highest honors, was, even at the moment when he undertook his last and most important service, audaciously planning to assassinate him. How many have been dragged down to ruin, and to eternal death by the companions with which they have surrounded themselves! Many an one has said, as Shakespeare makes Falstaff say:

"Company, villainous company, hath been the spoil of me."

Elisha's reply to the inquiry of Ben-hadad has been characterized as enigmatic, "Go, say unto him, Thou mayest certainly recover," living thou shalt live, "howbeit the Lord hath showed me that he shall surely die." The Prophet, however, was propounding no riddle in speaking thus. He simply announced that the disease with which the king was afflicted was not mortal, that it would not result in his death. This was all that was required to answer the inquiry, "Shall I recover of this disease?" Elisha was not asked to give information, save with reference to this particular matter. He was not commissioned to apprize the king of his danger, besides it would have been useless to have attempted to do so by the man who had already resolved upon the king's death, and through whom only, perhaps, he could have communicated with the king who had unwittingly surrounded himself with those who made the attainment of his dearest object impossible.

The added statement, "howbeit the Lord hath showed me that he shall surely die," was addressed to Hazael, and constituted no part of the Prophet's answer to the inquiry of Ben-hadad. The purpose of Elisha in this seems to have been simply to make known to Hazael that his dark designs were not hidden from the eye of God. Ben-hadad was to die, not of the disease which preyed upon him, but by the hand of the assassin who, in mock humility, then stood before the Prophet. As "the man of God" uttered these words, he fixed his searching gaze upon the "bold, bad man," and kept it there until the blush of shame covered the face of the murderer at heart, and his countenance fell.

As with a prophet's vision, Elisha beheld the people of Israel rushing on to an awful doom, and saw in the man who stood before him the terrible scourge which God had provided wherewith to punish the sins of his people, he burst into tears. "And the man of God wept." Nor does he attempt to conceal from Hazael the cause of his tears. "And Hazael said, Why weepeth my lord? and he answered, Because I know the evil that thou wilt do unto the children of Israel."

The atrocities which the Prophet foresaw Hazael should be guilty of were simply such as have characterized Oriental warfare, both in ancient and comparatively modern times. The traitorous courtier affected to be greatly surprised by the recital of the bloody deeds of which he should be guilty, and in feigned humility exclaimed, "But what, is thy servant a dog, that he should do this great thing?" or, as it is in the revised version, "But what is thy servant, which is but a dog, that he should do this great thing?"

His brutal character is illustrated by the fact that he was not horrified, as some have supposed, by the assurance that he should thus revel in deeds of fiendish wickedness. In his estimation, such deeds as the Prophet foretold in tears were "great things," worthy the highest ambition. He does not even pretend to be shocked by the intimation that he shall become such a monster, but rather to question the possibility of his being able to win such renown. The question with him was not whether it would be right for him to do such things, but "how could a person of comparatively low condition like himself have such high influence upon the fate of nations?" (Kitto.)

"And Elisha answered, the Lord hath showed me that thou shalt be king over Syria." This we may believe was not spoken as a revelation to Hazael of what was to be, but rather as a more distinct intimation than had yet been given him, that his murderous designs had been revealed to the Prophet. Thus ended the interview between these two remarkable persons, as different in character as light is different from darkness. Never did they meet again in time, but they shall yet meet again, for all nations must stand before the judgment throne of God, that every man "may receive the things done in his body, according to that he hath done, whether it be good or bad." In that day an eternal separation shall be decreed between Elisha and Hazael as wide as the East is distant from the West.

Departing from Elisha, Hazael "came to his master; who said to him, What said Elisha to thee? And he answered, He told me that thou shouldest surely recover." This was but part of what Elisha had said. The other part, Hazael withheld; not through a kind desire to spare the king the pain and disappointment which such unwelcome news would naturally occasion, but because his murderous designs seemed to require it.

We sometimes, with well-meant but mistaken kindness, practice deception upon our loved ones when they are sick. We seek to conceal from them the seriousness of their condition, flatter them, it may be, with the assurance that their recovery is certain and will be speedy, whereas we know that such cannot be the case.

Reprehensible as is such a course, Hazael is not to be credited with even so much as this. No doubt it would have been gratifying to him to have been told by the Prophet that the king's sickness was mortal; but when told that he should certainly recover, he probably at once resolved upon his destruction. That he might be the more certain to succeed in this purpose, it was necessary that the king should be kept in darkness concerning his danger. To have told him all that the Prophet said, would doubtless have aroused his suspicion and have led him to adopt such measures to insure his safety, as would have proved fatal to the designs of the would-be regicide.

Hazael's plan was to produce in the mind of his intended victim a feeling of security, to lull him to rest. "How often does Satan, even at the present hour, practice precisely the same cunning and destructive stratagem. Is the sick man terrified at the thought of approaching dissolution? Satan fears lest this be followed by a heartfelt cry to God for mercy, a strong, deep feeling of repentance; and, like Hazael with Ben-hadad, he whispers in his ear, Thou shalt certainly recover. This sickness is not unto death. Be not alarmed, all will yet be well. Is the sinner partially awakened to a sense of his own dreadful situation? Does he see the opening gulf which his sins have prepared for him? Does he fear the justly awakened anger of God which he has so long despised? The same false and deluding comfort is presented to assuage his fears, and to calm his apprehensions. Thou shalt not surely die, for God doth know that thou art not so bad as thousands around you; dismiss, therefore, thy fears, eat, drink, and be merry. Beware of the tempter, under what form soever he presents himself, but fear him most of all when he counterfeits the Comforter when, disguised as an angel of light, he would carry peace and consolation to your heart." (Blunt.)

The fears of Ben-hadad were allayed by the false report submitted to him. Doubtless he commended and rewarded the supposed fidelity of him who had secured such a favorable response from the Prophet; and, beguiled by the assurance of a speedy recovery, he rested in conscious security. "And it came to pass on the morrow, that he took a thick cloth, and dipped it in water, and spread it on his face, so that he died: and Hazael reigned in his stead."

There is an ambiguity in the Hebrew text which has led some commentators to attempt to exonerate Hazael from the charge of murdering his master. Ewald, without assigning a reason, chooses to lay the guilt of the king's destruction upon an unnamed servant who attended him in the bath; and who, without any assigned or conceivable motive, smothered the king with a bathing-blanket. Others insist that, so far as the text shows, the king may have put the wet macber, the coverlet as in the revised version, on his own face for refreshment, and accidentally suffocated himself, surely a very improbable happening. Still another interpretation is that the king designedly destroyed his own life, a supposition difficult to reconcile with his having sent, but the day before, to inquire of the Prophet if he might recover of his disease. "As Hazael is the subject of departed, and came, and answered, in verse 14, so it is the natural subject of took, and dipped, and spread in verse 15." (Pulpit Commentary.)

The whole course of the story, coupled with the obvious ambition of Hazael to be king, an ambition which was doubtless inflamed by the Prophet's prediction that it should be realized; the motive which he would thus have for a crime so bold and cruel; the fact that he seems to have been the king's closest attendant, and was the greatest and only gainer by his death; and the cruel and bloodthirsty character which he afterwards displayed, doubtless warrant the verdict of all subsequent ages which fixes upon him the murder of one who was at once his benefactor and sovereign. Hazael reigned according to the word of the Prophet. The Divine purpose concerning him was fulfilled, but God did not sanction the method by which he reached the throne. Even though he had been anointed king of Syria, as he probably was, it gave him no warrant to commit so foul a crime. The assurance given him that he should be king, should have induced him to rest contented until God, in his own time and way, should have fulfilled the promise.

How striking the contrast, in circumstances somewhat similar, between the conduct of Hazael and that of David who, though he had been anointed king of Israel and solemnly assured that the throne should be his, yet refused to touch the Lord's anointed, though God had seemed to place it in his power to destroy Saul who had grievously wronged him, and had sought to take away his life. "It was David's joy as well as his honor that he waited the movements of Divine providence. He found no cause of sorrow, when the throne was reached at last, that he had no evil agency in Saul's casting down." (Lowrie.)

If Hazael had come to the throne free from the consciousness of guilt, his life would have been happier, and his reign more beneficent. "He might have held his subjects by such bonds of allegiance and authority as would allow him to choose his own policy. But the wrong of the commencement placed him in a false position, and forced him, perhaps, to new crimes to maintain his power. If he had accomplices, they must be kept quiet; possibly his safety lay in giving the people something to do in a new war with Israel." (Lowrie.)

However this may have been, Hazael visited upon Israel all the atrocities which Elisha had foretold of him. In the tenth chapter we read, "In those days the Lord began to cut Israel short: and Hazael smote them in all the coasts of Israel; from Jordan eastward." Again in the thirteenth chapter these statements occur, "And the anger of the Lord was kindled against Israel, and he delivered them into the hand of Hazael, king of Syria." "For the king of Syria had destroyed them, and had made them like the dust by threshing." "But Hazael, king of Syria, oppressed Israel all the days of Jehoahaz."

After a reign of perhaps more than fifty years, much of which time he was engaged in war, offensive and defensive, sometimes suffering defeat, more frequently victorious, Hazael, the murderer, the usurper, the destroyer of homes, the plunderer of cities, the devastator of provinces, was called to put off the crown, to lay aside the scepter that he might meet at the judgment bar of God the multitudes of his victims who had preceded him there. "So Hazael, king of Syria, died; and his son Ben-hadad reigned in his stead."

## CHAPTER XXVI.

### JEHU ANOINTED.

"Though the mills of God grind slowly, yet they grind exceeding small;
Though with patience he stands waiting, with exactness grinds he all." (Longfellow.)

JOHN concludes his history "of all that Jesus began both to do and teach," with these words, "There are also many others things which Jesus did, the which if they should be written every one, I suppose that even the world itself would not contain the books that should be written." Although so large a space is devoted to the record of the events and acts of the life of Elisha, it is doubtless true that we have but an epitome of all that the Lord did by him and for him. The events in connection with which Elisha's name is mentioned must have been embraced within a period not exceeding twenty-five years; yet his ministry, counting from his call to the prophetic office, must have exceeded sixty-five years. There are, therefore, at least forty years of his active life of which we have no record.

It cannot be supposed that the Prophet was idle during this long period; that these years brought neither joy nor sorrow, disappointment nor victory. Then, as now, there was need to battle continually against the forces of wickedness, and Elisha was not a man who would consent to a truce so long as duty called him to contend against the foe. As a true and faithful servant of God, he stood bravely at the post assigned him, until called to rest and to glory. Considered in its relation to the history of Israel, the narrative contained in the record we now consider is of great importance. In connection with a study of the life of Elisha, it is specially interesting, in view of the fact that it is the last record of official act on his part.

"And Elisha the Prophet called one of the children of the prophets, and said unto him, Gird up thy loins, and take this box of oil in thine hand, and go to Ramoth-gilead: and when thou comest thither, look thee out Jehu the son of Jehoshaphat the son of Nimshi, and go in, and make him arise up from among his brethren, and carry him into an inner chamber; then take the box of oil, and pour it on his head, and say, Thus saith the Lord, I have anointed thee king over Israel. Then open the door, and flee, and tarry not."

Who this messenger was, we do not know. He is simply spoken of as "one of the children of the prophets," by which we are to understand, doubtless, that he was a student in one of the schools of the prophets. There is a tradition, to which some Jewish writers refer, which identifies him as the Prophet Jonah, but there seems to be no foundation in fact for such a tradition. While the name of this messenger has been withheld, what he did will be spoken of to the end of time. "He was an obscure person, yet he set in motion a train of events of the most tragic significance." (Dr. Orr.)

"He was one of the humblest in Samaria; yet he carried a kingdom to Ramoth." (Krummacher.)

Hazael, now seated upon the throne of Syria, already

gave promise of fulfilling the prediction of Elisha concerning him. He had already shown himself to be a warrior prince, and his ambitious designs had brought him in conflict with Israel. A great battle had just been fought under the walls of Ramoth-gilead. It would seem that victory finally inclined to the side of Israel, but not until king Joram had been wounded. Leaving his victorious army to the command of Jehu, who probably outranked his fellow-captains, the king had gone back to Jezreel to be healed of his wound. It was during the absence of the king from the army, that Elisha commissioned this child of the prophets to anoint Jehu to be king of Israel.

Twenty years, at least, previous to the sending forth of this messenger, Elijah, as he lodged in the cave at Horeb, had received a command from the Lord to anoint Hazael to be king over Syria, Jehu to be king over Israel, and Elisha to be prophet in his stead. This command he seems to have obeyed in person no further than it related to Elisha, upon whom, as his successor in the prophetic office, was laid the duty of executing its remaining provisions. God's purposes may seem to be long delayed at times, yet they shall not fail of fulfillment. God says, "My counsel shall stand, and I will do all my pleasure." "I have spoken it, I will also bring it to pass; I have purposed it, I will also do it."

"Why did not Elisha go in person to anoint Jehu as he seems to have done in the case of Hazael? It has been suggested that "He was no longer able in person to undertake the journey to Ramoth-gilead, but deputed a younger and more able representative to achieve the high and important enterprise." (Blunt.)

But Elisha lived for almost fifty years after this event, consequently he could not have been old and decrepit at this time. A better explanation of the Prophet's conduct is that this method was chosen in order to avoid publicity. "It was important that no man should know the errand of the messenger; that the reigning family should be taken wholly by surprise, so that the shedding of innocent blood might be prevented. Elisha was too well known in Israel to allow that he should journey toward the camp from which the king was absent. Immediate conjecture would spread abroad of the Prophet's designs, and the words of Elijah were too well remembered to make the interpretation of Elisha's visit favorable to the present king." (Lowrie.)

A messenger whose character and errand would be unsuspected was therefore sent. It is interesting to note the directions which Elisha gave to this messenger. When General Wayne submitted to General Washington his plan for a certain important movement of the forces under his command, Washington, observing that no line of retreat had been indicated, inquired what provision had been made in case a retreat should become necessary. To this the intrepid Wayne replied that he did not consider retreat as among the possibilities. Elisha makes no provision in his instructions to his messenger for delay or failure. A certain work is to be done in the name of the Lord, and he expects that this young man will proceed with it, leaving it to God to take care of contingencies and to remove obstacles which may be encountered. He is directed to prepare himself for action. "Gird up thy loins." There is a preparation to be made for God's service, a getting ready for action.

The messenger was further directed to take with him a certain box or flask of oil, doubtless the holy anointing oil of the sanctuary, and, thus equipped, he was to go to Ramoth-gilead, and there seek out Jehu, who was probably known to him, and having conducted him into an inner chamber, he was to pour the oil on his head, and in this manner anoint him to be king. The design of the injunction to conduct Jehu into an inner chamber was doubtless to prevent any information of the transaction from reaching the ear of the king at Jezreel; to insure the personal safety of the messenger; and to prevent any interference with him in the performance of the duty with which he was charged. Not only is this messenger given direction as to what he is to do, but the very words which he is to speak are communicated to him.

God's servants are thoroughly furnished for every service which he requires at their hands. If they fail or in any way come short of duty, the fault is not with God. Though engaged in a great warfare, the Christian is not at his own charges. He is not left to his own resources to devise ways and means of serving God. Called upon to enthrone Jesus, the Son of God, as Lord and King in his own heart, to honor him in all his ways, to advance the interests of his kingdom in the world, he is given explicit directions as to how he shall act and what he shall speak. "All scripture is given by inspiration of God, and is profitable for doctrine, for reproof, for correction, for instruction in righteousness: that the man of God may be perfect, thoroughly furnished unto all good works."

To the Prophet Jonah, God said, as he called him a

second time to go to Nineveh, "Preach unto it the preaching that I bid thee." As the servant of Jesus the Christ, we have a definite message to deliver to the world. The words we are to speak have been put into our mouths. "As ye go, preach, saying, The kingdom of heaven is at hand." "Go ye into all the world, and preach the gospel." "Preach the word."

"Go, preach my gospel! saith the Lord;
Bid the whole earth my grace receive;
He shall be saved that trusts my word;
He shall be lost that won't believe.

Teach all the nations my commands;
I'm with you till the world shall end;
All power is trusted to my hands,
I can destroy, and I defend."

Having anointed Jehu, the prophet messenger was to charge him with the execution of God's purpose concerning the house of Ahab, then open the door and flee. Though the duty with which this young man was charged must have seemed to him profoundly solemn and extremely perilous, yet he hesitated not to obey the Prophet's direction. "He accepts the subordinate position assigned him readily and cheerfully. He is content to obliterate himself, and to play the part of a tool or instrument." (Pulpit Commentary.)

How commendable is such a spirit! To be willing to serve God whenever called, and wherever called, is to have in us the "mind which was also in Christ Jesus." "Who being in the form of God, thought it not robbery to be equal with God: but made himself of no reputation. and took upon him the form of a servant, and was made in the likeness of men." O that all who profess to love and to serve Christ had in them that spirit which would make them willing to be lost sight of, to become as nothing, that he might be all and in all.

Receiving the Prophet's instructions without questioning, this messenger obeyed them to the minutest detail. While he was careful to do all that he was directed to do, he was equally careful not to transcend his instructions in any particular. He did not feel himself competent to improve upon the Prophet's plan. Sometimes we fall into the error of attempting to improve upon God's methods of doing things. Sometimes we are guilty of attempting to supplement by our own righteousness, the perfect righteousness of Christ. Sometimes we read into the word of God that which it was never designed to teach. Overstepping the limit of that which God requires of us may prove, in certain circumstances, to be as dishonoring to him as the act of wilfull disobedience. To each of us, as the follower of Christ, a message to our fellow-men has been committed. To those who hear it, this message must prove a savor of life unto life, or of death unto death. How important that we should be faithful in its transmission! The Master whose we are and whom we serve, expects us to be faithful. The vast interests involved, even the eternal destiny of immortal souls, demand that we be faithful.

Having performed his duty, the Prophet's messenger opened the door and fled, as he had been directed. There comes to our mind, by way of contrast, the strange story of the man of God who came from Judah by word of the Lord to cry against the altar of Bethel. Forbidden to eat bread or to drink water in that once sacred city, he was induced to disregard the Divine injunction, and was slain by a lion. What the consequences might have been had the messenger tarried in Ramoth-gilead, instead of hastening away, we can but conjecture. Had his flight been less precipitate, he would doubtless have been detained by the order of Jehu to let none go forth nor escape out of the city. Not only was his personal freedom, and, perhaps, his personal safety insured by his flight, but the cause of true religion was saved from the dishonor, which might otherwise have been put upon it, of being made to appear to lend its sanction to the treacherous and cruel conduct of Jehu, who might have sought to "make use of him as he made use of Jehonadab, by putting him in the chariot beside him.

"Of all dangers to which religion can be exposed, one of the greatest is that it be made subservient to worldly purposes. This will be attempted both in private and in public. Even Jehu will endeavor to have a prophet in his chariot. Worldly men will try to make use of our religion for promoting their own objects." (Edersheim.)

Let us as Christian men and women seek to avoid the entanglements of the world. Let us, as we are exhorted, "Abstain from all appearance of evil." We should not fail to note the fact, indicated in this record, that God claims the right to make and to unmake kings.

The Prophet's messenger was authorized to say to Jehu, "Thus saith the Lord, I have anointed thee king over Israel." So far as we know, Jehu was the first king anointed over the ten tribes by Divine appointment. Under the name of wisdom, God says, "By me kings reign, and princes decree justice. By me princes rule, and nobles, even all the judges of the earth." In Daniel these words occur, "He removeth kings, and setteth up kings." "Jehu was made king by the authority of God, who had taken the kingdom from the house of Ahab, and had given it to him. At the same time, "we are to distinguish between the motives which actuated Jehu in his conspiracy against Joram, and the providential purpose which, as God's instrument, he was raised up to fulfill." (Pulpit Commentary.)

In establishing himself upon the throne of Israel, Jehu received no impulse from without, but acted in accordance with his own treacherous and cruel nature. Yet in so acting he fulfilled the Divine purpose concerning the wicked house of Ahab. "Jehu is expressly ordered by God to smite, i. e., destroy utterly, the whole house of Ahab. This command he carried out; and his obedience to it obtained for him the temporal reward that his children to the fourth generation should sit on the throne of Israel. Yet still his conduct in destroying the house of Ahab is spoken of by the Prophet Hosea as a sin, and God declares by Hosea's mouth, that he will avenge the blood of Jezreel upon the house of Jehu.

It is naturally asked, How could Jehu's shedding this blood, at God's command and in fulfillment of his will, be a sin? And it is rightly answered, Because, if we do the will of God for any end of our own, for anything except God, we do in fact our own will, not God's. It is not lawful for Jehu to depose and slay the king his master, except at the express command of God. For any other end, and done otherwise than at God's express command, such an act is sin." (Pulpit Commentary.) "God rules in the army of heaven and among the inhabitants of the earth," and "he maketh the wrath of man to praise him," yet this fact does not justify wickedness on man's part. Do we as citizens of this nation realize that our rulers are Divinely appointed? that whether our political views prevail or not in our elections; that although unscrupulous men may scheme and plot, and in their base selfishness and dishonesty may perpetrate all sorts of fraud, nevertheless the Divine purpose concerning us as a nation is accomplished? Observe the Divine law of retribution as illustrated in the destruction visited upon the house of Ahab. That we may better do so, it is necessary to recall some of the deeds of wickedness perpetrated during the reign of this family. Although idolatry had been fastened upon Israel by the action of Jeroboam in setting up the golden calves in Bethel and Dan, a fresh impetus was given to idolatrous zeal in the introduction of Baal worship by the house of Ahab, the slaying of the prophets of the Lord, and the throwing down of his altars. Notable among their acts of cruelty and injustice, was the murder of Naboth and the confiscation of his vineyard. Twenty years previous to the events, the record of which we now consider, as Ahab went to take possession of the murdered Naboth's estate, Elijah had confronted him, and had declared to him the judgment which should come upon him and upon his still more wicked consort. "In the place where dogs licked the blood of Naboth shall dogs lick thy blood, even thine." "The dogs shall eat Jezebel by the wall of Jezreel." The record is that "when Ahab heard these words, that he rent his clothes, and put sackcloth upon his flesh, and fasted, and lay in sackcloth, and went softly." And God said to Elijah, "Seest thou how Ahab humbleth himself before me? because he humbleth himself before me, I will not bring the evil in his days; but in his son's days will I bring the evil upon his house." Never was a prophetic prediction more accurately and fearfully fulfilled. Punishment is sure to follow sin. It may be delayed, but it cannot be averted. Four hundred years passed before the sin of Amalek against Israel received punishment. For twenty years the sin of Ahab against Naboth had been permitted to go unpunished, but the day of reckoning came at last, and the sentence which God had pronounced was fully executed. "And can you doubt but that God, who if we may so express it, so studiously, so carefully provided for the fulfillment of his own word as regards these threatenings and these individuals, will not as certainly ensure the accomplishment of every threatening and against every individual? I know not a more fearful or a more painful thought, than the inevitable certainty of God's predicted judgments. If the impenitent sinner could only read the records of days gone by; if the man who has never yet fled to the Rock that is higher than we, and sought pardon from an offended God through the blood of Jesus, would only observe the manner in which every threatened evil that God has spoken, has infallibly come to pass, he would not be able to rest in his bed this night, until he had sought and found a Savior." (Blunt.) As we have seen, God had decreed the place in which his righteous judgment should be inflicted upon the house of Ahab. "In the place where dogs licked the blood of Naboth shall dogs lick thy blood, even thine." And so it fell out. "Joram himself gave the order to make ready, in order, without knowing or wishing it, to ride out to the place where Naboth's blood was crying for vengeance, and where ruin was prepared for him." (Berleb Bible.) It was so ordered that he met Jehu and was by him shot to death, "in the portion of Naboth the Jezreelite." The prediction concerning the wicked Jezebel, "The dogs shall eat Jezebel by the wall of Jezreel," was not less signally fulfilled. Thrown from her window, she was trodden under foot, and afterwards devoured by ravenous dogs. There is some times a correspondence between the manner in which a sin is committed, and the manner of its punishment. Jacob deceived his father Isaac, and is in turn cruelly deceived, and imposed upon, by his own sons. The treachery of Jezebel had caused the death of Naboth, but treachery finally overtook and destroyed both her and her house.

Let us learn from this narrative how terrible a thing it is to have God as our enemy. Well has the Apostle said, "It is a fearful thing to fall into the hands of the living God." We may thwart the designs of human enemies against us; we may by flight or concealment escape the hands of human justice, if we have committed a crime; but we cannot escape from God. Having decreed the extermination of the house of Ahab, God so ordered it that "swiftly and unconsciously to themselves, all the actors in the last scene were brought to their places." "If the king of Judah had remained at home, it is probable that Jehu would not have molested him. But his coming to Jezreel was providentially ordered that, as he was of the kindred of Ahab and shared his crimes, he might partake of the judgments denounced upon that house. Again it was the ordering of Providence that Jehu met and destroyed the forty and two brethren of the king of Judah at the shearing house." Sin unrepented of, must be punished in the person of the sinner. May God give us that repentance for sin which needeth not to be repented of; that faith which seeks and finds purification from sin in the cleansing blood of the Son of God.

"There's many a cross in the way we go,
And we may not choose but take it,
Yet evermore holdeth this truth the same:
That our life is what we make it.

Still into our hands come the somber threads
And bright ones,—the gift of heaven—
But what we weave is the pattern we choose
To make from the threads that are given."
(Kate W. Hamilton.)

## CHAPTER XXVII.

### ENTERING INTO REST.

"How beautiful it is for a man to die
Upon the walls of Zion; to be called,
Like a watch-worn and weary sentinel,
To put his armour off, and rest in heaven."

(Willis.)

WE HAVE followed Elisha from the fields of Abelmeholah, where Elijah found him at the plow and called him to the prophetic office, through an unusually long and useful career. We have observed his unfeigned piety, how closely he walked with God, and the comfort and joy which were his, even in the time of trial, and in the presence of danger. His courage, fortitude, and faithfulness appeal to the most generous impulses of the soul. Nor have we failed, I trust, as we have followed the inspired record of Elisha's life, to note the striking resemblance which he bore, in character and work, to our Lord. The account of the miracles which he wrought, multiplying the loaves, cleansing the leper, raising the dead to life; the testimony born to his amiableness of character and kindness of heart; his readiness to comfort the distressed and sorrowing, to heal rather than to wound, to speak gently rather than harshly, read like portions of the Gospel. Little less than fifty years must have elapsed since the anointing of Jehu, the event in connection with which, Elisha was last mentioned, and the events, the record of which we now consider.

That these many years of the Prophet's life were uneventful, and spent in idleness, we cannot believe. During the greater portion, at least, of this period, he must have been specially active in teaching the people, and his influence must have proved increasingly potent. "Fifty years of holy living and humble praying, in such a man as he, were not spent in vain, even though no earthly record was made of them."

We now come to contemplate the close of the life of this illustrious servant of God. He must have been at least ninety years old when the summons came to put off the armor, to lay down the weapons of warfare, that he might receive the victor's crown; to be divested of the faded and worn garments of earth, that he might wear the livery of heaven, be clothed with the white robes of the redeemed. "Now Elisha was fallen sick of his sickness whereof he died." Death has been called the king of terrors. This appellation is doubtless suggested by the fear of death which men universally entertain. Few persons like to think of dying. Even the most devout Christian may sometimes recoil from the thought of the dark river which separates the present from the unseen world. To most persons a death-bed has no attractions. Only a sense of duty, and the instinct of love suffice to draw us to the bedside of the dying. And yet how profound and impressive are the lessons which may be learned as we witness the closing scenes of a human life; as we listen to the last faint whispers of those who are passing to the other shore. In such circumstances, we cannot fail to be impressed with the fact of man's mortality, and of the transcending importance of things spiritual and eternal, as compared with the earthly and perishing. Let us draw near to the death-bed of Elisha that we may be instructed.

Observe the absence of fear or alarm on the part of the dying Prophet. Though the hand of death is upon him, there is a serenity of mind and manner which speaks of perfect assurance with reference to the future. Whatever may have been his feelings in former years concerning death, it had no power to terrify him now. Looking forward to him who was to come, and who through death was to destroy him who had the power of death, Elisha was delivered from the fear of death. As he lay upon his death-bed, he could look back upon a long life which, by grace, had been devoted faithfully to the service of God, and his soul was filled with peace. Like Paul, he could say, "I have fought a good fight, I have finished my course, I have kept the faith: henceforth there is laid up for me a crown of righteousness which the Lord, the righteous judge, shall give me at that day." So to live that we shall have the consciousness of the Lord's approval, should be the great purpose of life with each one of us. May our desire and prayer ever be, "Let me die the death of the righteous, and let my last end be like his."

"Oh for the death of those
Who slumber in the Lord;
Oh be like theirs my last repose,
Like theirs my last reward."
(J. Montgomery.)

To die as the righteous, to enjoy in death the peace and hope of the righteous, we must live the life of the righteous. To win God's approval, is to win success, though we may lose all else that men prize and seek after. To fail to win God's approval at the last, is to make shipwreck of life, though we might obtain every other object of human desire. Peace in the hour of death is not to be obtained by the possession of vast estate, or the enjoyment of worldly honor and renown.

"They that trust in treasured gold,
They that boast of wealth untold,
None can bid his brother live,
None to God a ransom give."

Another thing to be observed, is the childlike resignation which characterized Elisha in the last hours of his life. There is no murmuring, no complaining. He had faith to be healed, yet he would not dictate to God in the matter; yes, he had such unbounded, unquestioning faith, that he was willing to trust God, to leave his case entirely in God's hands. Though now an old man, Elisha doubtless had plans for the future which he must leave unexecuted, yet he expresses no regret that it is so. With the same prompt and cheerful obedience with which he assumed the duties of the prophetic office, he now laid them down. Oh, for a larger measure of this spirit of resignation to the Lord's will, as expressed in his word and providence! Oh, that that mind were more fully in us which was also in Christ Jesus, that with him we might be able at all times to say unto our heavenly Father, "Not my will, but thine be done." Had Elisha's piety been less genuine, he might have been disposed to murmur against the manner in which he was called to rest from his labors. Elijah, his master, had been borne from earth in the chariot of fire, swept splendidly into the skies, while, perhaps, still in the vigor of his years. Elisha, however, who had received a double portion of his spirit, lived to a great age, and doubtless came to feel the burden and the infirmities of old age. Although he had wrought so many mighty miracles, there was no miracle wrought in removing him to the heavenly home; no special distinction was shown him in his departure from earth. No visible chariots came to bear him away. "After long and weary toil, he must pass, weary and alone, through the valley of the shadow of death." (Edersheim.) He who had raised the dead to life, must himself die as ordinary men die. But Elisha knew that the angels of God, invisible to human eyes, should bear him in safety to the heavenly home, and he sought no greater honor. After all was he less honored in his entering into glory than his master had been? Is the honor shown to the humblest saint, in his translation from earth to heaven, in any important sense less marked than that which was shown to Elijah? Lazarus, the beggar, was borne by the angels to Abraham's bosom. What greater honor than this, to have the angels as our escort to our Father's home? But if there was contrast between the closing hours of the earthly life of Elijah and the life of Elisha, there were likewise points of similarity. To the last moment the thoughts of Elijah seem to have dwelt upon the work which had been given him to do. His last hours upon earth were spent in journeying from city to city to visit the schools of the prophets, and his last act was "one of faith and power," when he divided the waters of the Jordan. His last words were a prediction of what should be after his departure. To the last moment Elisha was interested in the affairs of the people of Israel. His last act was also "one of faith and power" when his trembling hand gave strength and brought blessing ere it was stilled by death; and his last words were a prophecy of things to come.

We many times fail to appreciate the blessings which the beneficent heavenly Father bestows upon us until, temporarily or permanently, we are deprived of them. No one knows so well how to appreciate the blessing of health as the confirmed invalid whose body is tortured with pain and wasted by sickness. Our friends are never so dear to us as when we are called to give them up. The parent who has been most indifferent, even cruel it may be, toward his children, may most deeply sorrow when bereft of them. The child who has been most heedless of the wishes and instructions of loving parents, may most keenly lament their taking away. The worth of a wise and good man to the community, to the state, is never fully appreciated until he has ceased from his labors. He may have been opposed and vilified while living, but when he is dead, we extol his virtues and rear the proud monument to perpetuate the memory of his deeds.

Joash, who was king of Israel at the time of the death of Elisha, was an idolatrous prince. The record concerning him is, "And he did evil in the sight of the Lord; he departed not from the sins of Jeroboam the son of Nebat, who made Israel sin: but he walked therein." It does not appear that once during all the previous years of his reign he had visited Elisha, that he had sought his counsel at any time, or that in any respect he had conformed his life to his teachings. The inference is that while he did not directly oppose or persecute the Prophet, he had nothing to do with him, took no notice of him. But when informed of his sickness, the youthful king, fearing, doubtless, that death would be the result, hastened to the bedside of the Prophet; and when he beheld him, wasted and worn, and was persuaded that his worst fears must soon be realized, he gave expression to the intense grief which he felt, in the exact words which had come to the lips of the now dying Prophet when, long years before, standing eastward of the Jordan, he had beheld his beloved master borne toward his resting place on high. "My father, my father, the chariot of Israel, and the horsemen thereof." Did Joash designedly quote the words of Elisha as he wept over his face or was it a mere coincidence? Perhaps the former is the correct view. He may have been familiar with the circumstances attending the translation of Elijah, and have alluded to it in this way to indicate that his sense of the loss which he and Israel should sustain in the departure of Elisha, was as profound as that which Elisha himself had experienced when bereft of his master. "The smallest movement for good is recognized and approved and often rewarded by the Almighty." (Blunt.) Hence it was that Elisha, before resting from his earthly labors, was permitted, by symbol and word, to give to king Joash who had thus honored him in his last hours, the assurance that he should be victorious over the cruel enemies of his country. Once again the prophetic influence was upon him, once again the prophetic fire gleamed in his eyes, and he thus addressed the king. "Take bow and arrows." The direction was complied with at once, the king probably receiving the weapon and the arrows from his armor-bearer. Again the Prophet spoke, "Put thine hand upon the bow," literally, let thine hand ride upon the bow. The command was doubtless to fit an arrow upon the string and to draw the bow as in the act of shooting. This was done, and then the Prophet, raising himself by supernatural strength from his bed, placed his withered hand upon the king's hands, and, when by his direction "the window eastward" had been opened, he gave command to shoot. As the arrow sped through the air, probably in the direction of Aphek, where the Syrians may have been encamped at the time, he gave the explanation of the symbolic act in these words of assurance to the king. "The arrow of the Lord's deliverance from Syria: for thou shalt smite the Syrians in Aphek, till thou hast consumed them." The design of the Prophet in placing his hands upon the hands of the king was doubtless to impress upon the mind of the young monarch that the victories which he was to win would be due, not to his own prowess or strength, but to Divine interposition in his behalf. "Without the assistance of Elisha, Joash would have drawn the bow in vain. Strong as is the monarch, he must learn that the blessing is simply and entirely from God; that the Prophet's nerveless hand laid upon his, shall impart a strength, and secure a triumph, which all the vigor of all the bowmen of Israel could not have purchased; so truly had he said, "The chariot of Israel, and the horsemen thereof." (Blunt.)

How important that we should remember this truth

in our conflicts with the spiritual foes which beset us round about. In our own strength we must prove unequal to the contest which is forced upon us. "For we wrestle not against flesh and blood, but against principalities, against powers, against the rulers of the darkness of this world, against spiritual wickedness in high places." God has said, "Not by might, nor by power, but by my spirit." Let us learn to trust in him, and to invoke his aid continually. Thus shall our bow abide in strength, and the arms of our hands be made strong "by the hands of the mighty God of Jacob." But Elisha had yet an important direction to give the king. A second symbolical act was to be performed, designed, it would seem, to test his faith, zeal, and perseverance. "And he said, Take the arrows. And he took them. And he said unto the king of Israel, Smite upon the ground. And he smote thrice, and stayed." Perhaps the majority of Bible readers have understood the Prophet's direction to the king to be to shoot the arrows upon the ground. It seems more probable, however, that the direction was to grasp in a bunch the arrows that remained in the king's quiver, after the one had been shot away, and with them to smite the ground as though smiting a prostrate foe. But whatever may have been the act required, "the man of God was wroth" with the king, because he had so little zeal in the thing commanded that he ceased when he had smitten the ground but thrice. "Thou shouldest have smitten five or six times;" he indignantly exclaims, "Then hadst thou smitten Syria till thou hadst consumed it: whereas now thou shalt smite Syria but thrice." To the two blind men who, upon one occasion, sought his mercy, our Lord said, as he touched their eyes, "According to your faith be it unto you." So it was in the case of Joash, king of Israel. His victories over the enemies of his country were according to his faith; so that instead of smiting them until he had consumed them, he could triumph over them but three times. Had he possessed the faith and the accompanying zeal to have smitten with the arrows but two or three times more, or until the Prophet had bidden him desist, he might have brought his enemies into complete subjection, but, lacking this faith and earnestness, he could be but partially successful. Is it not true that our limited victories over sin and the slowness of our progress in the Christian life and Christian experience are due to "an evil heart of unbelief" and to consequent indifference and carelessness? Is it not true that many times we are content to smite but thrice, whereas our safety requires that we should smite "five or six times" or more? "We overcome, it may be, a few evil habits, we conquer a few besetting sins, we advance a little way against our spiritual foes, and then we rest contented with our victories, and sit down quietly with the feeling of the man in the gospel, Soul take thine ease, and never attempt with all our heart and mind and strength to press onward and attain to the stature of the fullness of Christ." (Blunt.)

Against multitudes who are living to-day it must be charged, as against the children of Israel, "They turned back and tempted God, and limited the Holy One of Israel." God was ready to bless, but "they kept not the covenant of God, and refused to walk in his law," hence they received punishment instead of blessing. It is recorded that when, shortly after he had entered upon his public ministry, our Lord "came into his own country," "he did not many mighty works there" or, as Mark expresses it, "he could there do no mighty works," "because of their unbelief." God cannot bestow the fulness of blessing upon faithlessness and indifference. Of this truth Elisha was fully cognizant, hence his angry feelings toward king Joash. In the spirit of highest patriotism, the aged Prophet earnestly desired that his beloved country might be wholly freed from the oppression of her enemies. "He saw the greatness of the opportunity, the abundance of favor which God was ready to grant," and with indignation beheld how the blessing was, in large measure, forfeited by the king's "want of receptiveness."

Have not we as parents, as the companions of others, as members of the church, robbed our children, our companions, it may be husband or wife, brother or sister, our brethren in Christ, of a large measure of the blessings which God is willing to bestow upon them, by our indifference and carelessness in seeking spiritual blessings. In an important sense, every man is his brother's keeper. "None of us liveth to himself, and no man dieth to himself." In choosing for ourselves we are at the same time choosing for others. Those of our household, of the circle of our friendship and acquaintance, of the church of which we may be a member, will be brought nearer to God or denied some measure of his blessing according as we are zealous in seeking the blessing or stay our hand because of lack of faith and the indifference which doubt produces. A godless husband too often means a godless wife, and vice versa; godless parents, godless children. "The last scene of the Prophet's life is very briefly narrated by the inspired penman. And such is usually the case in the book of God. With the exception of Jacob, Joseph, and Daniel, there is scarcely an instance in which any particulars of a death-bed are recorded. There are more than twenty instances in each of which the solemn event is described in the original by a single word 'he died' as if to teach us that it is of comparatively small importance in what manner men die. The question is, how have they lived? It is not, what are the frames and feelings, often greatly deceptive, which manifest themselves during the last few painful, and it may be, almost delirious hours of mortal sickness, that will, generally speaking, avail any of us. The serious consideration is, what is the state of our hearts, what are the words of our mouths, the actions of our lives, while health and strength are our own, and the fear of death is distant. If men would only look at these important features now, with the feelings with which they will one day view them; if they would only examine themselves now, with half the anxiety, the self-suspicion, the misgivings with which they will scrutinize their conduct when the last great enemy approaches, and the veil now hanging between them and the eternal world is slowly drawn up, death would be robbed of his terrors." (Blunt.)

We do not know where Elisha spent the last days of his earthly life. Jerome says that his sepulcher was near Samaria. If this be true, and we have no reason to call it in question, it is probable that the Prophet was in Samaria at the time of his death. It matters little, however, where we die, if only we are prepared to die. John Howard, when parting with a friend previous to starting for Egypt where it seemed probable that he would die of the plague, said, "We shall soon meet in heaven, and the way thither is as near from Grand Cairo as from London." There is comfort in the blessed assurance that, if faithful, we shall reach our Father's home in his own good time; that the way thither is as near from one spot of earth as from another; that the cottage of the pauper is as safe a starting point for the land of immortality, if the heart be right with God, as the mansion of the rich or the palace of the king. Then why should we be so anxious about this present life? Why worry unduly over providing a home in which to end our days? Oh, that the words of the Master might have greater power with each one of us! "Seek ye first the kingdom of God, and his righteousness; and all these things shall be added unto you," that we could learn to do our duty as God reveals it to us, and trust him for the future, assured that his gracious will concerning us shall be accomplished. Not only are we ignorant as to the place of Elisha's death; but also, as already intimated, of the circumstances in which his death occurred. It would seem reasonable to suppose that the excitement occasioned by the king's visit, and the effort required to assist the king in shooting the arrow as he directed, would tend to exhaust the little strength which the Prophet yet retained, and thus hasten the end. But we are not told how long he survived the interview with the king. No mention is made of the friends, many or few, who stood around him when alone, and yet not alone, he entered the valley of the shadow of death. But while we must be content to remain in ignorance concerning the place and circumstances of Elisha's death, the event is replete with instruction for us. "There was in the mode of Elisha's departure from earth, a trial of grace far more difficult than we can discern in the mode of Elijah's departure." (Lowrie.)

Passive obedience is not less necessary to the development of true Christian character, not less important in the sight of God, than active obedience, while its exercise may be much more difficult. In the trials which God sometimes calls his servants to endure, as well as by their death, God would teach us the lesson of patient submission to his will. "For this purpose, doubtless, Paul languished in a Roman prison when so many harvest fields lay inviting him. So many another noble confessor has been silenced when he would gladly speak the praise of God with unceasing tongue. By such examples God bids us reflect that there are lessons of silence and suffering not less important for the glory of God, than any active zeal in his service. It is harder to suffer than to labor, harder to be patient than zealous, harder to exercise faith when things stand still than when we see that the Lord's cause prospers. Many a prison cell, and many a sick chamber has glorified the grace of God as truly, and perhaps as acceptably, as Paul's preaching or Elijah's chariot of fire." (Lowrie.)

"And Elisha died and they buried him." The statement that the body of Elisha was buried might seem at first thought to be unnecessary. It might be said, of course they would bury him. But it does not necessarily follow that because the Prophet died he should be buried. Dogs devoured the body of the wicked queen Jezebel. It is true that it seems to have been the prevailing custom among the Jews to bury their dead. "Nothing was considered so dishonorable and horrible as to have to lie unburied, the prey of dogs, hyenas, and vultures." It was a requirement of the Mosaic law to bury even those who were put to death for the commission of crime. But the burning of dead bodies or the denial of burial, was a practice not unknown among the people of Israel. The seven sons of Saul whom David delivered to the Gibeonites to be hanged for the sin of Saul against the inhabitants of Gebeah, were not suffered to be buried for the space of six months. One of the most pathetic pictures in all history is that of Rizpah keeping watch over her slain, suffering neither the birds of the air to rest on them by day, nor the beasts of the field to disturb them by night. In fulfillment of the words of prophecy, king Josiah burned men's bones upon the altar at Bethel to pollute it. Such treatment of the dead was designed, however, either as a punishment of crime or as a mark of contempt and dishonor or was adopted as a necessary measure for security in time of pestilence or war. The fact, then, that Elisha was buried is an evidence of the honor in which he was held. Even in idolatrous Israel the respect for Elisha was such that he was accorded an honorable buriel. Who "they" were that buried him we are not told; probably it was the sons of the prophets. Josephus says, "He also obtained a magnificent funeral, such an one, indeed, as it was fit a person so beloved of God should have." But the plain, brief statement of the inspired record seems like a rebuke to the pageantry and extravagance which so often distinguishes the funeral cortege of earth's departed greatness. If there were princely burial robes, a costly bier, and profuse floral offerings; if there were tears and loud lamentations at the tomb, the inspired historian did not deem them of sufficient importance to be mentioned in the record.

Years, it may be, had passed since loving hands closed the door of Elisha's tomb, probably "a squared or vaulted chamber cut in the native rock," when it was rudely torn open. The circumstances are thus briefly told, "And it came to pass as they were burying a man, that, behold, they spied a band of men; and they cast the man into the sepulcher of Elisha." Who the dead man was, who they were that carried him to the grave, we do not know, nor is it material that we should know. Josephus says, "It also happened that at that time certain robbers cast a man, whom they had slain, into Elisha's grave, and upon his dead body coming close to Elisha's body, it revived again." But this does not seem to accord with the narrative before us. From the statement that "the bands of the Moabites invaded the land at the coming in of the year," it has been inferred that the supposed hostile band, whose approach occasioned such consternation among those who composed this funeral procession, was a part of the invading force. However this may have been, those who bore the dead to the grave, fearing violence, doubtless, at the hands of the approaching band, and concluding that they had not sufficient time to reach the place of burial before the foe would be upon them, hastily removed the closing stone from the door of the tomb nearest at hand, and placing the body upon the bones therein reposing precipitately fled for safety. It proved to be the tomb of Elisha that had thus been disturbed. "And when the man was let down and touched the bones of Elisha, he revived, and stood upon his feet." It is proper to observe that this marvelous miracle affords no sanction whatever for the silly, offensive, and idolatrous teachings and practices of the Papal church in reference to the reputed bones of saints. Those who bore this dead man to his grave, did not visit the tomb of Elisha with any thought that their dead might be restored to life. "The instance proves nothing in behalf of the relics of saints and their misuse in the Romish church, for it was not the bones of Elisha, but the power of God, which made this dead man live. The church did not then dig up the bones of Elisha, and have never since dug them up, much less encased them in gold and silver, and given them to the people to kiss and to reverence, as is done under the Papacy, in order to gain favor with God, for which there is neither precept nor example in the Scriptures." (Stark.) This mighty miracle was designed not to inculcate and to foster superstitious and idolatrous notions and practices, but as a Divine testimony to the faithfulness with which Elisha had served God in life, a confirmation of the truth that his official words and deeds were inspired of God. Of him it may truly be affirmed, "He, being dead, yet speaketh."

"Rise, O my soul! pursue the path
By ancient worthies trod;
Aspiring, view those holy men
Who lived and walked with God.

Though dead, they speak in reason's ear
And in example live;
Their faith and hope and mighty deeds
Still fresh instruction give.

Lord may I ever keep in view
The patterns thou hast given,
And ne'er forsake the blessed path
Which led them safe to heaven.

www.ingramcontent.com/pod-product-compliance
Lightning Source LLC
La Vergne TN
LVHW020526100826
845148LV00010B/1355